THE CASE FOR SINGLE MOTHERHOOD

THE CASE FOR SINGLE MOTHERHOOD

Contemporary Maternal Identities and Family Formations

KATHERINE ELIZABETH MACK

THE UNIVERSITY OF ALABAMA PRESS
Tuscaloosa

The University of Alabama Press
Tuscaloosa, Alabama 35487-0380
uapress.ua.edu

Typeface: Adobe Text Pro

Cover image: Visual Generation/Adobe Stock
Cover design: Lori Lynch

Cataloging-in-Publication data is available from the Library of Congress.
ISBN: 978-0-8173-2154-3 (cloth)
ISBN: 978-0-8173-6112-9 (paper)
E-ISBN: 978-0-8173-9472-1

FOR KARIN COSTELLO AND DEENA GOLDSTONE

CONTENTS

ACKNOWLEDGMENTS

Writing a book, like mothering, is a collective endeavor. The dedication of this volume expresses my gratitude to the two most significant mothers involved in this project: Karin Costello and Deena Goldstone. Absent their nurturing and role modeling, I would not be the person I am. Nor would I have pursued motherhood as a single woman, a pursuit that led to the birth not only of my three beloved children—Andrew/Andrés, Marcelo, and Beatrice/Beatríz—but also of this book.

The book you are holding overlaps with my new project, a memoir about motherhood, family, and community, in that they both examine the paucity and constraints of labels and the language of relations. In the paragraphs that follow, I name individuals only once, though some could and should be listed several times, and I group them somewhat arbitrarily. While good enough, my authorial decisions don't feel exactly right to me. In this sense, these acknowledgments testify to the challenge of expressing the affective ties that bind us. With those caveats in place:

I began this project as an assistant professor of English at the University of Colorado in Colorado Springs. At its completion, I am a professor, having served as department chair along the way. During the many twists and turns of this journey, colleagues provided support (of various kinds), prodding, and critique. I am grateful to work with people I trust and respect and on whom I rely as much for friendship as for pedagogical, intellectual, and administrative camaraderie. Among many, Ann Amicucci, Steve Carter, Minette Church, Jackie Crouch, Larry Eames, Spencer Harris, Christina Jimenez, Rebecca Laroche, Christina Martinez, Michelle Neely (RIP), Jeffrey Montez de Oca, Kirsten Ortega, Raphael Sassower, Jeffrey Scholes, Emily Skop, Stephany Spaulding, Sonja Tanner, and Glen Whitehead deserve special mention.

I am deeply grateful to my mentors. Susan Jarratt introduced me to rhetoric, showed me the breadth of rhetorical studies, and taught me to think rhetorically. She has supported me professionally and personally from graduate school to the present. Susan expects and fosters careful, incisive, and ethical thinking in the writers lucky enough to count her as a mentor. I am fortunate to count myself among them. Jonathan Alexander's oeuvre alone provokes and inspires, but here I want to acknowledge his personal warmth, bravery, and enthusiasm: Jonathan makes me feel that I can and should write not only the next sentence but also many more. I owe thanks as well to the leaders of the two Rhetoric Society of America workshops that helped to shape my approach to this project: Jen Borda, Jess Enoch, Cheryl Glenn, and Sara Hayden. Jess Enoch also provided valuable feedback on an early draft of the book prospectus through the manuscript mentoring program of the Coalition of Feminist Scholars in the History of Rhetoric and Composition. For two decades now, Shevaun Watson has been a sounding board about the profession, rhetorical concepts, and institutional politics.

Marjorie Jolles is the principal interlocutor and reader of all my writing projects. Many strengths of this book stem from her thoughtfulness, generosity (discussing ideas from their most embryonic to fullest expression; commenting on every draft; proposing different, often more felicitous phrasing; suggesting new sources, frequently with the link or PDF attached), and deep knowledge of feminism and feminist philosophy.

My writing group partners, Jill Swinicecki and Tracy Whalen, provided encouragement and feedback that both clarified and deepened the arguments I advance. Our collaboration feels like an ongoing graduate seminar in rhetoric with the sharpest and kindest of classmates. Kudos to the Rhetoric Society of America's Career Retreat for Associate Professors for bringing us together and to Lynee Lewis Gaillet, in particular, for helping us set the wheels of our group in motion and being a trusted source of professional advice. Hera Mcleod and Aisha Jenkins, the founders of Mocha SMC, had a generative exchange with me about this project. I appreciate their time and effort.

My "framily" sustains me emotionally while also pushing me toward productive critique of maternal and familial pieties. Our lifelong conversations inform and shape the arguments of this book. For thirty years, Marcela Díaz—my children's radical *madrina*—and Priti Patel have helped me weather life's inevitable ups and downs and everything in between. Mona Megumi Cousino, Andrew Dibben, Cindy Maguire, Jimena Oliver, and Canción Soto also play an integral role in my surviving "this thing we call life."

Though I am not partnered, I am not raising my children alone. Thank you to Wendy Crispino, Dyan de Gaudio, Karin Dietrich, Hope Forti, Bruce Hamilton, Griffin Jones, Vicky McLaughlin, Laura McWhirter, Ericka and Johnny Povinelli, Patti Smithsonian, John Standish, and Steve Wood and the Concrete Couch staff for giving so much of your time and energy to my children. Your presence in our lives demonstrates how expansive the concept and feeling of "family" can be. Thank you as well to the faculty and staff of Buena Vista Montessori Elementary School. Because I knew my children were under your loving care and stimulating tutelage, I could burrow into my research and writing.

Adrian Ortega, you have helped me to discover new parts of myself and to awaken those that lay dormant for a period. Thank you for showing me that being a mother enhances other aspects of my identity.

I am grateful for my loving and supportive family, a term I define expansively: my aforementioned mothers, Karin Costello and Deena Goldstone; my late father, Alan Mack; my other father, Edward Costello; Martin Sweeney; the Costello-McGlynn, Goldberg, and Mack-Fett pods. Kristy and Henrik, I am humbled and inspired by the parental example you set. Dominik and Tatiana, I am amazed by your ongoing becoming and delighted that I have had the opportunity to witness it from the very beginning. Inspired by Claire A. Nivola's wonderful book *Star Child*, I finally want to thank *my* star children, Andrew/és, Marcelo, and Beatrice. Thank you for choosing me as your mother. Without you, this book would not exist, and my life would be filled with immeasurably less joy, laughter, and wonder. You expand my mind, heart, and soul on the daily.

Dan Waterman, my editor, has been an attentive and thoughtful guide throughout the publication process. He and the rest of the team at the University of Alabama Press made the process of bringing this book to press as seamless as it could be. I appreciate Heather Bergh's and Melissa Crowley's editorial assistance on early drafts of this manuscript; Joanna Jacobs's and Irina du Quenoy's meticulous and incisive editing of later drafts; and Bonny McLaughlin's work on the index, supported by a grant from the College of Letters, Arts, and Science dean's office and the Patricia Gray Endowment Fund. I am also deeply grateful to my two anonymous reviewers for seeing the value of my project and for their detailed insights and suggestions for revision; this volume is stronger as a result.

An early version of the material in chapter 1 on Jane Mattes's *Single Mothers by Choice* appeared in "I Am Murphy Brown: Race and Class in the Rhetorics of Single Mothers by Choice," *Rhetoric Review* 39, no. 3 (2020): 287–302.

I chose motherhood three times over, my children are the joyful center of my life, and I am sustained in my mothering by an abundance of support and resources. And, yet, at times, mothering still pushes me to my limits. This book goes to press at a moment when many women and people who can gestate face increasing obstacles around their reproductive health and choices. In the conclusion, I argue for the necessity and urgency of a reproductive justice framework that will support our ability to become mothers and to flourish in our motherhood when (and *if*) we decide to become mothers. This autonomy over our bodies and futures is an essential human right. I am grateful to have been able to exercise it, aware of the privileges that made doing so possible, and committed to a future in which all of us can say the same.

ABBREVIATIONS

ART	assisted reproductive technology
CM	choice mom
ESM	elective single mother
IVF	in vitro fertilization
LGBTQIA+	lesbian, gay, bisexual, transgender, queer / questioning, intersex, asexual and others
NGO	nongovernmental organization
RJ	reproductive justice
RJT	reproductive justice theory
SMC	single mother by choice

INTRODUCTION

Legitimizing Single Motherhood through Rhetorics of Choice, Desire, and Intentionality

I was single and nearing the end of the first trimester of my first pregnancy when Marcela, the *madrina* (godmother) of my son-to-be, came to Colorado Springs for the weekend. Marcela lives her politics both through her work as a grassroots organizer and through her quotidian interactions with others. In response to an announcement of a pending marriage, she has been known to ask, "Why are you getting married?" rather than offer the pro forma "Congratulations!" Likewise, when a woman announces a pregnancy, she will ask, "Are you going to keep it?," so as to keep all reproductive choices on the table. Marcela also insists on seeing strength, confidence, and self-determination in others, as if she can will those qualities into being through her assertions. Thus it was that on a walk through my neighborhood, we had a heated conversation in which she insisted, "You always wanted to have a child on your own. You've never wanted to have the husband, two point two kids, golden retriever, and white picket fence life. We're feminists! Being a single mother is the best way to have a family. You don't have to negotiate or compromise on your parenting decisions. Remember, too, that the vast majority of women around the world raise children on their own. So what you're doing is hardly unconventional."

While the academics who have written about elective single mothers (ESMs) do not know me personally,[1] they would challenge Marcela's characterization of the particular population of mothers in which I find myself as excitedly bucking convention. In *Single by Chance, Mothers by Choice*, Rosanna Hertz admits that she expected that the ESMs she interviewed "would be at the leading edge of a woman's movement." On the contrary, she found that they were "far from crusaders."[2] Hertz explains: "I found a category of women who denied that they were at the leading edge of anything and who assiduously shunned the spotlight. They aspired to acceptance in a middle-class milieu and alignment with conventional definitions of mother, child, and family."[3] Later, she states succinctly, "These women did not view themselves as trailblazers, much less as revolutionaries."[4] Another sociologist, Jane Bock, claims similarly that "they appear to be 'unwilling warriors' who, on the one hand, stress the importance of having the option of single motherhood, yet, on the other hand, cling to hegemonic fantasies of normative family structures."[5] Susanna Graham likewise calls into question the use of the word "choice" to describe ESMs' pursuit of motherhood, writing, "These women are not outwardly *rejecting* the nuclear ideal but instead reworking their ideas about motherhood and relationships in an aim to *salvage* at least some of the nuclear ideal they had imagined for themselves."[6] In other words, ESMs do not "choose" single motherhood; instead they resign themselves to it. They seek the nuclear ideal and maintain their belief in its superiority. Graham reports that "the majority of the participants experienced grief in giving up the prospect of a nuclear family, both for themselves and their future child. Elective single motherhood was never the plan but an option that had to be incorporated into their life trajectory."[7] According to these scholars' accounts, ESMs hope to form nuclear families, mourn their inability to do so, and, in the discourse of trauma, must "come to terms" with the unintended direction their lives have taken.

Here we have a mirrored contrast. Both Marcela and the scholars cited started off with idealistic feminist assumptions and aspirations that framed the ways they interpreted the words and experiences of actual ESMs as well as the conclusions they drew about them. Both also seem disappointed that real ESMs do not live up to a certain version of the feminist dream. For my part, I felt as uneasy reading the scholarly interpretations of elective single motherhood as I did when listening to Marcela's remarks. Did their conclusions sit poorly with me because they misrepresented my emotions and experience? In what ways did their framing of elective single motherhood strike me as misguided? This book represents my efforts to answer those questions. While it began as an attempt to understand and articulate my own experience of single motherhood, it evolved into an opportunity to examine how the phenomenon of elective single motherhood illuminates and indexes the flux of late twentieth- and early twenty-first-century North Americans' understanding and enactment of gender and family and their imbrication with race, class, and sexuality.

I came to realize that my discomfort stemmed in part from my rhetorical mindset and approach. I do not take the words of anyone, especially from a marginal position, as absolute, unchanging, and wholly transparent representations of their feelings or worldview. My assumption is that, whether in private exchanges, interviews, guidebooks, memoirs, documentaries, or blogs, single mothers, intentionally or not, respond differently to specific situations and audiences at particular moments in time and place. We are situated, responsive, and dynamic. Studying elective single motherhood from this rhetorical perspective entails a shift in framework from individual *identity*—"reluctant revolutionaries" or "unwilling warriors"—to rhetorical *stance*, one that is situated and mobilizes the "available means."[8] This approach sidesteps the application of labels and their implied judgment, focusing instead on revealing the context of and strategy behind ESM rhetorics and their effects, however conscious or intentional. This approach also recognizes that the various participants in any exchange—friends, interviewer and interviewee, artists, readers, and viewers—mutually create a representation of single motherhood via the questions posed and the give-and-take of dialogue. As we experience, we interpret, construct, and represent our experience for ourselves and others. Historian Joan Scott explains this simultaneity: "Experience is at once always already an interpretation *and* something that needs to be interpreted."[9] Equally important, our utterances can be both strategic and expressive of actual beliefs. A single mother—self-identified as elective or not—may be defending and legitimizing her status to the outside world while working toward understanding her own ambivalent and ambiguous feelings about the family she has created. A both/and interpretive strategy illuminates these mothers' negotiation of complex political and personal circumstances. For determining what one really wants—as opposed to the culturally dominant definition of a "good life"—is a lifelong process, one that evolves, at times dramatically, in response to cultural and material conditions and that a single conversation or survey, and even an extended interview, cannot capture. Finally, this process is profoundly rhetorical; we strive to articulate the lifestyles and goals toward which we aspire so as to understand them better and make attaining them more likely.[10]

Guided by these assumptions, *The Case for Single Motherhood* examines the rhetorical construction of elective single motherhood in self-sponsored texts by women who identify with (and contest) the label from the early 1990s through the present day. Created in the early 1990s, this distinct category has since then been complicated and contested by the women whom it ostensibly encompasses. To be sure, women pursued elective single motherhood prior to the 1990s. As Boyd et al. observe, "It would be wrong to draw a stark dividing line between an earlier period when women might become pregnant 'by chance' and decide to raise the child as a single mother and a more modern period when they become 'single mothers by choice.'"[11] Moreover, political, economic, and social conditions have long encouraged single motherhood in many communities in the United States. In the mid-1990s, however, the ESM—a white, heterosexual, professional, able-bodied, cis-gender woman in her mid to late thirties—became a recognizable and privileged identity in the public imaginary. Until recently, the majority of the women who identify as ESMs and create texts about the experience fit this description. Though their racial, sexual, and class status conditioned their experience of motherhood, these factors went unmarked in their writings. This unmarking is problematic, as "addressing underprivilege requires identifying and dismantling overprivilege."[12] Most germane to this project, "analyzing the relationships between people who are reproductively privileged and those who are disadvantaged is key to understanding the systems of difference and inequality and to illuminate the experiences of each group of people (and the individuals within them) who seek to control their destinies."[13] Analysis of the legitimizing tactics of ESMs, individuals comprising an ostensibly distinct and lauded category of single mother, thus fosters the aim of understanding, contesting, and dismantling stigmatizing racist and classist critiques of "bad" single mothers. With that aim in mind, *The Case for Single Motherhood* identifies the cultural, historical, and discursive forces that led to the creation and definition of the category of ESM and evaluates its rhetorical power as well as the exclusions and hierarchies it effects.

This book originated in personal experience and critical reflection. During my first pregnancy, when I was grappling with the seismic identity shifts that many new parents experience, I uncritically described myself as a Single Mother by Choice (SMC). Upon further investigation of the SMC label and identity construct, I became curious about its genesis, increasingly uncomfortable with its history and exclusions, and, finally, eager to discover complications and challenges to it. *The Case for Single Motherhood* is the fruit of this research, a scholarly project born of this grappling with, and finally resistance to, the Single Mother by Choice and Choice Mom labels that sought to name and claim me. Eventually, I found that some ESMs contest and resignify this identity and redeploy our maternal experience to foster progressive goals. As these mother rhetors demonstrate, being on the margins of dominant norms and identities can be a source of strength and vision. Admittedly, the archive of ESM-composed texts that I assemble here is selective and self-interested. Most ESMs do not conceive of themselves as radicals, trailblazers, or revolutionaries. Some, however, do, and their arguments about the significance of their motherhood—especially those made by mothers of color and younger mothers who were not imagined within the original ESM identity—warrant attention. Finally, because ESMs are still primarily a privileged group of women, they receive outsized attention for the challenges they pose to the idealized nuclear family model.[14] As a result, their representations of themselves and of their families have the potential to shape the way North Americans think about and do family. This book, then, offers both a critical analysis of maternal legitimizing in our recent rhetorical past and serves as an inventional resource for thinking about how we can, and why we should, legitimize single motherhood differently today, or perhaps not at all.

The Legitimacy Continuum

Legitimacy takes on particular force in this study because of the term's frequent use in reference to mothers and children. Historian Rickie Solinger asks, "Who gets to be a 'legitimate' mother in the United States? . . . What do race and class have to do with 'legitimate' and 'illegitimate' maternity? What do the government, the church, the community, and the family have to do with deciding and *enforcing* answers to these questions? How have answers changed over time? And perhaps more important, how does the maternal 'legitimacy' of some persons depend on and guarantee the *illegitimacy* of others?"[15] *The Case for Single Motherhood* uses rhetorical heuristics and critical methods to answer Solinger's questions and, in so doing, reveals the inevitable and inherent rhetoricity of legitimacy work. Legitimacy provides rhetorically rich terrain because it has two meanings that are simultaneously related and conflictual. On the one hand, legitimacy means in conformity with or circumscribed by the law. An "illegitimate" child is one born outside of the law, that is, outside of marriage, historically the only institution in the United States into which a child could be born and enjoy legal status. On the other hand, legitimacy refers to the defense or justification of an action, stance, or lifestyle that may or may not be legal. In these cases, legitimizing encompasses efforts to secure legal status and/or social and moral approval for the action, stance, or lifestyle in question. This latter meaning of legitimacy can entail the rhetorical efforts to secure the first: conformity with the law. In some instances, however, the legal status is not in question, and yet the action, stance, or lifestyle still lacks approval and thus requires defense or justification. Contemporary single mother families offer a case in point. While unmarried mothers and their children now enjoy legal status, they still fall outside social norms. For this reason, they continue to legitimize in both senses—to defend and to justify—themselves and their families.

Legitimizing, like normalization, is a rhetorical process that "operates through persuasion and negotiation."[16] While legitimizing is inherently defensive, since we legitimize only that which requires defense, it occurs on a continuum from negative to affirmative. Negative legitimizing responds to criticism, even if the criticism is only implied, and adheres to the framework and language of critics, which typically conform to dominant norms around the issue in question. The legitimizing of elective single motherhood in the early 1990s was primarily negative, as it adhered to the language and frameworks of critics of single motherhood. Rather than changing the framework by which they were evaluated, this first generation of ESMs sought to demonstrate that they were not qualitatively different from partnered mothers. In this sense, their legitimizing left the framework of the critics intact and further disparaged those single mothers who could not adhere to the dominant standards of "good motherhood."[17] Affirmative legitimizing, in contrast, confronts, and may even challenge, assumptions and dominant frameworks. In so doing, it reframes forms, norms, and practices and offers alternative vocabularies, perspectives, and modes of being. By the aughts, elective single motherhood legitimizing was more affirmative and inclusive. While ESMs were still on the defensive, they asserted the benefits of solo mothering. Instead of stating, "We're not so different from you," they asserted, "We are different from you, and that's a good thing!" In both instances, the rhetorical scene involved a generalized other: the partnered mother. What changed over this time span was the evaluative terms of that rhetorical relationship. ESM legitimizing of the 1990s sought to assimilate while that of the aughts moved toward a celebration of difference, mirroring the enduring feminist theoretical debate of "equality vs. difference" or "sameness vs. difference."

The legitimacy continuum draws on and extends insights from queer theory. First, at its core, queer theory has a critical relationship to norms and normativity, engaging as it does in a "thorough resistance to regimes of the normal."[18] Queer theory resists norms because norms stigmatize those who do not conform to them and squelch efforts and impulses to think and live outside their narrow conscriptions. In the words of Lauren Berlant and Jay Prosser, "When norms feel like laws, they constitute a social pedagogy of the rules for belonging and intelligibility whose narrowness threatens people's capacity to invent ways to attach to the world."[19] Our relations with and the effects of "the normal," however, are complicated. Norms enable and constitute as much as they constrain and restrain. Furthermore, conventionalizing—one mode of adhering to norms—is not necessarily or always synonymous with normativizing: "Sometimes conventionality is a defense against norms too, a way to induce proximity without assimilation [or] of creating another, counterconventional, space."[20] Legitimizing, no matter its location on the legitimacy continuum, entails a range of engagement with norms and normativity; as we legitimize, we negotiate, comply, adhere, reinforce, destabilize, alter, resist, and so on. Indeed, "we are better suited to imagine normalization not as something to be escaped, but to be maneuvered around, through, and with."[21] Moreover, competing normative frameworks exist, which creates irresolvable pressures for individuals and also produces "the tension necessary for normalization to continue."[22] The legitimacy continuum illuminates the complex dynamics and surprising effects of the legitimacy dance, underscoring that while norms and normative frameworks are inescapable, they are not wholly prescriptive or determinative.

Second, questions of intimacy and relationality lie at the heart of both queer theory and ESM legitimizing. Queer theorists ponder practices and forms of intimacy that "queer" the institutions traditionally associated with intimacy or occur outside of them entirely. As Michael Warner observes, queer life entails "a welter of intimacies outside the framework of professions and institutions and ordinary social obligations."[23] Some queer theorists seek to amplify the discourse of family, defining "queer" families as those "groups of individuals who define each other as family and share a strong emotional and/or financial commitment to each other, whether or not they cohabit, are related by blood, law, or adoption, have children, or are recognized by the law."[24] Others, such as J. Jack Halberstam, find the language of family stifling: "The focus on family is misleading and mistaken, and, ultimately, it blots out a far more compelling story about cooperation, collectivity and non-heterosexual, non-reproductive behaviors."[25] Halberstam thus urges a "'forgetting of family' in a number of different scenarios in order to allow for the possibility of other modes of relating, belonging, caring, and so on."[26] Still others, like rhetorician Dana Cloud, worry about the focus on intimacy of any kind, noting that queer theory "poses utopian experiments in intimate fulfillment . . . in lieu of a collective political struggle."[27] These interrogations of both the variety of forms and the limitations of intimacy help to illuminate the contours of ESM legitimizing and to deepen analysis of its potential political effects. ESM legitimizing, in turn, furthers understanding of the ways that discourse reflects and enacts new modes of intimacy and family formation. Like queer families, ESM families challenge normative reproduction. Most ESMs decouple heterosexual sex and reproduction in order to have children, thus unavoidably undermining reproduction's "stability and assumed naturalness."[28] Moreover, ESM families typically include people whose membership is not premised on blood or marriage, akin to the "chosen families" in the queer community.[29] Though most ESMs do not consciously theorize their lives, their writings provide new vocabularies and frameworks to describe familial identities and relationships, thereby addressing the "linguistic inconceivability" of queer life.[30]

The analysis of ESMs' writings in the following chapters reveals both the plasticity and constraints of contemporary discourses on family and the legitimizing that constructs and sustains it. To begin, I contextualize the efforts to legitimize elective single motherhood at the end of the twentieth century within the then-dominant conservative discourse of "family values." I go on to show that despite the growing acceptance of certain forms of family diversity in the early aughts, the stigma around single motherhood endures. The rhetorical constructs "Single Mother by Choice" and "Choice Mother" respond to the enduring stigma by drawing both on certain persistent axioms of family values and on postfeminist discourses of choice that are raced and classed. In the conclusion, I explain how this study addresses lacunae in rhetorical scholarship on motherhood and family, provide an outline of the arguments in each chapter, and, in the spirit of ethical feminist rhetorical scholarship, share more about my social location and path to single motherhood.

Family Values

No matter its location on the continuum, legitimizing engages with the discourses and *doxa* in circulation. By the 1990s, when the ESM construct began to take form, "family values" was "common-sense orthodoxy" and thus constituted the grounds of ESM legitimizing.[31] As a concept and rhetorical construct, family values was the fruit of the "ongoing collaboration" between new social conservatives and neoliberals who, despite their different motivations, shared a sense of crisis related to the social and cultural revolutions of the 1960s, specifically the breakdown of the so-called traditional family.[32] In some respects, new social conservatives and neoliberals were responding to a real shift in US familial culture. As family historian Stephanie Coontz demonstrates, "The 1950s was a profamily period if there ever was one. Rates of divorce and illegitimacy were half what they [were in the early 1990s]; marriage was almost universally praised; the family everywhere was hailed as the most basic unit in society; and a massive baby boom, among all classes and ethnic groups, made America a 'child-centric' society."[33] However, as Coontz underscores, the 1950s family was in no sense "traditional." It was, instead, "a historical fluke, based on a unique and temporary conjuncture of economic, social, and political factors," and, furthermore, "a qualitatively new phenomenon," as "at the end of the 1940s, all the trends characterizing the rest of the twentieth century suddenly reversed themselves."[34] The emotional expectations of the 1950s family were also novel: "The emphasis on producing a whole world of satisfaction, amusement, and inventiveness within the nuclear family had no precedents."[35] Most importantly, for many US Americans, the reality of 1950s life was more complex and certainly less rosy than select statistics and media representations of the period—like the TV sitcoms *Leave It to Beaver, The Adventures of Ozzie and Harriet,* and *Father Knows Best*—suggest. Many white families entered the middle class, but not all.[36] Black Americans, Mexican Americans, and Puerto Ricans faced systemic segregation and terror campaigns in addition to being "almost entirely excluded from the gains and privileges accorded white middle-class American families."[37] Finally, the heterosexual and gendered profamily culture of the 1950s required varying degrees of coercion, repression, and inequality, even for those who seemingly conformed to its strictures.[38] Nevertheless, the notion of "the traditional family" (and the happiness and stability it confers) lingers even today in the popular imaginary and "holds a special place in the American psyche."[39] The "traditional family" is a myth not only because it blends fantasy and reality but also because it exerts rhetorical force, reinforcing notions of right and wrong and attempting to guide our behavior.[40] The phrase itself serves as a potent rhetorical resource, "function[ing] as an ideological construction and as a fundamental principle of social organization."[41]

Indeed, the traditional family figured centrally in both new social conservative and neoliberal ideologies, though for different reasons. New social conservatives' concerns about the breakdown of the traditional family centered on changes to norms around gender and sexuality resulting from the growing number of "fatherless" homes and declining rates of marriage. Ventriloquizing the perspective of new social conservatives, which they then critique, scholars Jyl J. Josephson and Cynthia Burack state, "The problem with diverse families is that they cannot serve the functions of maintaining gender differentiation, order, authority and of curtailing unruly social practices."[42] In defense of the so-called traditional family, new social conservatives rallied against abortion, feminism, gay rights, pornography, and drug use while also contesting the efforts of organizations such as the National Organization for Women, the American Civil Liberties Union, and the National Education Association.[43]

Neoliberals, meanwhile, worried about the socioeconomic effects of the breakdown of the traditional family, not its cultural ramifications. Their concerns centered on the "enormous social [and economic] costs that [would] derive from the breakdown of the stable Fordist family . . . and the fact that these costs [would] accrue to the government and taxpayer rather than the private family."[44] The neoliberal solution to the familial crisis was to propose policies placing the responsibility for familial maintenance onto individual families, thereby using the powers of the state to "reestablish the private family as the primary source of economic security and a comprehensive alternative to the welfare state."[45] The goal was to "offload the costs and responsibilities of social reproduction onto families, women, and especially mothers."[46] This solution was consistent with broader neoliberal aims of "elevat[ing] . . . market forces, reduced government, 'choice,' and 'personal responsibility'" in all areas of life, an ideological, economic, and policy paradigm that theorist Wendy Brown describes as "*extending and disseminating market values to all institutions and social action.*"[47]

Family values rhetoric incorporated these distinct, yet intertwined, ideologies, as well as their intersecting goals.[48] It centered the autonomous nuclear family, impervious to socioeconomic forces beyond itself. Indeed, the Moral Majority's 1988 "Family Manifesto" declared, "We proclaim that it is good for the family to be as self-reliant as possible." Though conceptualized and coined by extremists, both new conservative and neoliberal, family values rhetoric was "capacious enough to accommodate Americans of differing theological orientations and political commitments yet specific enough to provide a common vision for leaders, activists, and fellow travelers."[49]

As a concept, family values emphasized the importance of married parents, who were assumed to be opposite-sex, cisgender, and heterosexual. The Moral Majority's manifesto is explicit: "We proclaim that children should be nurtured and raised by their own married parents."[50] These parents were to serve as models of binary gender roles and heterosexuality with their implied divisions of labor and patriarchal expectations of mothers'/wives' subordination to fathers/husbands.[51] Family values thus gave rhetorical heft to the belief that "family, marriage, and parenting are . . . the natural domain of heterosexuals only" and, therefore, "a primary site of heterosexual privilege."[52] Sociologist David Popenhoe asserted what he called a "confirmed empirical generalization" about the value of such "intact" households: "In three decades of work as a social scientist, I know of few other bodies of data in which the weight of evidence is so decisively on one side of the issue: on the whole, for children, two-parent families are preferable to single-parent families and stepfamilies."[53] Like those of self-reliance, family values axioms regarding two-parent households idealized a family formation that was not equally attainable by all Americans, and, in some instances, not equally desired. Communities of various racial and ethnic backgrounds and histories forged different ways of sustaining familial bonds in response to conditions, like slavery and discriminatory immigration policies, that sundered families, thereby making single-parent, extended family, and alloparent households the norm in some contexts.[54]

Advocates of family values admonished as much as they encouraged, "scapegoating [certain] private families—especially those headed by single parents, racial minorities, and the poor—for structural social problems."[55] In an article in the *Atlantic* titled "Dan Quayle Was Right," Barbara Dafoe Whitehead averred, "The dissolution of two-parent families, though it may benefit the adults involved, is harmful to many children and dramatically undermines our society."[56] Whitehead's was not an isolated voice. Paeans to married two-parent families appeared across the political spectrum. Sociologist Judith Stacey despaired that "Republicans and Democrats alike now compete to promote their politics in the name of the family—meaning one particular kind of family."[57] Indeed, in 1993, then-President Bill Clinton asked rhetorically, "Remember the Dan Quayle speech? There were a lot of very good things in that speech. Would we be a better-off society if babies were born to married couples? You bet we would."[58] After 1995 efforts on behalf of marriage and the two-parent family spread across America and began to take on the characteristics of a social movement.[59] While these calls for marriage were wrapped up in moralizing and talk of the psychological needs of the child, they also reflected the "ongoing collaboration" of social conservatives and neoliberalism in that marriage served the financial interests of the state and taxpayers by enabling the financial burden of parenthood to be shifted to individual workers and the private family.[60] Indeed, on August 22, 1996, President Clinton signed the Personal Responsibility and Work Opportunity Reconciliation Act, which assumed that "marriage is the foundation of a successful society, teen pregnancy is terrible for children, the welfare rolls are growing, and the goal of cutting AFDC [Aid to Families with Dependent Children] is to combat unmarried motherhood."[61] Single mothers, especially young ones, were its primary targets. With this act, welfare became a "federal apparatus for policing the private family responsibilities of the poor."[62] The irony is that "welfare reform" made achieving the family form idealized by family values nearly impossible. As Laura Briggs notes, "'Welfare reform' was both a symptom and a cause of changes in the middle-class family: nobody could stay home with the kids anymore and there could be no expectation of public support."[63]

Proponents of family values rhetoric also decried the absence of fathers—who were imagined as white, cisgender, heterosexual, and, most importantly, gainfully employed and thus adequate providers—and argued for their necessity in the upbringing of presumably heterosexual cisgender sons and daughters without the assistance of the state. While racialized conceptions of masculinity implicitly inform discourses about fathers, essentialist and binary beliefs about gender and sexuality explicitly underwrote the roles family values proponents assigned to men and women.[64] The "Family Manifesto" declares, "Sexual differentiation extends to psychological traits which set natural constraints on gender roles. Hence, in a family with children requiring nurture, the role of the male is most effectively that of provider."[65] In his 1995 bestseller, *Fatherless America: Confronting Our Most Urgent Social Problem*, David Blankenhorn—a secular evangelist for family values—declared bluntly that fatherlessness was "the major cause of declining child well-being, and the underlying source of our most important social problems."[66] Blankenhorn delineated the particular contributions of fathers to families: "physical protection," "material resources," "day-to-day nurturing," and "'paternal cultural transmission': a father's distinctive capacity to contribute to the identity, character, and competence of his children."[67]

Not surprisingly, technological breakthroughs that enabled women, among them ESMs, to become pregnant via various forms of assisted reproductive technology (ART) concerned advocates of family values. The "Family Manifesto" states bluntly, "We reject the technologization of reproduction."[68] The existence of the "Sperm Father," Blankenhorn argued, "eviscerates not only fatherhood but also the idea of fatherhood, the possibility of fatherhood."[69] Such concern "carries the masculinist fear that the new woman's independence demonstrates the irrelevance of men."[70] In point of fact, artificial insemination, or "artificial impregnation" as it was initially referred to, was developed in the last decades of the nineteenth century to help *heterosexual married* women with infertile husbands get pregnant.[71] Medical protocols and laws "enshrined the role of the physicians" in insemination, a level of control that extended even to the selection of the donor.[72] According to Kara Swanson, "It was the doctors who chose which vials of frozen sperm to purchase from a sperm bank and use for each patient."[73] With only a few notable exceptions, sperm banks sold only to doctors and "most doctors refused to inseminate any unmarried woman," leaving unmarried women, straight or lesbian, as well as lesbian couples, unable to access either semen or insemination.[74] Further complicating access was the fact that, for most of the twentieth century, insemination occurred under a mantle of intentional silence. Most doctors felt that legal fathers and their donor-inseminated offspring would benefit from, at the very least, privacy, but, in some cases, total ignorance about the nature of their genetic relationship, a concern stemming from the desire to maintain the fiction of the man's fertility and the facade of a "normal" biological family.[75] The potentially damaging legal consequences for children conceived through donor insemination, alongside widespread moral and religious opposition to the practice, contributed to the cloud of secrecy.[76] Given the consensus around the need for total discretion, record keeping and the creation of institutions to manage the storage of sperm developed slowly.[77]

A combination of factors in the final decades of the twentieth century led to increased knowledge about and access to the practice of insemination as well as to exponential growth of the for-profit fertility industry. These included reduced stigma around infertility, the threat of AIDS, and the gay and women's liberation movements and the corresponding rise in women-run feminist health clinics.[78] By the late 1980s, the sperm bank industry was booming and sperm had become a "desired commodity that [was] bought by banks and sold directly to users without medical control over allocation."[79] Artificial insemination became just one option among a rapidly expanding repertoire of assisted reproductive technologies. Scientists had been attempting in vitro fertilization (IVF), whereby an egg is fertilized in a laboratory and the resulting embryo is transferred to a womb for gestation, with nonhuman animals since the 1870s and with human eggs and sperm since the

1940s, but it was the successful birth and subsequent good health of Louise Brown, the first child born of IVF in 1978, that galvanized interest in and demand for the practice.[80] In the mid-1980s, success with egg and embryo cryopreservation (freezing) and with surrogacy further expanded the assisted reproduction frontier.[81] To be clear, most assisted reproductive practices are expensive, and, in the majority of US states, they are not covered by insurance. Thus, this mind-boggling range of reproductive services was available only to those with deep pockets or access to credit. For those lucky few, it became increasingly possible to pursue (at least partially) genetic children that they otherwise would not have had. The proliferation of these heretofore unfamiliar and unavailable practices raised the alarm among many in the conservative right.

Finally, and most significantly for this project, the construct of family values assumed that a certain kind of mother was essential to a family's well-being. Though the ideal mother it envisioned was heterosexual, married, and presumedly fertile and thus did not need to avail herself of reproductive technologies, ART's enabling of the pursuit of biological motherhood aligned with family values' conceptualization of the ideal mother in one significant way: maternal intensity, both in the becoming and the being. This intensive maternal construct constituted one strand of the backlash against the gains of the 1970s women's movement.[82] As record numbers of women in the United States began to work outside the home, divorce laws were liberalized, new legislation protected women against discrimination in the workplace, and more women ran for and won political office, popular media and commercial culture suggested suggested that women's true happiness lay in heterosexual marriage and a particular kind of motherhood.[83] Known variously as "intensive mothering," "patriarchal motherhood," and the "new Momism," the central tenets of this maternal vision held that "no woman is truly complete or fulfilled unless she has kids, that women remain the best primary caretakers of children, and that to be a remotely decent mother, a woman has to devote her entire physical, psychological, emotional, and intellectual being, to her children."[84] This maternal construct directed women to find meaning and fulfillment in the home; further, it suggested that domestic life could ameliorate social problems. As rhetorical critic Dana Cloud notes sardonically in her analysis of family values, "the solution to poverty and suffering—even starvation—is not material aid but maternal love."[85] In keeping with neoliberalism, the individualistic and privatized mother envisioned by this construct required nothing of the systems or institutions within which she, her children, and families circulated and on which they necessarily relied. This mother was also, presumably, a woman with privileges—economic, racial, cisgender, heterosexual, among others—that enabled her to choose domestic life and to heal others through her maternal presence. As Reid-Brinkley states, "not all women have equal access to the rhetorical saliency of the motherhood frame.[86] The "false universalism" of this construct occluded the differential effects of race, class, sexual orientation, and other identity markers on actual women's maternal opportunities and experiences.[87]

By the 1990s family values had to accommodate at least some of the socioeconomic and corresponding cultural shifts achieved by the women's movement. While still maintaining its socially conservative core axioms—the need for families to be self-reliant, to be headed by two married (ideally opposite-sex) parents, and to uphold essentialist norms of femininity and masculinity—the new version of family values embraced the professionally ambitious woman, but with one significant caveat: she must maintain her intensive maternal responsibilities at home. D. Lynn O'Brien Hallstein describes the "double-entanglement" in which career-driven mothers found themselves: "Post-second wave neoliberal mothering *now* coexists with *unchanged* values in the private sphere in relation to gender and family life management and responsibilities that continue to suggest that women still have primary responsibility for childrearing and family-life management."[88] Neoliberal ideals of "choice" and "personal responsibility" dovetailed with feminist ideals of independence and self-sufficiency, all working in tandem to create the mindset of 1990s mothers, who "assume they must solve any difficulties they face as mothers on their own [and] have been disciplined to assume that the problems they do face result from their own poor choices."[89] While neoliberal intensive motherhood generated stresses and tensions for all mothers, its messages and demands came as no surprise to poor women, especially those of color, who have been told consistently that their bad choices create the challenges and obstacles they face.[90] To ESMs, however, this maternal ideology offered fodder for legitimizing, as they could point to their aggressive pursuit of "choice" motherhood as evidence both of their maternal desire and of their competency. In this way, they could reframe, or, at a minimum, deflect attention from, the ways in which their family form deviated from the ideal family that family values envisioned.

Family Diversity Today

The ascendance of "family values" coincided, not coincidentally, with the proliferation of diverse family forms and practices. As Self notes, "Americans went about creating a vast array of different kinds of families . . . at the same time a political movement advocating social policies based on a narrow, obsolete, and uncommon model of the family gained traction."[91] In a

2010 report, Pew researchers describe the changes in the American family since 1960 as a "quiet revolution": "A variety of new arrangements have emerged, giving rise to a broader and evolving definition of what constitutes a family."[92] These new arrangements include blended, interracial, child-free, and polyamorous families; same-sex, gender-queer, unmarried, single, and openly adoptive parents; and families who embrace differently abled children. Family historian Stephanie Coontz wrote *The Way We Really Are* to address nonacademic readers who were confused about the disjuncture between the ostensibly ideal "traditional" family—married mother and father and their biological children—and the form and practices of actual American families past and present. Paralleling the proliferation and increased visibility in popular culture of diverse families were significant demographic shifts: the marriage age was rising among all groups, and, in the late eighties, it surpassed the age at which Middle American women, defined as those with a high school degree and maybe some college, gave birth to their first child.[93] The still dominant rhetoric of "family values" did not reflect these changes in family forms and practices.

Some conservative ideologues and politicians still proclaim the superiority of the nuclear family, but the fact of family diversity cannot be denied, and, due to LGBTQIA+ activism, the discourse of family values now recognizes it.[94] The aforementioned demographic shifts only intensified in the first decades of the aughts. There are increasingly more families formed by relationship breakdown and reformation; this phenomenon is accompanied by that of what psychologist Susan Golombok describes as "new families." "New families" are either entirely innovative, made possible by reproductive technologies, or merely newly visible, due to growing acceptance of so-called alternative families resulting from the LGBTQIA+ movement and progressive neoliberalism. The existence of these "new families" testifies to the fundamental shift away from nuclear family structures.[95] Popular culture offers a variety of takes on both diverse and new families, such as those on television series such as *Parenthood, Modern Family, Switched at Birth, Single Parents, One Day at a Time, Fuller House,* and *The Fosters.* Though we have yet to have a single or childfree presidential candidate, down-ticket politicians (or their families, for example that of Sarah Palin) do not always square with the nuclear model; nor do they take great pains to hide this fact. Former president Donald Trump's decidedly complicated familial history underscores this shift in US Americans' expectations of family. Journalists refer to Vice President Kamala Harris's family as "groundbreaking" because she has no biological children, is a stepmother, and is married to a man who states publicly and repeatedly that "I'm just gonna do what I always do . . . I'm going to support her."[96] In the legal realm, what Linda McClain refers to as the "diversity" model now dominates family law.[97] Reality has eclipsed fantasy, and Americans' ideologies of family are beginning to reflect these new circumstances. "It would seem that Americans subscribe to humanist and sociological notions of family rather than those that are conservative, archetypal, and prescriptive," writes Self.[98] More anecdotally, in my Rhetorics of the Family class at the University of Colorado in Colorado Springs, hardly a hotbed of radical leftist sentiments, the vast majority of my students identify as proponents of family diversity.

Despite the increased acceptance of certain forms of family diversity, some living arrangements and family forms continue to make US Americans uneasy. These include the growing number of solo dwellers, single adults, and childfree couples. Scholars in queer, feminist, critical race, and intersectional studies have long pondered the significance and consequences of family formations, living arrangements, and affective bonds, such as these, that are deemed "deviant" and "nonnormative." *The Case for Single Motherhood* draws on this deep scholarly tradition while also riding a crest of contemporary general interest publications that address ambivalence about these demographic trends and whose popularity suggests that as white, straight, and middle-class US Americans deviate from "the norm," these practices receive more attention, and, in some instances, more social approval. In *Living Alone*, Erik Klinenberg counters those who consider the fact that one in seven North American adults live alone "as an unmitigated social problem, a sign of narcissism, fragmentation, and a diminished public life."[99] Klinenberg draws on extensive qualitative and quantitative data to conclude that "living alone has *not* led to the 'decomposition' of collective life and the end of meaningful social commitments."[100] Bella DePaulo's *Singled Out* addresses parallel misgivings about the pernicious influence of single people on collective life. She argues that the "intentional communities" formed by single people "are more likely to think about human connectedness in a way that is further-reaching and less predictable."[101] The growing numbers of US Americans who decide to remain childfree or to postpone parenthood provoke similarly strong responses. The president of the US organization Negative Population Growth celebrates the fact that "American women are delaying the birth of their first child, they are having fewer children overall, and many are going childless for their lifetime."[102] Amy Blackstone's *Childfree by Choice* examines the stigmas the childfree face, especially women, but also emphasizes the joys and independence associated with her and husband's announcement "We were {not} having a baby!"[103] Meanwhile, the author of *The Rise of Post-Familialism: Humanity's Future?* defines "family" as parents, children, and extended kin and expresses concern about the practical and cultural effects of low fertility, namely that we will become more of a "'now' society, geared towards consuming or recreating today, as opposed to nurturing and sacrificing for tomorrow."[104] This characterization of the childfree as superficial hedonists is pervasive and ubiquitous, so much so that an essay collection that seeks to contest it is ironically titled *Selfish, Shallow, and Self-Absorbed: Sixteen Writers on the Decision NOT to Have Kids.*

The Persistent Stigmatization of Single Motherhood

While US Americans are ambivalent about many of the discussed changes to family form and practice, single motherhood, which weaves together disparate strands of these demographic shifts, continues to outright disturb the vast majority of the US population. Adrienne Rich's observation in 1976 still rings true today: "Motherhood is admirable . . . only so long as mother and child are attached to a legal father: Motherhood out of wedlock, or under the welfare system, or lesbian motherhood, are [*sic*] harassed, humiliated, or neglected. In the 1970s in the United States, with 26 million children of wage-earning others, 8 million in female-headed households, the late nineteenth-century stereotype of the 'mother at home' is still assumed as the norm—a 'norm' that has, outside of a small middle-class minority never existed."[105] Nearly fifty years later, the rates of working mothers and single-parent households that Rich identifies have only intensified, and yet the discomfort around single motherhood remains. A 2011 Pew research study found that "of all the changes in family structure, the one that draws the strongest negative reaction is single parenthood. An overwhelming majority (69%) say the trend toward more single women having children without a male partner to help raise them is a bad thing for society. And a majority (61%) still believe that a child needs both a mother and a father to grow up happily."[106] A 2013 Pew survey found only a slight decrease in disapproval ratings: "When it comes to the rising share of single mothers, the public takes a mostly negative view. About six-in-ten adults (64%) say the growing number of children born to unmarried mothers is a big problem." All single mothers contend with, and some internalize, this deep and persistent stigma. A central argument of this book is that this stigma has impelled ESMs' classed and raced attempt to distinguish themselves from other, "bad," single mothers.

ESMs' efforts, ongoing since the 1990s, to change the pejorative narrative about non-nuclear families parallel those of the LGBTQIA+ community, with whom ESMs share the experience of forming and sustaining families that do not hew to the heterosexual norm. In this sense, ESMs, irrespective of their sexual identity, are "queer." For, regardless of their path to motherhood—anything from an "oops" pregnancy to adoption to donor egg, donor sperm, and a surrogate—ESM families do not include a father in any conventional sense or a paternal narrative beyond "a nice man gave me 'seed' to make you." Just as significant to ESMs' queer identity is the visibility of their difference from the two-parent heterosexual familial norm. When children are young, ESMs can "pass" as divorced, widowed, or exes of some sort, but eventually they must "come out" as ESMs, if only to their child(ren). This visibility distinguishes ESMs from single mothers who were, at some point, partnered or married and whose children have a father, no matter how distanced or absent, as well as some form of conventional paternal narrative, even if it is one of abandonment. Furthermore, if these single mothers have biological children, people assume that they had heterosexual (penetrative) sex, forestalling inquiry about *how* the child came to be. Some ESMs, like me, also have a queer sensibility, which refers to one's approach to life and outlook on the world, not to others' perceptions and judgements or an identity per se. A queer sensibility questions heteronormative conventions, assumptions, and timelines; values a wide range of intimacies, including those that are ephemeral, or, according to some, perverse; and embraces nonbiological kinship.

As I discuss in more detail in chapter 4, the movements to legitimize the stigmatized identities and family formations of ESMs and LGBTQIA+ people share certain goals, strategies, and discursive tactics. However, the movement toward LGBTQIA+ equality has necessarily been both legal and cultural, as laws until recently explicitly forbade gay marriage and policies restricted LGBTQIA+ couples from becoming and/or being recognized as parents. In contrast, the resistance faced by ESMs has been primarily cultural. While some fertility clinics and adoption services refuse services to unmarried women, US law cannot explicitly prevent a woman—no matter her sexual identity—from becoming a mother. Single mothers, however, do face strong social censure, and the law has not always provided equal protection to their children. As Jodi Vandenberg-Davis notes, "Not until the 1960s and early 1970s did the Supreme Court rule that children born to single mothers are entitled to equal protection under the law, including the right to child support from their fathers."[107] ESMs have thus had to wage a rhetorical battle in which they seek to persuade themselves and others of the legitimacy of their family formations.

This quest for legitimacy stimulated the creation of the ESM identity and associated labels. In this sense, the identity is rhetorically motivated and fashioned. The actual line dividing ESMs from other single mothers is blurry at best, and ESM labels—like Single Mother by Choice (SMC) and Choice Mom (CM)—are thus more rhetorical than denotative: they seek to distinguish and affirm a subset of single mothers. They do so by emphasizing the mindset of the ESM. Intentionality is the key feature of that mindset, and, according to some, it matters more to the ESM identity than the mother's relationship status. In *Retrospective: Eighteen Years as a Choice Mom*, Mikki Morrissette, founder of the organization Choice Moms and writer of the eponymous guidebook, explains, "I coined the term 'Choice Mom' as an alternative to 'single mother by choice' because I believed the emphasis should be on women choosing to be mothers—being single is the happenstance."[108] Whatever the emphasis, the labels SMC and CM capitalize on the positive associations of "choice" in liberalism, neoliberalism, and some versions of feminism as well as support for white women's reproduction.[109] As Rickie Solinger explains, "'Choice' also became a symbol of middle-class women's arrival as independent consumers. Middle-class women could afford to choose. They had earned the right to choose motherhood, if they liked . . . Poor women had not earned the right to choose."[110] The truth, however, is that single mothers rhetorically excluded from the ESM identity are also, at least somewhat, intentional and their children "chosen." Teen mothers and mothers who receive public assistance opt to keep a pregnancy rather than terminate, despite the likelihood that they will parent without the active participation of the child's father. Additionally, even before conception, there is intentionality in mothers not typically included within the ESM label. In their study of poor unmarried mothers, Edin and Kefalas found that "the majority of children were the result of *neither* explicit planning *nor* contraceptive failure. Most conceptions were described in terms that placed them between these two ends of the continuum—between planned and accidental."[111] Moreover, like ESMs, the mothers in Edin and Kefalas's study desired motherhood above all else: "They judged children to be a necessity, an absolutely essential part of a young woman's life, the chief source of identity and meaning."[112] Again, like ESMs, these mothers are purposeful and demonstrate agency. As Edin and Kefalas observe, "The[ir] choice to mother in the context of personal difficulty is an affirmation of their strength, determination, and desire to offer care for another."[113] In a similar vein, Coontz writes about the economic independence and collective childrearing practices of single Black mothers, noting, "There is good reason to believe that these are healthy, not pathological, qualities."[114]

Intentionality, however, is not coterminous with planning. ESMs typically do a great deal of short- and long-term planning prior to the birth or adoption of their child. That elective single mothers *can* plan is a privilege; they have the material and psychological resources to do so. Angela, a single mother interviewed by Edin, comments on that planning and lays bare the assumed whiteness of the construct: "Someday I'm going to *plan* my pregnancies like . . . *white* women do. You know, like Murphy Brown! You have your fancy car, . . . your fancy house, your career all set, and *then* maybe you'll have a baby!"[115] As Angela's comments make clear, despite its actual diversity, the ESM identity is overdetermined by middle-class white womanhood, and the women who label themselves as such draw, consciously or not, on the cultural capital contained therein. Edin and Kefalas hear condemnation in Angela's comments about elective single motherhood; in their interpretation, Angela implies that the advance planning of Murphy Brown mothers marks them as "selfish and unnatural."[116] Rather than condemnation, I hear both envy and critique of ESMs' class and racial privilege, which makes their planning and achievement of these middle-class milestones possible. As Elizabeth C. Britt observes, "Middle-class white women in America to some degree share the expectation that life will proceed fairly predictably, that they have some measure of control over their destinies, and that hard work will be rewarded with success."[117] The guidebooks and websites under analysis in this book serve ESMs' desire to plan and suggest the centrality of this planning to their identity. These texts simultaneously address and call into being a certain kind of rational reader who understands herself as agentic and resourceful. As a liberal subject, she enjoys the freedom to construct her life and to choose among the many options available to her. She inhabits "ready-made hierarchal worlds of sense in which individuals form intentions, make choices, [and] carry out actions."[118] The textual genres that facilitate this mode of agency and way of being in the world, like guidebooks, affirm and reinforce the values of intentionality, planning, and responsibility upon which ESMs pride themselves.

These texts also point to the absence of common knowledge and cultural norms of single motherhood in the white middle-class culture to which self-designated ESMs aspire. ESMs find themselves on the defensive, needing to demonstrate that their families are stable and sound in a cultural context—that of white middle-class America—that finds them deficient. They understand that they are violating, and, according to some, flouting community norms. Those ESMs whose rhetorics fall on the negative end of the legitimacy continuum internalize the concerns about their children being raised by a single mother. They seek advice and support to pursue a deviant lifestyle choice for which they have few models. They hope to demonstrate that they can be "good mothers" according to dominant models of good motherhood. In contrast, those whose rhetorics fall on the affirmative end of the legitimacy continuum draw on their experience of single motherhood to theorize "good motherhood" anew. Their single motherhood is a source of strength and inspiration, and their rhetorical legitimizing imaginative and visionary. The rhetorical efforts of this latter group, while small in number, have the potential to alter dominant norms of family and are thus worthy of attention. The ways these mothers emotionally, intellectually, and practically project themselves into maternity despite the constraints on their maternal imaginary showcase rhetoric as an art of invention, "capable of creating new versions of the real and the valuable."[119] As Jacqueline Royster and Gesa Kirsch observe, "thinking broadly and deeply about what is there, not there, and could be there instead" is one of the critical goals of feminist rhetorical scholarship.[120] Here rhetoric's visionary powers dovetail with those of intersectional theory, which likewise fosters and celebrates a "resistant imaginary" that seeks to imagine otherwise.[121]

Extending Rhetorical Scholarship on Family and Motherhood

There is a robust and growing transdisciplinary body of scholarship on motherhood dating from the 1986 publication of Adrienne Rich's seminal *Of Woman Born: Motherhood as Experience and Institution.* Rich marks the difference between "the *potential relationship* of any woman to her powers of reproduction and to children . . . and the *institution* [of motherhood], which aims at ensuring that that potential—and all women—shall remain under male control."[122] Her insights laid the groundwork for scholars to examine the varied effects and significance of motherhood, and, as importantly, to investigate how maternal experiences can diverge from, and potentially contest, the "*institution.*" Rhetorical heuristics, theories, and methods illuminate how discourse constructs both the "*institution*" and "potential relationships." D. Lynn O'Brien Hallstein defines "mothering rhetorics" as both "the rhetorics of reproduction (rhetorics about the reproductive function of women/mothers) and reproducing rhetorics (the rhetorical reproduction of ideological systems and the logics of contemporary culture)" and calls for scholarship on these rhetorics' "historical and contemporary permutations."[123] Given that identity, location, and social context enable and shape "mothering rhetorics" as well as their expressions, consequences, and rhetorical power, understanding motherhood's rhetorical significance requires an intersectional perspective. In *Rhetorics of Motherhood*, Lindal Buchanan calls for precisely this kind of intersectional rhetorical work, which focuses on "who has rhetorical recourse to motherhood, how maternal appeals are crafted, what they communicate about gender [and other axes of identity], and when they serve or subvert women's interests."[124] Heeding the necessity of an intersectional approach, *The Case for Single Motherhood* deepens and extends scholarship on motherhood and demonstrates what its study yields for rhetorical studies in four ways.

First, the legitimacy continuum illuminates the rhetorical mechanisms that construct maternal hierarchies. Naming is a critical component of legitimacy work. Star Medzerian Vanguri proposes a "rhetorical onomastics, an approach to name study that examines the social and political motives for and consequences of naming via the interactions of the namer and the named."[125] Karma Chávez and Cindy L. Griffin bring intersectional concerns with power and privilege to bear on naming. They ask, "Who is being named, what name is being given or offered, who has the power to do so, and what privileges exist that sanction this naming?"[126] The monikers SMC and CM labor to distinguish and affirm some single mothers, underscoring the point that the lines dividing the broad category of single mothers are rhetorical, not denotative, and could thus be drawn otherwise. ESM legitimizing tactics require, if only implicitly, the stigmatizing of other, ostensibly distinct, single mothers whom their legitimacy rhetorics exclude and whose rhetorical existence enables the privileged category of the ESM. These excluded single mothers motivate and shape the ESM rhetorical construct, just as ESM legitimizing further reinforces their illegitimacy.

Second, *The Case for Single Motherhood* contributes to feminist rhetorical efforts to crack "the code of Motherhood," which "subsume[s] the specificity and uniqueness of groups and individuals."[127] In addition to demonstrating single mothers' differential access to the rhetorical resources of the maternal—single mothers do not have equal access to "the code"—my work illuminates the diversity within the ESM community. Popular representations of ESMs, like the feature films *The Switch*, *Baby Mama*, *Back-Up Plan*, and *The Single Moms Club*, do not capture their demographic or perspectival complexity. They represent ESMs as culturally white, heterosexual, middle-class professionals in their late thirties and forties who are either hell-bent on becoming mothers (and so pursue motherhood as single women) or are single mothers who yearn for a man to complete their families.[128] While some ESMs fit this profile, not all do. Scholars, including myself, have critiqued these films' inaccurate and troubling representations.[129] In their attempts to arrive at general conclusions about this population of mothers, many scholars also flatten out the diversity of women who identify as ESMs. Rosanna Hertz's conclusion in *Single by Chance, Mothers by Choice* captures the dominant scholarly perspective: "I found a category of women who denied that they were at the leading edge of anything and who assiduously shunned the spotlight. They aspired to acceptance in middle-class milieu and alignment with conventional definitions of mother, child, and family."[130] While such denials do appear in the archive of ESM rhetorics, so do a range of positions on the social and political significance of elective single motherhood.

Third, *The Case for Single Motherhood* expands the archive of rhetorical studies. Existing scholarship focuses on women who have been deemed infertile; women who are already mothers, from pregnancy through birth and after; or women in varying stages of motherhood.[131] In contrast to these studies, *The Case for Single Motherhood* examines how women envision themselves as mothers-to-be and their deliberations about who can and should mother. It thereby amends Buchanan's appeal by examining who has *imaginative* "recourse to motherhood" as well.[132] The archive of women's envisioning assembled in this project reveals spoken and unspoken assumptions about who deserves to be a mother and about what assets, qualities, or life circumstances are necessary to mother well.

This book's focus on ESMs' "self-sponsored" writing, rather than on texts that represent and address them, also expands the archive. ESMs' self-sponsored texts provide insight into the complex processes by which women project themselves into motherhood, undertake the identity work and rhetorical self-fashioning that becoming a mother entails, and negotiate dominant ideologies of motherhood and family. Self-sponsored writing is "writing that belongs to the writer, not to an institution."[133] The term "capture[s] writers' practices that are personally and socially oriented" as well as "the agency at work in these acts of literacy."[134] Of most significance to this project is the fact that self-sponsored texts are self-initiated and voluntary. Desire may motivate some academic and workplace writing, but it *always* motivates self-sponsored texts. Absent that desire, the writer would simply not write. While self-sponsored texts are often personally oriented, they are not synonymous with life writing where the topic is always a self, either one's own or someone else's. The topic of self-sponsored texts may be the self, but their defining characteristic is the writer's sense that she has something to say and the desire to say it. At present, those wishing to express themselves in this fashion enjoy abundant opportunities to fund, publish, and circulate self-sponsored texts in a way previously unimagined. Examples include e-platforms, such as Shebooks, the publisher of Rachel Lehmann-Haupt's *DIY Mom: A Solo Parenting Adventure*; self-funded and self-promoted documentaries, such as Nina Davenport's *First Comes Love*; blogs, such as the multiauthored blog hosted by the organization and website Single Mothers by Choice, as well as those published by websites such as HuffPost; and multimedia platforms like YouTube.[135] For this project, these self-sponsored texts are especially critical, given the assumptions about value and audience that guide mainstream publishers' decisions about which projects to support.

Fourth, *The Case for Single Motherhood* extends our understanding of "mothering rhetorics" by demonstrating the inextricable and dynamic relationship of "the rhetorics of reproduction" and "reproducing rhetorics." While all ESMs, and therefore their writings, are conditioned by the "ideological systems and logics of contemporary culture" and some outright reproduce them, others draw on their experience to complicate and contest these "systems" and "logics."[136] As this volume shows, some ESMs draw on their maternal experiences to critique the "*institution*" and its corresponding "systems" and "logics," envisioning maternity and motherhood anew.[137]

Theory and Methodology

I use theories of genre and ethos, as well as reading strategies drawn from scholars of intersectionality, to develop a heuristic with which to analyze how the ESM-composed texts examined in this book define elective single motherhood, cultivate identification with their readers, and legitimize single motherhood in ways that are raced, classed, and embedded in neoliberal logics. As Carolyn Miller asserts, genre theory enables cultural critique. She writes, "As a recurrent, significant action, a genre embodies an aspect of cultural rationality. For the critics, genres can serve both as an index to cultural patterns and as tools for exploring the achievements of particular speakers and writers."[138] The genres under analysis in this project—self-help guidebook, multiauthor blog, and memoir—exploded in popularity in the early 1990s,[139] just as the ESM construct took shape and became a recognizable kind of single mother. This simultaneity is not coincidental: these literatures of the self facilitated the making and transformation of the ESM construct, for, like all genres, they are constitutive and dynamic, "both organizing *and* generating kinds of texts and social actions."[140] My heuristic seeks to reveal how the genres of self in this study work to construct the ESM identity and establish the boundaries of the ESM community. To that end, I ask: What are the typical motives and expectations of self-help guidebooks, multiuser blogs, and memoirs? What kind of relationship does each of these genres establish with its readers, and what role do readers play in shaping that relationship? What is this genre's dominant rhetorical force? For the self-help guidebooks, is it suggesting, directing, and proposing? For the SMC blog, is it sharing and community-building? For the memoirs, is it world-building? And, finally, how do each of these genres' particular affordances enable and support the rhetorical work they aim to do?

To a great extent, the answers to these questions turn on the writer's ethos. Aristotle describes *ethos* as the appeal concerned with "moral character" through which rhetors seek to establish their "practical wisdom" (*phronesis*) and "virtue."[141] In literatures of the self, writers establish their ethos via their honest and truthful representation of their personal experiences. Readers believe, and, further, trust a writer who is able to "manifest the virtues most valued by the culture to and for which [they] speak."[142] This "to and for which" suggests that ethos is as much social and communal as it is personal, a construct grounded in place and relationships as much as it is in character and habits. As Nedra Reynolds observes, "considering the social construction of *ethos* . . . shifts its implications of responsibility from the individual to a negotiation or mediation between the rhetor and the community."[143] To be clear, readers can believe a writer and trust the veracity of their representation, but not find them virtuous. That is, belief is not synonymous with agreement or endorsement. When readers do agree and endorse, or, in rhetorical terms, when they *identify* with the experience and the communal values expressed, they form a relationship with the writer that undergirds and enhances the text's rhetorical pull, force, and power. As a rhetorical critic, then, I ask: How do these ESM authors construct their ethos in ways that resonate and build identification with some readers and exclude others? That is, in what ways does their ethos influence the rhetorical vector and force of their writing?

A writer's social location, particularly in literatures of the self, influences how they construct their ethos as well as its effects on their readers. Social location can encourage or discourage identification by marking points of connection and divergence. ESM-composed texts seek to identify with readers not only through similarities in experience, values, and goals but also through implied affiliations, especially those of race and class. While social location has overt markers, its rhetorical power in ethos more often lies in its suppressed or unstated premises, which function through what rhetoricians call enthymemes, a form of reasoning in which these premises are "assumed by [the] rhetor when inventing and by [the] audience when understanding the argument."[144] Whiteness continues to be an unstated or suppressed premise in most US discourses. As Krista Ratcliffe suggests, "whiteness is a rhetorical trope that lends itself well to a pairing with the enthymeme [because] unstated whiteness functions as an assumed norm, which haunts discourse on any topic."[145] Heeding Lisa Flores's injunction that rhetorical scholarship "signal and center the ways that race has made those histories [we study],"[146] I aim to highlight how whiteness in particular informs and influences the dynamic ESM construct and also shapes the writerly ethos and implied audiences of the ESM-composed texts I analyze in this study.

To achieve these critical and interpretive aims, I use strategies developed by theorists of intersectionality, an analytic sensibility and political praxis that originated in Black feminist thought and activism. Drawing on Kimberlé Crenshaw's metaphor of the "intersection,"[147] intersectionality "conceiv[es] of categories not as distinct but as always permeated by other categories, fluid and changing, always in the process of creating and being created by dynamics of power."[148] Attending to the formation of categories, and the power dynamics that shape them, is particularly important in this study of the ESM construct and identity, given its central argument: that ESM legitimizing requires, often implicitly, the construction and then stigmatizing of other, ostensibly distinct, categories of single mothers whom the ESM legitimizing rhetorics exclude.

To track this mutually constitutive dynamic of maternal legitimacy and illegitimacy in ESM rhetorics, I attend to the *enmeshment* of the ESM construct with that of other single mothers, particularly vis-à-vis the interlocking forces of raced and classed privilege and oppression. In this sense, intersectionality is critical in that it helps us "theorize the convergence, co-constitution, imbrication, or interwovenness of systems of oppression [or privilege]."[149] I also rely on intersectional reading strategies, such as "think[ing] beyond (or against the grain of) familiar boundaries or categories" and "plumb[ing] gaps and silences for suppressed meanings and implications,"[150] to further illuminate the enthymematic and subtextual dimensions of ESM legitimizing and its implied vectors of identification and exclusion.

Overview of Chapters

Chapter 1, "The Invention of the Single Mother by Choice," argues that ESMs created the category of *elective* single motherhood to avoid being grouped with other, highly stigmatized, single mothers. It analyzes how the first two guidebooks for this population of mothers—Jené Stonesifer's *When Baby Makes Two: Single Mothers by Chance or Choice* and Jane Mattes's *Single Mothers by Choice: A Guidebook for Single Women Who Are Considering or Have Chosen Motherhood*—defined ESM in ways that highlighted their differences from other single mothers and their alignment with at least some of the axioms of family values. This chapter highlights the role and power of definition and naming in legitimacy work. Subsequent chapters analyze the deliberations about the definition and significance of elective single motherhood by women who identify as such in self-sponsored texts from the early 2000s to the present day.

Chapter 2, "Rhetorical Sharing: Identity Policing and Community Building on the *Single Mothers by Choice* Blog," illustrates how rhetorical sharing—the consequential sharing of experiences and perspectives with others on the multiauthor blog sponsored by the SMC website—generates awareness of the diversity of maternal identities and perspectives within the SMC community and enables users to understand themselves and the effects of their decisions related to motherhood. I argue that this intimate deliberation on a public forum, not only the doing of single motherhood, fosters a range of ESM identities and stances. Rhetorical sharing leads some users to commit to their pursuit of single motherhood, some to doubt it, and many others who are already mothering to reframe becoming and being an ESM as desirable and empowering.

Chapter 3, "Contesting the Single Mother by Choice Construct in Memoir," explores how Nefertiti Austin's *Motherhood So White*, Robin Silbergleid's *Texas Girl*, Rachel Lehmann-Haupt's *DIY Mom*, and Alexandra

Soiseth's *Choosing You* variously define, contest, and reimagine the meaning of elective single motherhood. It argues that these memoirists' accounts of becoming an ESM are a mode of legitimizing, as they seek, ultimately, to justify who they are to themselves and to their readers. It further demonstrates how the genre of memoir provides an apt vehicle for this work of subject-formation and legitimation. Using the heuristic of the legitimacy continuum, this chapter examines how Austin's, Silbergleid's, and Lehmann-Haupt's memoirs challenge, while Soiseth's reinforces, dominant constructs of good motherhood and family. Despite the affirmative title, the legitimizing in Soiseth's *Choosing You* is defensive and apologetic, whereas Austin's, Silbergleid's, and Lehmann-Haupt's legitimizing counters *doxa* about motherhood and family and envisions new ways of creating and doing family.

Chapter 4, "Guiding in the Aughts: The Constrained Evolution of the Single Mother by Choice Identity," returns full circle, generically speaking, to consider two self-help guidebooks of the aughts, Mikki Morrissette's *Choosing Single Motherhood: The Thinking Woman's Guide* and Louise Sloan's *Knock Yourself Up—No Man? No Problem! A Tell-All Guide to Becoming a Single Mom.* This generic bookending illuminates continuities and shifts in the sociocultural context of ESM legitimizing, highlighting how the legitimizing of these most recent guidebooks reflects the more inclusive, yet still limited, cultural and political climate around family of the early aughts, exemplified by the slogan coined by LGBTQIA+ activists, "Love makes a family." Morrissette's and Sloan's shifting of the argumentative grounds upon which ESMs understand and legitimize their families suggests the potential for coalitional work driven by pride in nonnormative familial structures. However, their guidebooks also reflect the ongoing influence of the neoliberal paradigm on the ESM construct and the concomitant exclusions that paradigm effects.

The conclusion, "Beyond Legitimacy," questions the radical potential of the ESM construct, however defined, and, more broadly, the act of legitimizing itself. Building on John Schilb's notion of "rhetorical refusals" and guided by reproductive justice theory (RJT), it proposes that mothers—so-called ESMs but also others—adopt an *assumptive maternal stance,* one that centers their maternal experiences and thereby minimizes the tendency toward and, perhaps in some instances, obviates the need for, legitimizing and the prejudicial hierarchies such legitimizing inevitably creates and sustains.

My Story

If you'd asked me back when I was in high school whether I'd embrace single motherhood in 2012, the answer would've been an emphatic "No!" In my social milieu, straight *couples* had children. I didn't even know any intentionally single parents or queer couples with kids. Despite the abundance of television shows depicting divorced and blended families in the 1980s, on Thursday nights my father and I watched the nuclear families on *The Cosby Show* and *Family Ties*. As my reference to my father's and my Thursday night ritual suggests, I was intimately familiar with "broken" families. My parents got divorced in 1979, when I was five. By the time I was in high school, most of my friends had divorced parents, too. Our families were not anomalous—the divorce rate in the United States peaked in the late 1970s and early '80s—though perhaps there were more of them in my hometown, Los Angeles, than elsewhere in the country. The message I received during these years was contradictory: one should be married to a member of the opposite sex to have children but needn't stay married to raise them.

As already discussed, "family values" rhetoric crescendoed in the 1980s and '90s. According to its proponents, the health and success of a family requires heterosexual marriage and co-residential fathers. While my progressive mother verbally contested the sexist, racist, classist, and religious undertones of family values rhetoric and its connections to evangelical Christianity, her actions suggested how much this ideology influenced her. Only a year and a half after divorcing my father, she remarried, in part because she felt my stepfather embodied the male strength and stability that she, my sister, and I needed. I've heard her recall many times her memory of the first time my stepfather stood in the doorway of the home she bought after the divorce: "His shoulders were so broad he filled the space." My mother could not imagine her life without a man by her side, and she sincerely believed that children fared better with a residential father or father figure. Her childhood undoubtedly shaped her thinking; having been raised by a divorced mother in the 1950s, she grew up with the stigma associated with a "fatherless" home.

At the same time, my mother identified strongly as a feminist. Her work as an educator and writer mattered to her. So did motherhood. She had a devoted group of female friends, all professionals, several of whom married "late," which at that time (and still today), meant in their mid-to-late thirties. Deena, her best friend since middle school and whom I consider my "second mother," was saving money and speaking with potential fathers in the late 1970s so that she could have a child on her own. We didn't discuss her plans to pursue elective single motherhood until I was in my midtwenties, but Deena's independence and out-of-the-box thinking influenced other aspects of her life and provided a powerful model of single womanhood. While my mother's friends eventually married, the ongoing intensity of their bonds with one another demonstrated to me the importance of friendship, no matter one's marital status.

My father marched to the beat of his own drummer and encouraged me to do the same. He had girlfriends occasionally and even joined a dating service after my parents divorced, but it was clear that, for him, finding a romantic partner was not a priority. His life as a single man countered the mythology of marriage, the notion that "marriage delivers as its ultimate reward the most sought-after American prize: happiness. Not just garden-variety happiness, but deep and meaningful well-being. A sense of fulfillment that a single person cannot even fathom."[151] It never seemed to occur to my dad that he was bereft because he didn't have a girlfriend or wife, that "one all-purpose, all-important partner who can meet our every emotional and social need."[152] I do remember him saying, however, that he was eternally grateful to my mother for insisting that they have children. He had not thought that he wanted to be a father, and, until the divorce, had not appreciated us or spent much time being one. After the divorce, however, he devoted himself to my sister and me. He often said that he could not imagine his life without us, that we were hands-down the best thing that had ever happened to him, and that he felt sorry for people who didn't have children. Though this was not his intention, the message he conveyed was that children, not romantic love, were the key to happiness and fulfillment. This admittedly disputable claim took root in me.

Meanwhile, the marriages into which I had the most intimate view, my mother and father's and then my mother and my stepfather's, were difficult, hardly selling points for a coupled life. It is possible that my witnessing their marital turmoil made me leery of the institution. This response, however, would distinguish me from my peers. That is to say, if I responded to the marital turmoil that I witnessed by opting out of coupledom rather than opting into a committed marriage, I am an outlier in my social class. While marriage rates in the United States have declined overall since 1970, the rate of marriage for those who are educated and middle- or upper-income has remained steady. At the same time, the divorce rate has declined in the last thirty years, most dramatically, again, for those with a college education. To put it simply, the majority of my generational peers have gotten and stayed married: "Of college-educated people who married in the early 2000s, only about 11 percent divorced by their seventh anniversary, the last year for which data is available."[153] It would seem that the family values rhetoric we imbibed in the 1990s stuck, at least for some of us.

I attended Columbia University in New York City in the mid-1990s. *Sex and the City* first aired in 1998, the year after I graduated, but the city was already "serving as spouse, and, sometimes, true love" for educated professional single women during my college years.[154] While my largely female group of friends and I talked about romance, and most of us at that time identified as straight so we were talking about guys, that topic didn't dominate our conversations. We immersed ourselves in our studies, engaged politically, and explored the city. Some of us had boyfriends (myself included), but men were largely peripheral. Our female friendships formed the core of our college experience. I still find that I gravitate toward women who married later or who did not expect to marry at all. And my closest friends are those who are as apt to disappear for a while because of the work they are doing as they are because they fell in love.

Twenty-five years have passed since we graduated. Our friendships with one another have longer histories, and in some cases, have outlived our romances. Some of us are married; some aren't. One of the married ones jokes that she would never have considered dating her now-husband if she had not been living abroad, far from what I call "framily"—the friends that become family. She also insists that while she adores her husband and son and would not wish for a different life, she would have been as content had she not gotten married or become a mother, as she was quite fulfilled by her work as a human rights activist and as a friend, daughter, and sister. One of the unmarried friends, who is deeply engaged in her work, passionate about her framily, and has an active romantic life with men to whom she does not seek commitment, has frozen her eggs so that she can become a single mother in her midforties. My oldest sister, who was eager to marry but didn't meet the right man until she was in her early forties, wrote about her commitment to maintaining her friendships, and her husband's promise to respect them, in her wedding vows. Meanwhile, I became a single mother at age thirty-seven, a decision I could not imagine having made without the support of my "framily," including Marcela, my sons' godmother. My quite happily married friends work hard to sustain their friendships, and my unmarried friends do not pine for marriage, finding succor and sustenance in their friendships and in work. My admittedly unscientific sample underlines the truth of the assertion that "marriage and its ancillary, committed dating, are simply not the only relationships that sustain and help to give shape, direction, and passion to female life, at least not for all women."[155]

I don't mean to suggest that I did not have romantic relationships during these years, or that I did not entertain the hope that I would meet "the one." In an effort to do so, I expanded the pool of romantic possibilities to include those substantially older and younger; male and female; working-class and professional. When Paul, a man with whom I explored Rio de Janeiro in my late twenties, suggested that I, like many of his unmarried women friends back in London, was in fact content being single despite protestations to the contrary, I, well, protested. I had done the same when, a few years earlier, my aunt suggested that I would meet Mr. Right only when and if I truly wanted to do so. I had to admit, if only to myself, that I felt mildly panicked when my romantic other expected to take precedence over my friends; that I wondered how I would sustain a romance and my friendships; and, finally that, in my more honest moments, I asked myself which mattered more to me. It would take me more than a decade, however, to realize that such binaristic and hierarchical thinking about relationships was neither helpful nor reflective of what I actually experienced in relationships with the important people in my life, and further, that I was okay on my own, indeed that I was flourishing.

I had queer friends in high school and college, but straight assumptions, though I was not cognizant of them as such, governed my imaginary until I entered my mid-thirties. By this I mean that I assumed I would marry and have children, and that my relationships with my spouse and children would inevitably take priority over other bonds in my life, including those with my natal family and framily. Post-college life altered those assumptions. After graduating and moving back to Los Angeles, I lived in two historically gay neighborhoods: Los Feliz and Long Beach's "gay ghetto." I became friends with adults whose intimacies did not revolve around monogamous coupledom and who did not assume that romantic relationships necessarily lead to marriage and offspring. This exposure to queer intimacies cast both my current life and future expectations in a new light. I realized that I experienced fulfilling and varied intimacies and loneliness when I was single *and* when I was coupled. I found myself envisioning a fulfilling future that did not necessarily entail marriage. I still had to travel quite an emotional and intellectual distance to embrace the idea of single motherhood, but this realization about romantic partnership was a necessary first step on that path. I am still curious about the intimacy that develops within a committed romantic relationship and am open to experiencing it, but I no longer believe that it is intimacy's only or supreme form. Simply put, intimacy and family are not one-size-fits-all categories. As Bella DePaulo aptly states, "The overvaluing of couples places one meaning of the word *family* at the tips of our tongues, when other meanings are at least as deserving of that place of honor . . . Why is the question about 'family' so much more likely to be asked than one that, to me, is far more interesting: Who are the important people in your life?"[156]

As I got older, models of elective single motherhood surfaced—or I became more attentive to them. In my early twenties, I saw the Dutch film *Antonia's Line*, a feminist fairy tale of sorts. Danielle, daughter of the eponymous Antonia, decides to become a mother but not a wife or partner. While repairing a fence, she says to Antonia, "Mom, I want a baby," to which Antonia responds quizzically, "Whatever give you that idea?" and then asks, "How about a husband to go with it?," to which Danielle responds, "No, I don't think so." Danielle later makes the same point to Letta, her "sperm broker," stating, "We urgently needs the service of a man. Just to get me pregnant. I don't want him into the bargain. A child is all I want." Letta offers "the service" of one of her relatives, and Danielle gets pregnant in short order. With the exception of the village priest, no one comments on the origins of her pregnancy or on the structure of the family unit she has created. The understated representation of elective single motherhood in *Antonia's Line* suggests that it is, quite literally, unremarkable—just one path to motherhood. At the time, I did not consciously register Danielle's influence on me, but I did include *Antonia's Line* on my list of favorite movies. Upon reviewing it years later, I marveled at its representation of single motherhood and wondered if, on an unconscious level, I considered Danielle a role model.

At age twenty-six, the summer before I started graduate school, I read Barbara Kingsolver's essay collection *High Tide in Tucson*.[157] When I first read *High Tide*, the thought that I'd become a single mother myself—by choice to boot—hadn't occurred to me. Looking back, however, I believe that Kingsolver's essays planted a seed. Several of them concern her family's sojourn in the Canary Islands to escape the first Gulf War war-mania of the early 1990s. I remember being struck by the seeming ease with which Kingsolver packed up their lives and moved abroad. Scant references to Kingsolver's then-husband led me to mistakenly assume that she and her daughter traveled to Spain alone. Upon rereading the essays in early 2012 in anticipation of the birth of my firstborn, however, I noted that Kingsolver's husband and the father of her daughter did in fact accompany them to Spain; I just hadn't registered his presence. Perhaps I hadn't because other essays in the collection discuss single motherhood and challenge "family values," so dominant in the 1990s (and also personally relevant to Kingsolver, who eventually divorced the father of her daughter and thus became a single mother). That I unconsciously merged the essays about international travel and single motherhood suggests my attraction to the autonomy enjoyed by an unattached woman. I recall that only a few months after reading them, I told Emily, one of my childhood friends, that I would become a single mother if I had not partnered by the time I was in my late thirties. Emily told me that she wasn't surprised to hear this, as I had mentioned doing so when we were in our teens.

Fast-forward six years to December 2007. I was now thirty-three and at the tail end of my graduate studies. One day, Marcela and I watched a thirty-something Australian woman and her ten-year-old son lug duffel bags across a train platform in southern India. We ended up sharing the same compartment with them on the train and got to hear her story. She told us that she'd accidentally gotten pregnant. Both she and the father knew that they didn't want to stay together, but she decided to keep the baby. She always loved to travel and decided that she could and would combine being a mother with that passion. Fortunately, her son seemed to enjoy it as much as she. They had traveled in Africa several times, and this was their third trip to India. She told us that, as a young boy, her son would see a church in Australia and call it a mosque because, at that stage in his life, he'd seen more mosques than churches. Here was a real-life single mother leading a life that I could envision and desire.

Closer to home, Vida, Marcela's friend and roommate, provided another example of single motherhood and a source of inspiration. Vida and her daughter, Isabella, moved into Marcela's house in the fall of 2008, when Isabella was three, and lived there until 2013. Vida did not (and still does not) describe herself as an ESM, but "elective" is nevertheless an apt adjective to describe her. Having decided that it was not in her or her daughter's best interests to co-parent with her daughter's father, she immigrated from Monterrey, Mexico, to the United States, when Isabella was an infant, knowing that doing so would most likely sever their tie with Isabella's father. As an undocumented immigrant, then and now, Vida faces a distinctive set of circumstances and challenges, ones largely unrecognized in the literature in English about and by ESMs, which centers the mothering experience of citizens, whether of the United States or of select countries of the British Commonwealth. At the same time, our conversations reveal points of convergence in our thinking about and experience of motherhood, namely our desire to be mothers, partnered or not; our belief that children can thrive in a single-parent home; and, finally, our sense that our professional lives are as integral to our identity and well-being as motherhood. Despite the significant differences in our experiences of single motherhood, we recognize these points of overlap and affinity.

These fictional and real-life role models of single motherhood fell on ground made fertile by class and racial privilege. My father died in 2005 and left the bulk of his estate to my sister and me. Despite popular representations and assumptions to the contrary, not all ESMs are wealthy. However, the financial cushion provided by this inheritance has profoundly shaped *my* experience of motherhood. It enabled me to access artificial reproductive technologies and has ameliorated the practical challenges of single motherhood from conception onward. It now allows me to afford quality childcare and do the "self-care," if only in the form of an hour-long walk by myself on Saturdays and Sundays, that advocates insist all parents need, but that most cannot afford. This class privilege shields me from the stigma of single motherhood. I enjoy most of the perks of a dual income or high single income family, including the kudos accorded to parents who can afford to parent "well," whether in the form of enrichment activities or play therapy.[158] My whiteness is another privilege in the specific sense that I never worry that my single motherhood confirms prejudices about people of my race, a concern of some women of color, especially African Americans, who have long been single mothers by chance and by choice and roundly castigated by dominant white American culture for being so. As historian Linda Nicholson observes, ideologies of race, class, and age shape our perceptions of mothers. She writes, "A well-dressed, young, white woman alone with a baby will not be perceived as an 'unwed mother,' whereas an African-American woman from a range of classes may very well be."[159] Asha Bandele explains how blackness contributed to her fears about being perceived as a single mother when she became pregnant with Rashid, her then-husband who was incarcerated: "Being a black woman factored into the image piece: I mean, did I look like some statistic walking around pregnant with no man in sight?"[160] Indeed, in certain contexts, white professional women's decision to defer marriage and pursue single motherhood "can be understood as beneficial; they can be seen as social progress and perhaps part of a moment, or at least a glamorized trend."[161] In the United States in the third decade of the twenty-first century, I am considered (by some) to be hip and progressive, while low-income Latina and Black single mothers, especially if they are young, are deemed pathological.

These various threads came together in February 2008 during a job interview at the University of Colorado in Colorado Springs. My future colleague mentioned professors in the anthropology and biology departments who had had pursued motherhood as single women. She also noted that the university appreciated the role model these professors offered to the large number of single mother students at our university. This was a story told in passing, but one that would figure prominently in my self-imagining and eventual pursuit of motherhood as a single woman. Andrew was born in July 2012, Marcelo in January 2016, and Beatrice in December 2018. Together, we have created what Kath Weston calls, in her eponymous book about queer family formations, a "chosen family."

From the spring of 2011 (when I first decided to pursue motherhood) to Beatrice's first birthday in December 2019, I devoted much of my energy and attention to issues such as conception, pregnancy, birth, breastfeeding, and early child development milestones. In ways both trivial and consequential, my status as a lone parent influenced my engagement with these matters, and I found that writing by other ESMs, most of which focuses on the process of becoming a mother and the early years of parenting, provided helpful insights and guidance. In these early years, I took pride in my children's development, in the family traditions we created, and in the overall happy mood of our home. Though not consciously, I believe I celebrated our family in part to legitimize, both to myself and to others, my pursuit of single motherhood.

The subtext of the stories I shared with family and friends about happenings chez Mack was a cry: See, we are doing just fine!

Increasingly, my legitimizing efforts are directed more toward my children, and they reflect my engagement with and responses to their feelings about my choices around motherhood and our family structure. As they age, new issues surface, most of which defy immediate, practical responses, and many of which they will explore and negotiate with me, but also on their own and with others. In my children's early years, it was easier not to see, or simply to minimize, their separateness. How to determine where my body and emotions began and theirs ended? I would think, you grew inside me; you are growing now, because of the milk I provide, which you drink from my breast; you see the world I choose to share with you. All true, but not the whole story. As any observant parent knows, we control far less about our children's lives, even from the moment of conception, than we assume and than we might like. As Andrew Solomon avers, "There is no such thing as reproduction. When two people [or one!] decide to have a baby, they engage in an act of *production*."[162]

My growing realization of my children's separateness coincided with the emergence of new questions, ones in which my children and I have different investments and toward which we have different practical and emotional stances. How should I respond to their occasional expression of their desire to have a father? And, furthermore, what does "father" mean to them? How do they imagine this man—this father figure—would participate in and contribute to our family life? What kind of relationship should I/we/they pursue with their half-siblings, a.k.a. "diblings," and with my sons' biological father, whose identity I learned when the eldest was six years old? What message does my creation of our family as a single woman send to my children about parenthood, domesticity, and family? How might a romantic relationship figure in the family structure I have created, and how do I explain the nature of this relationship to my children? As my children and I weave the fabric of our family and discover ourselves within and outside of that unit, we explore these questions separately and together.

I recognize that many children and their caretakers, especially those doing family outside the nuclear model, grapple with these or similar questions. I continue to ponder to what extent our family's relatively unique origin story makes it *meaningfully* different from others, and if so, in what particular ways. In so doing, I grapple with human beings' paradoxical relationship to difference: "Ordinary people insist that they are really unique, while extraordinary people maintain that they are really just like everyone else."[163] This project demonstrates that ESMs, in their quest for legitimacy, do both: insist on their specialness in some contexts and maintain that they are just like partnered mothers in others. As the title of the conclusion of this project, "Beyond Legitimacy," suggests, I'm left wondering how ESMs might conceive and talk about themselves were they less concerned with legitimizing themselves, via comparisons to other mothers, and fully open to the possibilities of being and relating that elective single motherhood makes available. I look forward to pursuing that line of inquiry in my next book.

CHAPTER 1

THE INVENTION OF THE SINGLE MOTHER BY CHOICE

Strive to make your legacy one that includes your child's affirmation: "I may not have a dad, but I have the best mom I could ever imagine."

—Jené Stonesifer, *When Baby Makes Two*

[We are] single women who chose to become mothers; single mothers who are mature and responsible and who feel empowered rather than victimized.

—Jane Mattes, *Single Mothers by Choice*

On April 29, 1992, an all-white jury acquitted four white Los Angeles Police Department officers who had brutally beaten Rodney King, a Black man, whom they had stopped for speeding after a brief chase. The protests that erupted in south central Los Angeles in response to the verdict turned violent. Riots, arson, and looting continued for six days, a response to the injustice of the verdict, inequality, and systemic racism in the city and to the historically toxic relations between the Los Angeles Police department and Black and Latino communities. Despite division within the Republican party, the White House cleaved fast to analyses that attributed the events in Los Angeles to the failure of the Great Society programs of the 1960s and '70s. Then, in a curious turn, in a speech to the Commonwealth Club on May 19, then-Vice President Dan Quayle attributed the "lawless social anarchy" in Los Angeles "to the breakdown of the family structure, personal responsibility and social order in too many areas of our society" and declared that those who bear babies "irresponsibly" are "simply wrong."[1] In the peroration of the speech, Quayle made an aside to the decision of Murphy Brown, a white TV sitcom character, to pursue single motherhood: "It doesn't help matters when prime time TV has Murphy Brown—a character who supposedly epitomizes today's intelligent, highly paid, professional woman—mocking the importance of fathers, by bearing a child alone, and calling it just another 'lifestyle choice.'"[2] Despite the fact that most of Quayle's speech focused on the problems of the "underclass," it became known as "the Murphy Brown" speech.

Quayle's conflation of Black and white single mothers tacitly acknowledged demographic trends that disturbed some people in the United States. As critical race scholar Patricia Hill Collins observes, it was Quayle's "*mixture*, not mere juxtaposition, of images of white and black women's unmarried bodies: corrupt by virtue of their autonomy, their uncontrollability" that provoked such strong responses to the speech.[3] By creating and maintaining families without men, these mothers defied a patriarchal gendered order and revealed the increasing alignment of Black and white family structures that did not hew to the nuclear model. Quayle's was not an isolated voice. In a 1992 op-ed in the *New York Times*, sociologist David Popenhoe observed ominously, "Ponder this fact: the white family structure today is astonishingly similar to the black family structure in 1965." In 1993 Charles Murray, another sociologist, raised the alarm about a growing "white underclass."[4] Children's advocate Marian Wright Edelman likewise lamented this demographic trend: "Today, two-thirds of all black and one-fifth of all white babies are born to never-married mothers. And if it's wrong for a 13-year-old inner-city girl to have a baby without the benefit of marriage, it's wrong for the rich celebrities, too, and we ought to stop putting them on the cover of *People* magazine."[5] These unlikely bedfellows—Quayle, Popenhoe, Murray, and Edelman—together called attention to a phenomenon that had steadily increased since 1960: *white* unmarried motherhood. Collectively, their rhetoric framed "single motherhood [as] a Black cultural trait that [was] creeping into white homes."[6] Indeed, from 1968 to 1994, the fraction of births to white unmarried mothers grew from approximately 1 percent to 26 percent.[7] Murphy Brown mothers represented only a small portion of that 26 percent, but they generated outsized attention and opprobrium because they were largely middle-class white women bucking the dominant norms of family.[8] The effrontery of their motherhood was compounded by the fact that they were failing to adhere to white middle-class, presumably achievable, standards of motherhood and family; indeed, to some critics, they appeared to be flouting these standards.[9] These mothers thus found themselves doubly on the defensive, needing not only to legitimize the families they created as stable and sound in a cultural context that found them deficient but also to justify their having willfully and knowingly violated dominant norms. In 1992, then, Murphy Brown mothers stood at a crossroads: embrace their affiliation and potential alliance with other single mothers or mark their difference from them, while simultaneously demonstrating their alignment with the idealized "traditional" American family and the then-dominant discourse of "family values." Unfortunately, many opted for the latter through their construction and adoption of the label Single Mothers by Choice (SMC).

Names and labels are rhetorically motivated and rhetorically powerful.[10]

They establish and reinforce power differentials and hierarchies and thus frequently figure in legitimizing efforts. The women who came to call themselves SMCs understood the power of the name. Jane Mattes, the founder of the organization Single Mothers by Choice, recounts, "One of our lengthiest discussions involved what we should name the organization. We felt strongly that we wanted the name to convey that it was our choice and our decision to become single mothers."[11] The group's chosen name—SMC—emphasized their economic autonomy and ability to choose motherhood and avoided directly challenging prevailing axioms about the importance of fathers and two-parent homes. It marked SMC as virtuous mothers, able participants in the cultural logics of family values, despite their unmarried status. This chapter tracks the rhetorical fashioning of the SMC label and construct through an analysis of the first two guidebooks to elective single motherhood, both published in 1994: Jené Stonesifer's *When Baby Makes Two: Single Mothers by Chance or by Choice* and Jane Mattes's *Single Mothers by Choice: A Guidebook for Single Women Who Are Considering or Have Chosen Motherhood.* Stonesifer's and Mattes's guidebooks established the grounds and refined the meaning of the SMC label. I discuss Stonesifer's guidebook first, as it conveys the fuzziness of the lines separating the broad category "single mother" from groups like widows and divorcées and thereby highlights the rhetorical work necessary to establish and police the boundaries of the SMC construct. While Stonesifer devotes separate sections to single mothers "by chance" and "by choice," she suggests that it is the total absence of fathers in these single mother families that distinguishes them. Jane Mattes, in contrast, anchors the definition of the SMC on different grounds, and, in so doing, makes the identity more exclusive and resonant with postfeminist neoliberal rhetorics of the 1990s: For Mattes, autonomy and choice mark an SMC, not the absence of a father in the family she creates. Though Stonesifer and Mattes define the SMC differently, for each, the classed and raced "welfare queen" functions as the implicit foil for the single mothers they envision and address.

Compulsory motherhood, a maternal ideology that suggests that women *do* and *should* desire motherhood, that they will gain intense satisfaction from it, and, that those who do not become mothers are not "real" women, plays a critical role in SMC legitimizing.[12] For the most part, women of color in the United States have not experienced compulsory motherhood in the same way or to the same degree as white women. As rhetorician Natalie Fixmer-Oraiz observes, "The histories of women marginalized by and within heteronuclear white supremacist culture are decidedly dissimilar to compulsory motherhood, and in fact reveal the opposite—sustained, institutionalized efforts to curtail or prohibit fertility and motherhood."[13] The SMC name and identity bear the imprint of these divergent maternal histories and capitalize on the affordances of the ideology of compulsory motherhood for middle-class white women. Most immediately, the SMC construct was impelled by the specter of the single Black mother in the public imaginary in the last quarter of the twentieth century, which provided the foil against which SMCs, who were imagined as middle-class white women, defined and legitimized themselves.[14] In illuminating the construction and rhetorical aims of the SMC construct and revealing how its success depended on pejorative construction of the contemporary and historical single mothers who fell outside its ambit, I advance feminist rhetorical inquiry into the power of maternal rhetorics to further the interests of some women while, in so doing, undermining the interests of others. This analysis also highlights the dynamics of maternal rhetorics, whereby the legitimization of one group of mothers often depends on the delegitimization of others. The SMC construct was enabled and necessitated by, enmeshed with and dependent upon, the delegitimizing of other, less worthy, single mothers. Stonesifer's and Mattes's negative legitimizing thus demonstrates the reciprocal relationship between rhetors and the available means as it drew on prevailing family values rhetoric about "good" mothers and family, and, through the uptake of the axioms and claims of that rhetoric, reinforced it. Ultimately, their legitimizing only slightly expanded the existing tent of virtuous motherhood, leaving most of its class, race, and sexual exclusions intact.

Single Motherhood and Race in the Postwar Era

In the United States, all women's reproductive capacities have been controlled and directed, though in different ways and toward different ends. The discursive and material forces that have shaped and guided reproduction provided the "available means" for Stonesifer's and Mattes's legitimizing of the women who would come to call themselves SMCs. Until very recently, white, native-born, heterosexual, married middle-class women in the United States were expected to become mothers and thus contribute to the "white family imperative."[15] This targeted pronatalism found especially fertile ground in the sociopolitical culture of the postwar era.[16] According to historian Elaine Tyler May, "The ideology of domesticity, which centered on the nuclear family with children, came to embody the hope for the future of the nation and the ultimate achievement of happiness and personal fulfillment for its citizens."[17] During this time, the birthrates across all US populations grew, fueling what we now call the baby boom.[18] The childfree were seen as unpatriotic, "as downright un-American."[19] At the same time, the assumption that motherhood should occur within heterosexual marriage became explicit and emphasized. "The postwar definition of family strongly suggested a new definition of motherhood—that it could not be achieved without a husband, outside of a properly constructed family—as postwar 'womanhood' could not be achieved without a man."[20] Women who resisted marriage and motherhood altogether were suspect and "likely to be labeled neurotic and [thus] unfit for parenthood."[21] Unwed mothers, meanwhile, posed a different, though equally troubling, "threat to the healthy, procreating, consuming family, the bedrock of postwar society in the United States."[22] Historian Rickie Solinger demonstrates how "regardless of race, [unwed mothers] were defined and treated as deviants threatening to the social order. Single, pregnant girls and women of whatever race shared the debased status of illegitimate mother: a mother with no rights, or a female who had, according to the dominant culture, no right to be a mother."[23] Given this dominant perception and corresponding treatment of nonmarital pregnancy, legitimizing single motherhood, both to the women who were considering pursuing it and to society at large, posed a significant rhetorical challenge.

In the postwar era, social norms deemed motherhood outside of marriage unacceptable, no matter the race of the mother. As historian Rickie Solinger demonstrates in *Wake Up Little Susie: Single Pregnancy and Race before Roe v. Wade*, however, race and racism determined the particular experience of unwed mothers, the political significance of their pregnancies, and the social meaning assigned to the children they bore.[24] Biological, and later cultural, determinism shaped the public response to single Black mothers after 1945. State policies directed at Black women treated their unwed pregnancies as the inevitable result of their assumed hypersexuality and inability to form normative families: "Black unwed motherhood was often treated, publicly and politically, as a status devoid of affective, traditional, cultural, or historical dimensions; it was simply a biologically determined fact."[25] Most maternity homes excluded Black women, either explicitly in their policies or implicitly in practice.[26] The few truly integrated or Black-only maternity homes served relatively few Black mothers.[27] Because the adoption "market" favored white babies, and because Black people were leery about engaging with official systems and had long-standing informal practices of "taking in" nonbiological children and making them kin, Black babies were typically either raised by their biological mothers or adopted informally. [28] Long-standing networks of care and support in the Black community supported the bearing and raising of these children.[29] As welfare programs began to serve women of color in the 1960s, however, the state took on a more interventionist and activist role in Black family life. Black mothers were scapegoated, "blamed for the population explosion, for escalating welfare costs, for the existence of unwanted babies, and blamed for the tenacious grip of poverty on blacks in America."[30] As law professor Dorothy Roberts meticulously demonstrates, Black single motherhood, Black fertility, indeed Black life, came to be perceived as "major social problem[s]," best resolved through punitive measures, like child exclusions, euphemistically referred to as "family caps"; required birth control measures; and sterilization campaigns.[31] In a disgraceful simultaneity, these efforts to curtail the reproduction of poor women of all races and ethnicities coincided with the pronatalist directives aimed at white middle-class women: just as "white women's domesticity and motherhood were valorized and encouraged across a variety of contexts," poor women were "being subjected to forced sterilization or targeted by state family planning services."[32]

In sharp contrast, the postwar domestic ideology and corresponding practices offered white women who became pregnant outside of marriage a second chance. While maternity homes in the first decades of the twentieth century prepared unwed white mothers for lives as so-called ruined or outcast women, postwar maternity homes "prepar[ed] [them] to relinquish their illegitimate babies and groom[ed] them to resume the roles of normative young womanhood—coed, coquette, and bride."[33] That is, they aimed to erase the episode of unwed motherhood entirely. Indeed, the young women's unmarried status negated their motherhood: "White, unwed mothers became, by definition, unfit mothers, in fact, not mothers at all."[34] Newborn children were placed in closed adoptions and the young women were returned to their homes, ostensibly ready to have the "right" kind of family. This opportunity to return to the normative cultural fold, however, came with a high price tag: shame and erasure. As rhetorician Heather Brook Adams explains, "Shame was fueled to the unwed mother, who was expected to hide her pregnancy to preserve the reputation of her family, herself, and her unborn, 'illegitimate' child, who would be 'given' to a married couple."[35] The maternity homes thus promoted the "family agenda" of the era in two key ways. First, they increased the supply of adoptable white babies available to worthy parents (i.e., married white couples who were unable to conceive themselves). And, second, they "facilitate[d] an unwed mother's reconstruction."[36] For, by enabling the unwed mother to distance herself, quite literally, from the product of her errant ways, they permitted her to make herself anew: "The girl could undergo psychological treatment; she could change. She could escape being permanently defined by her error. With professional help, in a triumph of individualism, she could prevail over her past, her mistakes, her neuroses."[37] Thus remade, she became a woman ready for childbearing within the culturally sanctioned nuclear family. In this way, "Rhetorics of shame enact a rhetorical strategy for upholding 'Mother' as a god-term that articulates with culturally sanctioned concepts of home, morality, national and self-sacrifice."[38]

These norms shifted over time. By the last quarter of the twentieth century, the women's movement and sexual revolution had altered the material, and thus the rhetorical, landscape for all single mothers, though, as always, with different effects depending on their social location. Record numbers of women of all races, married and unmarried, including mothers, entered the paid workforce, undermining the claim that single mothers could not support a child.[39] At the same time, more liberal attitudes toward birth control, premarital sex, and female sexuality helped to decrease the shame and disgrace of single pregnancy. The labels used to describe single mothers evolved to reflect these shifts: "The more autonomous sounding term 'single mother' replace[d] the pitiful and old-fashioned sobriquet 'unwed mother.'"[40] Though the adjective "single" still indexed the importance of marital status and the assumption that partnered parenthood was the norm, "single" was a more neutral characterization of these mothers than "unwed."[41] Increasingly, white single mothers asserted control over the narrative and consequences of their "*oops* pregnancies."[42] White women who, a decade earlier, would have likely succumbed to pressures to relinquish their child for adoption began instead to claim their right to mother. As Sue-Ellen, a young single mother profiled in *Seventeen* asserted, "You don't understand: The baby is MINE. I'm going to get a job and raise my baby . . . I wanted the baby, and I wanted it for myself."[43] Though most of these mothers had experienced an unplanned pregnancy and were thus single "by chance," not "by choice," their increasing visibility and resistance to the stigma around their single motherhood created rhetorical openings the women who would come to identify as SMCs would seize.

Concern about the fiscal and social costs of increasing rates of single motherhood, in addition to long-standing moral concerns, made the inclusion of "choice" in the SMC moniker a rhetorically savvy decision. "Choice" marked SMC as both financially autonomous and virtuously maternal. As Rickie Solinger explains in *Beggars and Choosers*, her history of reproductive (in)justice in the decades following *Roe v. Wade*, "In an era of redefining motherhood, 'choice' became a very useful concept for sorting out good women from bad, responsible women from irresponsible women, independent women from dependent women."[44] The logic was circular and classist. "Good choosers" were mothers, like SMCs, who were personally responsible and financially independent and could thus afford motherhood. Conversely, the logic implied, "women who cannot afford to make choices are not fit to be mothers"—or to be mothers at all.[45] SMCs could be "fit" mothers because they had the material privileges necessary to raise their children without public assistance, and, therefore, they had the right to be mothers. In the end, then, "Despite the normalization of [some kinds] of single motherhood in these years, *real choice* remained elusive for those who lacked this cluster of resources."[46] "Choice" also underscored SMCs' maternal desire: good mothers wanted to mother. At a time characterized by cultural unease in some quarters about women's economic independence, sexual autonomy, and ability *not* to choose motherhood, SMCs' intent to mother mitigated concerns about their single-parent families and the threat they posed to traditional gender relations and roles.

Meanwhile, poor single mothers faced more obstacles in (re)directing the narratives of their single motherhood. Though the expansion of eligibility requirements made Aid for Dependent Children (ADC), commonly referred to as welfare, readily available to Black mothers only in the mid-1960s, they were swiftly and erroneously assumed to be the program's primary beneficiaries.[47] In short order, critiques of the program took on racialized, in addition to classist, dimensions.[48] Though Black mothers' righteous participation was evidence of their commitment to support their children, it was used against them, presented instead as proof of their dependency, social depravity, and lack of worth ethic."[49] Public discourse characterized Black welfare recipients not as devoted mothers and deserving recipients but as oversexed, prolifically fertile, and averse to labor and therefore reliant on welfare.[50] This racialized antiwelfare logic unspooled as follows: "Black unwed mothers were guilty of being without a man, thus in some way independent, or at least 'on the loose,' in way that violated gender norms. At the same time, they were guilty of being too dependent, their lives sustained by public assistance. In this way, they violated the ethic of self-reliance."[51] Within this framework, welfare recipients defied "all-American" fantasies of autonomy and self-sufficiency: "The welfare-dependent single mother is finally the synecdoche, the shortest possible shorthand, for the pathology of poor, urban, black culture."[52] She became "a standard feature of public discourse,"[53] depicted as "the agent of destruction, the creation of the pathological, black, urban, poor family from which all ills flow; a monster creating crack dealers, addicts, muggers, and rapists."[54] On Lindal Buchanan's continuum of "Good Mother" and "Devil Woman," the mother on welfare represented a particular iteration of the Devil Woman: though not childless, she was self-centered, materialistic, immoral, self-indulgent, and sensual.[55] The "welfare queen" thus provided an ideal foil to the SMC. SMCs could trumpet their financial autonomy, a position they achieved despite their single status, and thereby contrast themselves to those "other" single mother who had the gall not only to get pregnant out of wedlock but then to seek financial assistance from the state to support their mothering.

The neoliberal family values context of the last decades of the twentieth century thus provided rich, yet complicated, grounds for SMC legitimizing. The long-standing US emphasis on self-reliance, reinforced by neoliberal *doxa* of personal responsibility and autonomy, and enduring pronatalist sentiment directed at middle-class white women provided affordances with which SMCs could and did legitimize themselves. Nevertheless, their motherhood still violated persistent, essentialist, and racialized beliefs about gender and family, which existed alongside and in tension with the cultural changes brought about by the sexual revolution and women's movement. The lingering and "communicable" shame of single motherhood, which "functioned to maintain an ideal of morally pure motherhood recognized within the context of marriage," still informed and shaped SMC legitimizing.[56] For, by definition, SMCs were neither wives nor participants in "heteronuclear family formation[s]," which, alongside whiteness and wealth, undergirded "the capacity to be valued and publicly lauded for motherhood."[57] With deft rhetorical maneuvering, Jené Stonesifer and Jane Mattes sought to navigate the crosscurrents of this rhetorical maelstrom. Sadly, the definitional lifeboat they constructed reinforced the forces of classism and racism and excluded most single mothers.

Self-Help Guidebooks

Stonesifer and Mattes leveraged the rhetorical power of self-help, an ascendant genre in the 1990s, to further their distinguishing and legitimizing efforts.[58] Self-help literature "defines its readers as insufficient, as lacking some essential feature of adequacy . . . and then offers itself as the solution."[59] It urges readers "to chart their own courses, to 'master' their destinies, and to make themselves over.'"[60] The reader, now armed with the necessary know-how, then does the labor to make herself anew. Cultural critic Micki McGee describes this reader as a "belabored self"; she is the "subject and object of [her] own efforts at self-improvement."[61] Self-help literature takes many forms: guidebooks, how-to books, even some memoirs. What these forms have in common is their rhetorical aim: the construction of a different self, one that is able to become a different and better person, in some instances simply by reading the self-help text. The genre facilitated the therapeutic and self-making work of prospective SMCs and provided an ideal conduit for the SMC ideology, which emphasized the autonomy and agency of a self-reliant woman.

The readers of Stonesifer's and Mattes's guidebooks were ideal recipients of self-help rhetoric. They sought not only guidance regarding the practical matters of single motherhood but also emotional sustenance, as single motherhood, while increasingly prevalent in the 1990s, and, in some circles more tolerated, was not yet wholly culturally sanctioned. The very existence of these self-help texts constituted their readers as an acknowledged group, and, in so doing, provided reassurance to at least some of them. Stonesifer and Mattes aimed to help their readers envision and desire this still unorthodox path. They did so by acknowledging their concerns and then by demonstrating that their fears, if not unfounded, could be ameliorated by being the kind of mother their guidebooks prescribed. Ultimately, Stonesifer and Mattes aimed both to produce a certain kind of person—a single woman confident in her abilities to raise a child—and to shift societal attitudes toward this subset of single mothers. In this sense, they worked rhetorically and ideologically to legitimize individual single mothers and the institution of single motherhood within the strict parameters established by their guidebooks, and their legitimizing was directed both at single women who were considering motherhood and at their critics.[62] To these ends, they provided information and practical advice about how to *do* single motherhood and suggested that, *when done correctly*, it could be a positive experience for children and mothers, or at least not irreparably damaging.

Jené Stonesifer's 1994 *When Baby Makes Two: Single Mothers by Chance or by Choice*

In the 1990s the line dividing single mothers "by chance" and "by choice" was blurry, and the definition of a "Single Mother by Choice" still inchoate.[63] Stonesifer's inclusive title—its address to single mothers by "chance" and by "choice"—conveys that blurriness, though she does divide *When Baby Makes Two* into two parts: "Single Mothers by Chance" and "Single Mothers by Choice."[64] For Stonesifer, the unifying characteristic of her target readers is empirical: the absence of a father from the beginning of the child's life. This absence distinguishes single mothers by chance and by choice from divorcées and widows, whose children have (or had) relationships with their fathers. Stonesifer assumes that her target readers share an emotional bond generated by their profound dis-ease with that foundational absence. The father is the sun in the family universe she envisions; everything revolves around his involvement or lack thereof. Echoing the family values rhetoric of the day, she tells readers, "We must educate ourselves, acknowledging the special challenges of raising children in *fatherless* environments."[65] Stonesifer's rhetoric both echoed and indexed family values' emphasis on the importance of heterosexual and cis-gendered role models for children and the heightened concerns around "fatherlessness" that dominated public discourse in the 1990s. *When Baby Makes Two* thus falls on the negative end of the legitimacy continuum. That is, Stonesifer's legitimizing works within, and thereby reinforces, dominant conceptions of the ideal family and motherhood experience in the 1990s, rather than transforming them.

To build her ethos, Stonesifer underscores that she shares her readers' concerns about "fatherlessness" and single mother families. Throughout *When Baby Makes Two*, she fixates on the potential ramifications on children of growing up in a home without a father and advises her readers to make the best out of a bad situation: "Strive to make your legacy one that includes your child's affirmation: 'I may not have a dad, but I have the best mom I could ever imagine.'"[66] Stonesifer hails her readers—good single mothers who share her preoccupations about "the father issue"—and encourages them to maintain the father fixation. She emphasizes that worthy single mothers, like her, do everything within their power to compensate for their deficient family formation. She defends *When Baby Makes Two*, and, by extension, the mothers it aims to legitimize, by noting their conservative morality: "Nothing here, however, is intended to advocate irresponsible sexual relations or to undermine the importance of fathers."[67] For Stonesifer, it seems, good single mothers must and should experience a degree of guilt, regret, and contrition. This affective relationship toward single motherhood, either by "chance" or by "choice," is a mode of legitimizing: showing contrition mitigates single mothers' violation of white middle-class norms of family and motherhood.

Stonesifer does not state her social location nor that of the intended readers of *When Baby Makes Two*. For the most part, their whiteness and middle-class status is assumed and thus unmarked, as whiteness and middle-class status typically are.[68] In one regard, however, Stonesifer's racialized thinking is explicit. She characterizes adoption as a competitive venture, the goal of which is a white child: "The fact is, most adoptive parents hope to adopt white infants, and as a result, the odds are extremely competitive."[69] She thus advises her readers, "Both fertility and your chances of adopting a healthy Caucasian infant decline steadily after age 40. Get the ball rolling."[70] Stonesifer prepares her readers for the possibility that they will not get their desired white baby, while trying not to squash their hopes entirely: "A bit more flexibility and open-mindedness with regard to a type of child may be necessary for a single mother. That is not to say that you won't be able to find a healthy white newborn."[71] Stonesifer does not examine the origins or the implications of these desires for a white child, be they the creation of a racially homogenous family (if the adoptive mother is white), a valuing of whiteness and a desire to propagate it, or something else. The racial desire is assumed, and the advice Stonesifer offers guided by it. Whiteness thus infuses *When Baby Makes Two*'s construct of the single mother both "by choice" and "by chance."

Because Stonesifer's target readers are middle-class white women, their anxieties stem from the personal shame and financial stresses of single motherhood, not from concerns about being read as "welfare queens." Sadness and shame are the dominant notes of Stonesifer's rhetoric. Single motherhood was definitively not Plan A for her, nor was it, she speculates, for the majority of her readers. Stonesifer advises single mothers "by chance" about how to inform unsuspecting fathers about the pregnancy, how to deal with their reactions, and, ultimately, how to accept the family they end up having.[72] She shares her own experience as a "by chance" single mother to connect with her "by chance" readers, who, she assumes, were as dismayed as she was to find themselves pregnant, and, as she did, fear their families' and friends' negative judgement. Stonesifer recounts that she found herself unexpectedly pregnant when she was only one year out of college, still living with her parents, and holding two part-time jobs. She explains that "the idea of an abortion in this instance filled [her] with dread," so she decided to keep the baby, despite the father having told her that he was "not ready to be a father."[73] Though decades separate Stonesifer from the white mothers in the 1960s who despaired about the "social ostracism and loss of reputation" occasioned by a nonmarital pregnancy, her initial response to her unsought pregnancy echoes theirs.[74] She recalls, "My concerns about a future with an infant had less to do with making ends meet than with the possible reactions of those around me—my parents, my older brothers, friends of our family, the doctor for whom my mother worked, and one set of neighbors in particular—the two little girls who lived next to my parents and who looked up to me. I worried about how the parents next door would explain my circumstances to their children . . . would I now be looked upon as someone who was 'bad'?"[75] Consistent with these concerns, Stonesifer offers *When Baby Makes Two* as a "support group meeting" and "survival guide."[76] Typically, "support groups" and "survival guides" exist for those undergoing not only a challenging but also an undesired experience. Stonesifer's diction reflects her belief in the dominant narrative that single motherhood is not desired, more challenging than parenting with a partner, and thus ideally avoided. Why else would one need a "support group" or "survival guide"? The implication is that, given other options, no woman would in fact *choose* single motherhood.

Nevertheless, Stonesifer seeks to persuade her readers—and give them the tools for self-persuasion—that a surprise pregnancy *can* be a positive turn of events, though it was not initially planned or desired. To this end, she uses the metaphor of a "tunnel," asserting that "the light at the end of the tunnel *will* come, rest assured."[77] While Stonesifer acknowledges her readers' "numb despair" and "resentment,"[78] she argues that they must eventually transition from being "victims" to "survivors," as did she, and, in so doing, reap the unexpected rewards of their pregnancy. She asserts, "Some [victims] remain fixed in their anguish and despair. Others [survivors] grow from the jolt of pregnancy and find personal attributes that they didn't know existed. They fully experience the blessings of their pregnancy and motherhood."[79] The epilogue of *When Baby Makes Two,* a quote from Psalms 127:3, echoes this Christian language and sentiment: "Children are a gift from God; they are his reward." This Christian pronatalist rhetoric works to legitimize Stonesifer's target reader as well—a woman seeking to cultivate her maternal desire or already feeling it—given that "many Americans were not happy to see women apparently slighting their 'maternal instincts' to follow untrustworthy, individualistic impulses."[80]

Furthermore, though Stonesifer addresses single women who proactively pursue motherhood—single mothers "by choice"—she assumes that single motherhood was "plan B" for them as well. She ventriloquizes what she imagines to be the thoughts and feelings of a single mother by choice: "It wasn't supposed to be this way. Mary and other single mothers realize that even before they seriously consider flipping through a sperm bank catalog or taking in a child who may bear no physical resemblance to them."[81] Though Stonesifer does not articulate precisely what she means by "this way," the implication is that these mothers would have preferred to become biological mothers in the context of a romantic partnership. Her rhetoric assumes that the ideal family is one imagined by proponents of family values: two heterosexual parents with biological offspring. Stonesifer, however, is not all doom and gloom. Her tone shifts in later subsections of the book. In "Joys of Single Motherhood by Choice," she discusses the spiritual alignment that some SMCs feel when they actively pursue motherhood. She refers to "the joy of taking action," "turning the process into a pleasure," and "having your dream come true."[82] She titles another subsection "Who Needs Men? The Thrill of Being Self-Sufficient."[83] However, the underlying premise of her guidebook—that single mothers "by choice" must turn lemons into lemonade, just like single mothers "by chance"—does not change. Stonesifer's tent of virtuous motherhood remains open only to single mothers who are grateful for their motherhood but who, on some level, remain wistful about their single status. Their motherhood is a "blessing," but single motherhood, no matter their path to it, forever remains Plan B.

Jane Mattes's *Single Mothers by Choice: A Guidebook for Single Women Who Are Considering or Have Chosen Motherhood*

Though Jane Mattes shares some of Jené Stonesifer's discomfort around the ramifications of single motherhood on children, the SMC she envisions is nevertheless confident about the viability of her family, not wistful and contrite. Initially, like Stonesifer's, Mattes's definition of an SMC is grounded on the absence of a co-parent and could include either a single mother "by choice" or "by chance," as long as she starts out single. She writes, "A single mother by choice is a woman who starts out raising her child *without a partner*. She may or may not marry later on, but at the outset she is parenting alone. This definition excludes unmarried couples, heterosexual or homosexual, because although they are not legally married, they will be coparenting, and it also excludes women who became mothers while they were married and then later were widowed or divorced."[84] Over the course of the guidebook, however, Mattes refines this definition, which would include many stigmatized single mothers, like teen mothers and those who receive public assistance, whose very presence enabled and necessitated the creation of the SMC. Ultimately, Mattes's tent of virtuous motherhood encompasses only single mothers who are financially autonomous, a definition that distinguishes them from "bad mothers" and legitimizes them by demonstrating their ability to adhere to neoliberal norms. Like Stonesifer, her negative legitimizing shores up the then-dominant discourse of family values and its axioms about "good" motherhood and family.

Single Mothers by Choice recounts the origin story of the eponymous organization. In 1981 Mattes, a psychotherapist, was in the process of adopting a child as a single woman when she accidentally became pregnant with a man who was uninterested in being a parent. Nevertheless, Mattes decided to keep the baby.[85] Finding herself struggling with the demands of caring for an infant as a single woman, she formed a support group for mothers in situations analogous to hers.[86] A New York *Daily News* article about the group generated interest in their meetings.[87] Shortly thereafter, a *New York Times* piece about the group was picked up by newspapers across the country.[88] In response to the surge of interest that this publicity generated, Mattes determined that they "would have to get more organized;" Single Mothers by Choice became "a nonprofit corporation in 1982."[89] According to Mattes, it was Quayle's reference to Murphy Brown in 1992, however, that stimulated a veritable tidal wave of interest in the organization: "Thanks to [Quayle's] decision to make an issue about single motherhood, we were flooded with media attention, and requests for information about our group tripled."[90] She explains that she wrote *Single Mothers by Choice* "to share some of what I have learned from all these personal and professional experiences with the hope that it can be of use to others."[91] Her guidebook has sold forty thousand copies and is still in print.[92] Consistent with the conventions of the genre, Mattes provides information, advice, and directions about how to manage this unfamiliar experience, and, in so doing, performs the rhetorical work of defining, defending, and legitimizing SMCs as a putatively distinct population of single mothers.

Mattes addresses two groups of readers: women considering single motherhood and their critics. Like Stonesifer, she describes how she had to overcome sadness and shame about forming a single parent family. The details she includes in her biographical portrait depict her evolution from guilt-ridden angst to quiet confidence. In the introduction, she shares, "My guilt was palpable: I was doing something that I considered forbidden and I felt I would be lucky to escape with only minor injuries—emotional, if not physical . . . [I was] so nervous about my decision that I had nightmares in which outraged people threw stones at me."[93] Mattes's revelation functions rhetorically by emphasizing how deeply she, like her target readers, had internalized the dominant cultural attitude toward middle-class white single mothers. She goes on to say that in her "more realistic moments," she "simply feared" being ostracized: that is, that being a single mother would ruin her career as a psychotherapist, that her family would disown her and the child, and that her friends would abandon her to the situation she had chosen.[94] Mattes attributes her feelings to the fact that she was raised in what she calls a "traditional" family, a descriptor she does not define but that implies the nuclear family organized according to patriarchal and heterosexual logics. She also mentions that her first job was at a maternity home to which unmarried teenage girls were sent "to hide their pregnancies."[95] Significantly, she fails to mention that, except for rare exceptions, as discussed earlier, only *white* unmarried mothers were sent—or, depending on one's perspective, had the opportunity to go to—these homes. While Mattes's ethos does not preclude readers of color and queer readers from identifying with her and adopting the SMC label, it does reveal her vision of her target readership: other presumably white, middle-class, heterosexual women for whom single motherhood was antinormative, undesired, and censored.[96]

At the same time, Mattes's ethos makes her less threatening to critics of single mothers and models a stance that potential SMCs can adopt to ward off their criticism. While Mattes opted to become an SMC and advises other women to consider doing so as well, she emphasizes that she did not do so brazenly. She notes that, "It has not been an easy journey."[97] Her rhetoric throughout the guidebook is measured and works to minimize concerns that SMCs spell the demise of the "traditional" family and men's role within it. While being an SMC can be doable and even enjoyable, it is never, she suggests, Plan A. To the contrary, Mattes claims that SMCs would prefer to parent with a partner, if that were an option. In "Becoming a Single Mother by Conception," the chapter in which she reviews the options for and decisions entailed in becoming a biological mother, she states, "The key question is whether or not you can accept the *lack of perfection* of any of the solutions that are available to you."[98] She tells prospective SMCs, "To be happy being an SMC you need to come to terms with giving up your dream of parenting your child from the beginning with a loving partner."[99] Mattes implies that it is only SMCs' ardent desire to become mothers, itself a confirmation of their femininity and a tenet of compulsory motherhood, that overrides their compunctions about doing so in this less-than-ideal manner and allows them "to live with the inevitable ambivalence of this kind of *compromise*."[100] As discussed previously, low-income single mothers of color, depicted in public discourse as unapologetic creators of "deviant" families, serve as implicit foils to the conventionally feminine and apologetic SMC that Mattes envisions and constructs rhetorically. While acknowledging that many two-parent families do not function well—"We now also know that [the traditional family] was not perfect"—Mattes does not challenge the claim that when they function well, they are the best structure in which to raise children: "We all surely would agree that having a child in a family with two loving parents is the ideal situation."[101] She resorts to the passive voice to make a tentative claim about the viability of non-nuclear families—"The fact that children can be raised successfully in other kinds of families is now becoming more accepted"—and stresses the importance of communicating to children that "a family does not have to fit the traditional model in order to be acceptable."[102] However, just as increasing acceptance of family diversity does not necessarily signify approval or affirmation, to deem unconventional families "acceptable" is hardly a rousing endorsement.

Mattes's engagement with concerns about fatherlessness aligns her and prospective SMCs with the gendered and sexualized assumptions of family values. She simultaneously acquiesces to and dispels fears that SMCs might spell "the end of men" by emphasizing the centrality of men both to SMCs and to their children. Though Mattes states that SMCs "include both straight and gay women in our numbers," the reader she imagines and addresses is heterosexual.[103] She writes, "Most of us were raised with the dream of falling in love with a wonderful *man*, getting married, and raising a child in a loving relationship," and later in a section about socializing as an SMC notes that "we also need to make sure that we give ourselves time to look for and enjoy the company of *men*."[104] As for the children of SMCs, she claims emphatically that they *will* wonder about the absence of a father: "Your child inevitably will go through periods of confusion about 'the daddy issue.'"[105] Mattes softens what she assumes will be the blow of that assertion by adding, "A child *can* grow up and do fine without having a dad. It may at times be confusing, but it doesn't have to be devastating."[106] Her reasoning about the significance of fathers likewise conveys her essentialist beliefs about gender and sexuality: "Traditionally in our society, mothers have been seen as representing nurturing and protection in the home, while fathers represent excitement and separation from the security of home and mother."[107] Mattes's "our" is white and middle-class, the heirs of the "cult of domesticity," which entailed the separation of public and private spheres and strict gender roles; it excludes most working-class, immigrant, and people of color for whom working outside of the home was and is the norm. In making the case for men's significance to children, Mattes also assumes innate, stable gender identities and heterosexuality. She asserts, "A boy needs a relationship with a man for masculine identification, whereas a girl needs it for the experience of loving and being loved by a man."[108] Here heterosexuality describes not only sexual orientation but also enacts (ostensibly essential) sexual difference. In addition to begging further questions—If gender and sexuality are innate and essential, why the need for gendered and sexualized enculturation? In what way(s) do men parent boys and girls differently than women?—Mattes's comments underscore that SMCs do not aim to challenge gender roles or heteronormativity by having children without men. She must offer these reassurances about gender and sexuality, however, precisely because most SMCs *do* decouple heterosexual sex and reproduction to make their families. In so doing, their families unavoidably undermine reproduction's "stability and assumed naturalness."[109] Mattes's legitimizing aims to downplay the threat that SMC families inevitably pose to the nuclear family and "natural" reproduction.

To distinguish SMC from stigmatized single mothers and further mark their adherence to family values, Mattes emphasizes their *intention* to parent alone as well as the consciousness and conscientiousness they bring to motherhood. In recounting the history of the organization she founded, she relates the founding members' desire to highlight this intentionality in the name: "We felt strongly that we wanted the name to clearly convey that it was our choice and our decision to become single mothers . . . Some of us made the choice before conceiving, and some, like me, decided after having conceived, but we all *chose* motherhood at some point."[110] Mattes positions SMCs as "good" choosers, autonomous and agentic, as "single women who chose to become mothers; single mothers who are mature and responsible and who feel empowered rather than victimized."[111] She acknowledges the rhetorical power of the neoliberal tenets of the SMC identity in her comments about the medical profession's increasing receptivity to facilitating motherhood for certain single women: "The medical profession is fairly positive about *mature, responsible* single women trying to get pregnant by insemination."[112] According to Mattes, these "mature, responsible" SMCs make "good" decisions, exercise self-control, and are self-reliant. She informs her readers, "You cannot responsibly bring a child into the world unless you know that you have sufficient money to support the two of you and provide for your basic needs."[113] Here she implicitly contrasts SMCs to single mothers who did not choose single motherhood and who are, presumedly, immature, careless, and financially unstable.[114] Read within the anti-welfare rhetorical context of the 1990s, Mattes's statement also implicitly condemns those single mothers who *do* receive public assistance. As legal activist Benita Miller observes, SMCs "distinguish themselves from [poor mothers] based on their education and economic status, often making it plain that they don't have to rely on public funds to raise their children."[115] This rhetorical strategy has troubling consequences. Cultural critic Jane Juffer explains how SMCs' assertions of autonomy "put more pressure on the low-income single mother to distance herself from dependency to gain respect."[116] By emphasizing their self-reliance, SMCs "reject the support for caring that they and other mothers could use because they fear being stigmatized as dependent. They attempt to transcend social conditions rather than arguing for the resources that would help themselves and many other single mothers."[117]

Mattes's reassurances about the viability of SMC families seem inadequate to her goal of legitimizing, but there is a rhetorical strategy behind her seemingly lukewarm defense. Her acknowledgment, like Stonesifer's, that SMCs create less-than-ideal homes, coupled with her assertions that they thus must do everything in their power to understand and mitigate these deficiencies, again like Stonesifer, casts them in a favorable light; though not explicitly wistful and contrite, Mattes's SMC is still aware of the problems of single motherhood, and she works hard to address them. Mattes's essentialist comments about gender and sexuality align SMCs with family values and quell concerns that they seek to challenge them, despite their decision to form non-nuclear families themselves. At the same time, her defense of SMCs enthymematically underscores their difference from unmarried mothers who thoughtlessly, and worse, shamelessly, create nonnormative families. In contrast to those other single mothers, Mattes implies, SMCs are eager to and do address their families' shortcomings. Her definitional work thus relies on moral distinctions and disidentifications from other single mothers; the "by Choice" in the SMC label actively marks a specific and privileged class, racial, gender, and sexual location.

Conclusions

In ways both implicit and explicit, Stonesifer's and Mattes's negative legitimizing developed and popularized an SMC construct that was racialized (white), classed (middle-upper), and sexualized (heterosexual). The rhetorical success of this construct is unsurprising, given that, in the 1990s, racialized antipathy toward single motherhood reached its zenith and neoliberal family values dominated discourse across the political spectrum. The SMC construct reinforced exclusive norms of motherhood and family and deepened the stigma experienced by those mothers who did or could not adhere to them and who were thus cast as "unfit, degraded, and illegitimate."[118] Indeed, SMCs' *ability* to leverage class and racial privilege to combat the stigma of single motherhood was inextricably tied to these other single mothers' *inability* to do so. By positioning SMCs as distinctive and legitimate single mothers, implicitly by virtue of their whiteness and heterosexuality and explicitly by virtue of their maternal desire, financial autonomy, and intentionality, Stonesifer and Mattes distinguished SMCs from within the growing number of single mothers in the 1990s. A different rhetoric might have enabled and supported coalitional legitimizing that would have supported the maternal rights and legitimacy of *all* single mothers, while still recognizing the differences in their experience.

CHAPTER TWO

RHETORICAL SHARING

Identity Policing and Community Building on the *Single Mothers by Choice* Blog

We're all pioneers and have to make our own paths for our families.

—Anonymous, *Single Mothers by Choice* blog

Taking the plunge (or bungy jumping as I used to call it to myself) to make the moves to have a child on your own is exhilarating and definitely becoming pregnant seems like a feminist crime that changes your life.

—Ali, *Single Mothers by Choice* blog

On April 25, 2010, Jane Mattes launched the blog *Single Mothers by Choice* (*SMC*), which shares the name of the organization she founded in 1981. In her introductory post, Mattes calls attention to the mainstreaming of elective single motherhood: "What was back then a new concept (mature single women choosing to become single mothers? Most people didn't know anyone like us) is now a well-established trend in our society." Mattes goes on to assert a collective identity through the pronoun "we"—"we're better understood"—that she then elaborates: "We're not radical feminists, we're not anti-men, we're just women who want to make an active decision about having or adopting a baby before it's too late."[1] Here Mattes presents elective single motherhood as decidedly apolitical, an exercise of women's agency to pursue the socially sanctioned role of mother *sans* the feminist roar. Becoming an elective single mother and claiming the SMC label thus does not entail joining the "sisterhood." Mattes's definitional claims also seem to admonish future *SMC* bloggers to focus on their desire to become mothers, rather than on the ways that those desires call into question societal norms about family form and practice. In framing elective single motherhood this way, Mattes downplays its radical potential, and, as she did in her 1994 guidebook, assumes that visitors to the website and users on the *SMC* blog are, at least primarily, women for whom being a single mother is, at best, a second-choice route to motherhood.

Mattes's claims about SMC identity, and her subtle attempt to squash claims suggesting otherwise, provoked an immediate and vigorous response. On May 13, 2010, OuthistoryBlogger commented, "But some of us are radical feminists! I would say we come from a broad range of political perspectives, rather than characterizing us all as 'not radical feminists.'" This exchange crystalizes two of the central questions driving this study: *Who is included in the "we" of elective single motherhood, and how do the women who identify as such understand the significance of the various ESM labels and experience*? Inspired by OuthistoryBlogger's retort, this chapter examines *SMC* bloggers' deliberation about the definition, as well as the personal, social, and political consequences of elective single motherhood, from the launch of the blog in April 2010 until December 2014. These first four years of the blog's existence capture users' direct engagement with Mattes's claims and reveal the topoi—places of argument—that provoke the most interest and engagement. The *SMC* blog is dense with deliberations that are intimate, interactive, and influential, leading some users to commit to their pursuit of single motherhood, some to doubt it, and many others to explore their questions and concerns with what one user calls "SMC Wikipedia." I call this consequential exchange of perspectives and personal experience *rhetorical sharing*. Rhetorical sharing names the collaborative meaning-making that happens through the articulation of personal expression in sites of what Tasha N. Dubriwny calls "collective rhetoric," which are characterized by the presence of three elements: "an active and participatory audience, the deployment of an experiential epistemology, and the transformation of the meaning of individual experiences through the articulation of those experiences."[2] New media genres, like the *SMC* blog, add a novel dimension to "collective rhetoric": they enable rhetorical sharing among strangers.[3] On the blog, strangers, bonded initially only by their shared interest in elective single motherhood, engage in persuasion and identity-formation. These strangers' rhetorical sharing on the site fosters intimacy among them, provokes definitional work and metaphorical creativity, and nurtures agonistic deliberations about the individual and societal effects of single motherhood. Ultimately, rhetorical sharing on the *SMC* blog foments and sustains users' "rhetorical sel[ves]"—"a local and ongoing aesthetic formation, continually becoming and coming into being."[4] Tracking the various ways that users explain, define, legitimize, and constitute themselves as SMCs via their rhetorical sharing on the *SMC* blog illuminates the distinctive affordances of new media genres to contemporary sites of "collective rhetoric."[5] This analysis of users' rhetorical sharing on the blog also complicates representations of ESM by some ESMs themselves (like Mattes), the media, and certain scholars as conservative adherents to nuclear notions of family.

The Digital Era

The digital domain has played a pivotal role in the construction and experience of contemporary motherhood. Many, many mothers write online. The "mamasphere" refers to the cyber community generated by mothers' networked life writing.[6] Indeed, the rise of the web coincided with the dramatic rise of elective single motherhood. Choice Moms and Single Mothers by Choice, the two major organizations and eponymous guidebooks for ESMs in the United States, have extensive websites that provide information and support, build community, and sponsor various forms of life writing by ESMs. Both organize the ESM experience as a progression into parenthood, with tabs like "Thinking, Conceiving, Adopting, and, Parenting" (Choice Moms) and "thinking, trying, and mothering" (Single Mothers by Choice). Choice Moms sponsors several Yahoo discussion groups and invites readers to contribute material for the various e-books and podcasts that it produces, while Single Mothers by Choice publishes a quarterly e-newsletter distributed to paying subscribers. Single Mothers by Choice also hosts the blog from which I quote in this chapter. Its homepage features the beginning of the most recent post and a link to the blog in addition to the "Blog" tab on the page's banner. I focus on the *SMC* blog because it has neither admissions requirements nor guidelines for users' contributions. Unconstrained by membership fees and moderators' dictates, casual as well as committed visitors to the Single Mothers by Choice website can read and write freely on the blog. In this sense, the SMC blog is a host for self-sponsored writing.

Blogs, a particular form of online discourse, proliferated in the 1990s with the creation of user-friendly content-management systems.[7] Their content covers a wide range: some blogs are topical, while others function more like online diaries. Blogs are public and infinite in the sense that anyone can read and respond to them, but they feel intimate, like an exchange among close, though not necessarily like-minded, people. The proliferation of blogs by mothers has led to the coining of the term "mommyblogs" to describe those blogs that "capture *maternal* experiences, give mothers a voice, and foster conversation and participation in a community."[8] Blogs' defining characteristics are frequently updated time-stamped content and a reverse chronological structure in which the most recent posts are displayed first.[9] Most blogs now also have a "comment feature" that enables readers to comment on the original blog post and to respond to other readers' comments.[10] The comment function on a blog turns blog readers into co-authors of the text, thus eroding the distinction between readers and writers. An initial post might instigate a discussion, functioning as a "catalyst," but the thread of responses that ensues can move the discussion in unexpected directions and pursue themes that are suggested, but not fully developed, in the original post.[11] While the ease with which users can voice their experiences and respond to others on an open access blog works against the dominance of any single perspective, as with other types of digital activity, there are certain "material and social preconditions" for participation in the blogosphere.[12] These include "literacy, English literacy (the majority of blogs are written in English), regular access to a private or public Internet connection, basic computer skills and familiarity with the web browser environment, baseline knowledge . . . and enough free time to read, contribute to, or create a blog."[13] Once these preconditions are met, however, blogs are a particularly accessible online genre, as they "forego the institutionalization of communicative practices and offer spaces for writing that are more collaboratively constructed than other online spaces."[14]

Like any genre, blogs "survive to become recurrent and thus generic if the *kairos* also recurs or persists."[15] They reflect and reinforce a twenty-first-century focus on selfhood and identity, what Miller and Shepherd characterize "as some shared, recurrent need for cultivation and validation of the self."[16] The self-orientation of blogs has led some critics to deem blogging an activity of and for the self-absorbed. May Friedman recalls the widely negative perception of blogs about mothering in 2003, the year of her son's birth: they "were viewed as notoriously narcissistic at best, and abusive of the children they chronicled at worst."[17] In a related vein of critique, Judith Statman Tucker alleges that blogging, as a genre and activity, is uniquely prone to vacuity. She asserts, "The unspoken premise of blogging is that depth and context are expendable, because everyone understands what you're talking about and why it matters. In this paradigm, authority is derived from presentation, and substance is optional."[18] According to Tucker, blogs are all show, not occasions for sincere and serious deliberation. In Tucker, we hear echoes of Socrates's critique of rhetoric as not an art that produces knowledge but rather an experience "of producing delight and pleasure."[19] That is, blogs are essentially fluff—"bad" rhetoric's quintessential expression and medium and narcissistic to boot.

While some blogs do lack "depth and context," it is precisely bloggers' self-orientation that can promote critical self-reflection as well as engagement with matters that extend beyond the self.[20] Users' sense that they are simply sharing their personal experiences and perspectives, not making an argument that requires defense or rationale, paradoxically enables analysis and deliberation. Moreover, selfhood itself is an inherently rhetorical phenomenon, a lifelong process of self-persuasion and self-definition. The "rhetorical self" is necessarily "open to difference, to continual movement and transformation."[21] Reflection, whether conscious or not, figures centrally in the process of becoming; as Bradford Vivian notes, "The exercise of reflection—as a means of coming to know one's self—consists in persuading one's self to adopt particular styles of life from all those available in any given situation."[22] The reflective "rhetorical self" thus enjoys a symbiotic relationship with her environment, reflecting and responding to the "abundance or poverty of materials available at any given moment."[23] The *SMC* blog serves as a deep inventional resource by making available, via users' rhetorical sharing, an "abundance" of lifestyles and life paths to women whose immediate familial, social, and geographic contexts offer few or limited visions of motherhood and family. Users' rhetorical sharing also offers narrative frames that ascribe various moral, political, and cultural meanings to those visions. That is, users of the blog are exposed not just to alternative life paths but also to alternative characterizations of those life paths. Rhetorical sharing on the blog variously constructs, fortifies, and solidifies users' identities, underscoring the notion that one's "self is both co-created and amended by the self in relation to others."[24] The rhetorical scene of the *SMC* blog is thus simultaneously enabling and constraining. In the analysis that follows, I analyze the threads instigated by users' rhetorical sharing rather than isolating particular statements. In these threads, users engage in deep, nuanced, and contextualized thinking about elective single motherhood and construct their "rhetorical selves." In so doing, they simultaneously create a polyvocal "collective rhetoric," one that is sustained and deepened via their rhetorical sharing with strangers.[25]

Definitional Debates

This book contends that the labels used to name ESMs, namely Single Mother by Choice and Choice Mom, are more rhetorical than denotative. Definitional rhetorics are thus central in the self-sponsored texts by women who gather under them. The boundaries and elasticity of SMC identity are driving concerns on the *SMC* blog and identity claims figure centrally in users' rhetorical sharing. In a February 5, 2012, post titled "The Politics of Smcs," Robyn explains how participating in the face-to-face and online SMC community challenged her assumptions about SMC identity: "I thought that making such an 'unconventional' life choice would be a decision only left-leaning, primarily urban/coastal women would make. I could not have been more wrong. What I've found instead is an amazingly diverse community of women." Robyn goes on to define diversity in terms of politics, profession, race, ethnicity, and location, among other factors. She concludes, "This sisterhood is truly powerful." Whether SMC are demographically diverse is hard to determine. The frequently asked questions section on the website of the Single Mothers by Choice organization claims diversity along the same axes as Robyn. The section also states that the average age of SMC members is thirty-five, and that "nearly all" of them have completed college. An article on the Choice Mom website, titled "Where Are Choice Moms?," describes the dramatic rise in the number of visitors to the site and its global reach, but neither the article nor the website provide demographic data. Whether women who identify as Single Mothers by Choice or Choice Moms are actually diverse along these different axes matters less, however, than the fact that users, like Robyn, are motivated to claim and celebrate that they are. Highlighting diversity is a form of definitional work, one that conjures an imagined audience who finds such diversity valuable. Indeed, on August 23, 2016, another user responds simply to Robyn's post: "Lovely." Robyn's post also subtly underscores Mattes's claim that "we're not radical feminists," at least, she suggests, not all of us.

To claim SMCs' diversity, as Robyn does, is one matter; to call attention to the effects of difference on one's experience of single motherhood is another. In the first four years of the *SMC* blog's existence, only one thread explicitly introduced race and addressed how racial identity influences one's experience of single parenthood. It may be that whiteness so dominates the rhetorical space of the *SMC* blog that it precludes discussions that foreground race.[26] Or, it may be that women who come to the Single Mothers by Choice website, no matter their race, do so to address what they share with other self-identified SMCs—the commitment to pursue motherhood as single women—and so opt not to use the blog to call attention to that which distinguishes them.[27] An April 1, 2012, post titled "Keeping My Future Child Safe" is the only one that explicitly foregrounds race and the way it conditions the experience of single motherhood. The user begins by situating her reflection on her pregnancy in racial context: "I have just been so sad since the story of the Trayvon Martin case came out." Trayvon Martin, a young, unarmed Black man, was shot fatally by George Zimmerman, a volunteer neighborhood watchman, who claimed to be acting in self-defense. The incident instigated a national debate about "stand your ground" policies and the effects of implicit and explicit bias. It also took place as international awareness of police brutality grew in response to the mainstream media's increased attention to its ubiquity. The user explains how Martin's death provoked her to think differently about the gender of her future child. She had wanted a boy to carry on the family name but now wonders about her ability, as a single mother, to raise a Black boy in a racist society. She asks, "What if I don't teach this kid about how to act in front of police officers? How do I help him understand that he needs to be compliant around people who would find him 'suspicious,' even if he's done nothing wrong, without breaking his little spirit?" She attributes her concerns to the fact that she is a single mother, explaining, "This is really the first time I have felt the huge responsibility of doing this without a man in the house who may be able to explain life in a way that I simply cannot. Because although I am black, I'm not a black MAN, facing the unique concerns that exist for black men."

Users responded in deeply personal ways to the concerns raised by the writer of "Keeping My Future Child Safe." All state that they are "black" or "women of color," highlighting the assumption that users on the *SMC* blog are white unless otherwise identified. Their identity claims move the conversation "in ways that facilitate thinking together."[28] On April 20, 2012, Michelle asserts that "most women feel the same as you," a universal claim about mothers' concerns for their children's safety." She then adds, "I'm black, DD [dear daughter] is biracial." In asserting her identity, Michelle is likely signaling her awareness of the particular vulnerability of Black bodies in the United States. While most mothers are concerned about their children's safety, some threats menace all children while others are particular to the child's social location. Zenzeta first states that she was "comforted to see that there are other women of color who have made this choice [to be an SMC]," thus acknowledging how SMC identity is assumed to be white. She then identifies with the user's fears and elaborates on their relationship to blackness by lamenting (albeit controversially) "the lack of positive male role models in the black community." On April 8, Lorraine claims her kinship as a Black SMC and identifies with the user's uncertainties. She then encourages her to relinquish the shame she feels, as "the reason for the fear is not your fault." On April 2, Christina identifies emphatically, "I completely feel the same way as you," and goes on to state, "I believe you speak to the fear many black women (or women of color) have for their sons, nephews, and brothers." These users leverage their identity as fellow women of color to empathize and to reassure, and, in so doing, to create the conditions to voice and contend with concerns and challenges that face single mothers of Black boys. Grounded in statements of identification and empathy, users' rhetorical sharing fosters self-understanding and compassion in addition to opening up argumentative space for future discussions among users regarding the particular needs of Black boys in the United States.

Rhetorical sharing on the *SMC* blog, however, does not only or always provoke claims of identification and inclusion. In the thread analyzed below, users police the boundaries of SMC identity so as to include some mothers and exclude others. The Single Mothers by Choice website defines SMC as "single women who CHOSE to be the sole parent of their child (at least at the outset)." In a November 3, 2012, post, Emma Johnson, a self-described freelance business writer, asks provocatively, "But what is really to be a single mother by choice?" Johnson's decision to post on the *SMC* blog was bold. In the first lines, she states twice that she was married when her children were born. This fact would seem to negate her identity as an SMC. But Johnson goes on to say that she feels "a kinship with women who identify as Single Women by Choice." She troubles the adjective "single" by asking at what juncture one becomes single. In her case, she explains, she engaged in sexual relations with an emotionally unstable husband in the context of a marriage that was "likely to fail." Johnson uses the rhetoric of choice, emphasizing her intentionality to become pregnant with a second child by noting that she was aware of and opted not to use birth control or to pursue an abortion. She calls attention to the privilege of her position and the agency it bestows: "I am an educated white woman living in the western world. I've been educated about conception and have knowledge about my own cycle. I have the financial resources that afford me birth control and live in a culture that give me access to abortions." Hours later, in response to a comment on her post, Johnson reiterates her agency and concomitant intentionality regarding motherhood: "I don't pretend to be a SMC, but I do want to raise the question: aren't ALL mothers really mothers by some choice, particularly in the West where we have so much control over our bodies and personal lives." Johnson argues here that motherhood in developed, liberal nations is always a choice, seemingly unaware of, or simply uninterested, in women's vastly different experiences of motherhood "in the West" and the privileges inherent in maternal choice.

Johnson highlights her awareness of society's condemnation of unconventional mothers to suggest her affinity with SMCs. She states her concern that others will label her decision to pursue motherhood in an unstable relationship "stupid" or "selfish." She parries those critiques by implying or stating overtly the positive outcomes of elective single motherhood. First, she interrogates the meaning of partnership by asking whether mothers who co-parent with a substance abuser, philander, or "just generally a self-absorbed jerk" are truly co-parenting or are, in fact, functionally "single." She pushes against narrow definitions of parenthood and family by contrasting SMCs with a "rich extended family of relatives and friends" to "a married couple with few outside emotional resources." In so doing, she challenges the culturally validated nuclear definition of "family" and implies that the chosen families of SMCs nurture just as well, if not better. She also challenges the meaning of marriage and singlehood by suggesting that she was single even when she was married. Finally, Johnson muses about what constitutes a good environment for childrearing, referring to mothers "consciously bringing a child into poverty, or wartime or to a disintegrating marriage." Johnson is bold, provocative, and deliberatively agonistic: she explores and debates definitions just as much as she describes, in a purely expressivist mode, her own life.

Thirteen users respond with varying degrees of frustration to Johnson's exploratory response to her own question. Clearly something is at stake when they passionately demarcate the boundaries of the SMC identity, shouting on the screen via capital letters that they are "TRUE SMCs."[29] Their rhetorical sharing consolidates their identity as SMCs, exemplifying the concept of "identity-in-use," that is, one "shaped at the micro level through discursive negotiations and interactions that happen in conversation."[30] These users reject Johnson's claims of "kinship" and insist on the distinctiveness of the process of becoming and the state of being an SMC. For them, the SMC label marks a hard-earned personally and politically transformative process, one that neither other single mothers, nor mothers more generally, have earned. Theirs is a rhetoric of choice and desire. They argue that the intentionality and emotional toil entailed in their decision making distinguish them both from other single mothers and from partnered mothers for whom motherhood was not easy to achieve. In short, their suffering, motivated by powerful maternal desire, warrants the label SMC. Val observes, "The SMC route comes after some long hard soul searching, in in [*sic*] many cases at great expense" (November 4, 2012). Olivia refers to "the months/years of agonizing up-lead a prospective SMC must face" (November 4). Li repeats that she "planned, planned, planned" and relates that she "struggled with every emotion" and "gave blood, sweat and tears" to arrive at her decision to pursue single motherhood. Ultimately, she concludes, "The two kinds of single mothers . . . are, in their very core, quite different." (November 4). Michelle describes "the struggles we have gone thru" and characterizes Johnson's experiences as a single mother through divorce as "NOT AT ALL like what choice moms have gone thru and deal with every day" (November 12). Similarly, Leslie claims that "Most SMCs go through years of agonizing to decide if this is right for them" and states that the presence of Johnson's ex-husband as a co-parent makes her experience "not the same" (November 8). These users' references to their psychic angst and struggle imply their awareness of societal norms and the difficulty of breaking them. Only one, however, articulates the conflict explicitly. Li writes that she "fought to weigh my own desires against society's expectations and mandates," which she then specifies as "any choice [to pursue motherhood] within a couple relationship" (November 4). She proceeds to repeat, elaborate, and use all capital letters to clarify and emphasize her point about SMCs: "The deliberate, unconventional choice to become a mother as a single person is VERY different than any choice made within a couple relationship which conforms to societal expectations" (November 4). This chain of passionate negation evokes an image of locked arms, a barricade against interlopers to the SMC community as these users have defined it.

Only a few users counter Emma Johnson's claims of affinity among all single mothers by also asserting the uniquely positive attributes of SMCs and their families. In celebrating the virtues of ESM families, however, these users implicitly devalue both partnered mothers and single mothers whose path was not so explicitly intentional. Lily F writes, "As for us SMC, we have the true stability, consistency, peace that most married parents can only dream of" (November 10). Li argues along similar lines: "I am not concerned about explaining the beginnings of my child's life to her because they were intentional, happy, and very supported. She is loved by a whole community who we call family. There is no sadness or disappointment in it." Here Li exerts definitional agency by defining "family" as intentional—a chosen affective community that exceeds blood-based ties and legal relations. She continues by emphasizing SMCs' maternal desire: "The difference between single mothers by choice and single mothers by circumstance is that SMCs go in with eyes wide open and a happy heart. Single mothers by circumstance usually do not. They often have heavy hearts and I feel sorry for their pain." Li's definitional work is premised on two questionable assumptions: first, that a firm wall separates these two categories of mothers, as if choice does not figure in circumstance and vice-versa, and second, that the emotional experience of the single mother by choice is unique and happier. Of significance here, however, is not the soundness of her reasoning but rather her aggressive assertions of the boundaries of the SMC identity. According to these users, SMCs are agentic, autonomous, and intentional, not the victims of circumstance, and their children reap the benefits of their careful planning.

With a few exceptions, noted above, the majority of the users in the thread that unspools from Emma Johnson's post define SMCs as women who made an anguished choice. Their rhetorical sharing on the blog emphasizes their suffering and makes it central to their self-understanding. Their SMC identity, which requires constant defense and articulation of its distinctiveness, emerges and sustains itself through their rhetorical sharing. The latter highlights and celebrates the agency that result from their particular path to motherhood. For some, it also fosters pride in their decision to buck white middle-class conventions around family. Their identity consolidation, however, happens at the expense of mothers who do not meet the exacting standards of self-identified SMCs. By arguing that they are the only worthy recipients of the label SMC, these users implicitly denigrate women whose path to single motherhood was less obviously and consistently intentional, thereby reinforcing troubling assumptions of liberal agency.

Single Motherhood as Plan A

Other users on the SMC blog more subtly explore the interplay of choice and circumstance, as well as the emotional complexity, of their journey toward and experience of single motherhood. Their rhetorical sharing is reflective and nuanced and is directed internally as much as it is externally toward other users. Many ponder the typical characterization of single motherhood as a "Plan B." In the post that launched the *SMC* blog, Jane Mattes establishes a hierarchy of value in which Plan A—partnered motherhood—is preferable to Plan B—single motherhood. She implies that elective single motherhood is an option that women consider only when their biological clock begins to tick and is not what they have always wanted and envisioned.[31] Plan B thus necessarily entails the angst referenced by the users who responded to Emma Johnson, who describes SMCs as "just women who want to make an active decision about having or adopting a baby before it's too late." This framing of elective single motherhood as Plan B is ubiquitous; to wit, a 2004 documentary about elective single motherhood was titled *Plan B: Single Women Choosing Motherhood*. As I suggest in chapter 1's analysis of Jené Stonesifer's and Jane Mattes's 1994 guidebooks, claims that elective single motherhood is a Plan B can be understood as an example of negative legitimizing in which ESMs ward off critique by acknowledging that their families are not ideal, not even to them, thus giving credence to (or leaving unchallenged) *doxa* about the necessity of fathers, while suggesting that ESM families can at least be good enough.

Several users on the *SMC* blog, however, outright reject the characterization of elective single motherhood as a Plan B, claiming instead that single motherhood was their angst-free Plan A all along. A strong rhetoric of maternal desire also animates these users' posts. Their rhetorical sharing is affirmative, indeed triumphant, and it inspires and resonates with SMCs who are less secure and whose face-to-face community does not include other ESMs. They enact a form of suasion by example—"I did this, I am thriving, it is possible to do, just look at me!" After explaining that she was raised by a widowed and thus single mother, "SMC in Eastern Europe" asserts on July 22, 2010, "Becoming a single mother by choice was never Plan B for me . . . I never did picture mom, dad, and kids as the perfect family when I was a kid. Having a great mom was quite enough." "SMC in Eastern Europe" feels compelled not only to set the record straight but also to counter the negative connotations of the Plan B label. She adds, "Sometimes I want to shout it from the hilltops of this agricultural country—solo mothers do not need your pity, and my kids are very happy!" Similarly, on November 1, 2014, one user writes, "I feel like a bit of an exception. I didn't debate either question [whether to become an SMC or whether to have a second child] much. I always wanted to be a mother. I had few relationships, none of them long-term. I felt strong and capable of doing it alone." Several users celebrate the confident eloquence of this post. Hana's Mum writes, "Thanks for this beautifully written blog post," a sentiment Laraf123 echoes: "Yes, this was beautifully written and very relatable."

By avoiding the rhetoric of Plan A and Plan B altogether, the rhetorical sharing of other users offers alternative ways of envisioning and characterizing the path to single motherhood. One post stands out for the way the user, Janine, asserts unequivocally that single motherhood was and is the right choice for her while still acknowledging the destabilizing effects on her psyche of societal norms of family. Janine recounts feeling simultaneously confident and uncertain about her decision to become an SMC. "I had my twins three years ago and can still remember the anxieties and doubts that I allowed to plague me—and this is coming from someone who was (and still is) positive that I was doing the right thing," she writes. Sandra Lee Bartky's insight about ambivalence and feminist consciousness illuminates the seeming contradictions in Janine's post. Bartky observes, "Even the woman who has decided to be this new person and not that old one, can be tormented by recurring doubts."[32] Janine transitions from her account of her personal emotional journey to make an abstract statement about the "recurring doubts" that beset ESMs: "One of the hardest things to do is re-programming our thinking and letting go of all that we thought we knew about what it means to be a parent/mother/father and what it means to be a 'family.'" Here she attributes her paradoxical emotional state to the clash between her internal certainty about her decision to pursue single motherhood and a cultural context that holds up the nuclear family as the ideal. Human sociality makes us vulnerable to doubt when we act in countercultural ways. There is power, therefore, in naming the clash between one's internal desires and society's expectations and judgments. In articulating that clash, Janine begins to work through the tension that it generates. She goes on to state, "Undoubtedly raising children alone has been the single most hardest thing I've done but I AM doing it." Janine's use of the collective "our" to describe the "re-programming" that SMCs must undertake reinforces the sense of community on the *SMC* blog. SMCs are unified in their need to respond to this pressure to have a certain kind of family. This is definitional work: there is a specific "we" posited by her use of "our." She positions herself as one of the group by sharing her own insecurities. Janine's emphasis on the fact that she did and is doing it, underscored by the capital letters of "AM," celebrates her own achievements and also inspires other users to persevere. Here is a different variation of suasion by example. Unlike the triumphant claims of the SMCs who claim "Plan A all along," Janine declares, "I'm doing this despite my fears, and you can, too!" The flood of responses to her post testify to its influence. On August 24, Sarah thanks Janine: "Janine, thank you for what you said. In particular, thank you for saying, 'If being a mother is what your soul desires, then it is the right thing for you. Everything will fall into place.' It was exactly what I needed to hear . . . Your comment helped me remember that I need to do what is right for me and that everything else will fall into place. Thank you so much." As this thread demonstrates, rhetorical sharing allows users who are unwilling, unable, or not yet ready to articulate their internal conflicts to benefit from the psychic and rhetorical labor of women like Janine.

Still other users engage in rhetorical sharing on the blog to explain, articulate, and ultimately affirm for themselves as well as for their readers their circuitous route to single motherhood. They describe a process wherein they realized only belatedly that being a single mother was in fact their Plan A. On October 4, 2010, Joy, a self-described "feminist" and "single by choice," wrote, "Now, 4 months and 1 day into being a single parent at the age of 44, I know I did everything just right! . . . I should have stuck with Plan A all along!" Others, like Andrea, recount the evolution of her own thinking about and characterization of her experience in her post from January 12, 2011: "At first it bugged me because I saw this as such a 'Plan B,' but now I see it simply as my life's path, full of all sorts of experiences, both challenging and rewarding." Andrea goes on to explain why she rejects the implication that she "settled" for "Plan B": "I'm a MUCH stronger, more self-assured, confident person now and attribute that to having to really put my priorities on the line and stand behind them. I have become so confident in my decision that I don't feel like I 'settled'." On November 22, 2014, another user wrote, "While becoming a single mom once seemed like Plan B—after finding a man didn't work—I now realize this was my path all along. I was meant to be a single mom. I'm type A, I like having all the control. I like making all the decisions . . . I have no regrets. I'm glad I pursued a great career and had lots of fun doing it. I'm glad I traveled and dated in my 20s and early 30s . . . I am so grateful to be a single mother by choice." The accretion of details in this user's post supports her assertion that being a single mother was, though unbeknown to her initially, her Plan A. At the same time, her assertion "This was my path all along" illuminates the complexity of the rhetoric of "choice." One cannot simultaneously have planned every step and realize belatedly that one's path was meant to be. The former is active and premeditated, the other passive and reflective on the unexpected discoveries that result from the experience's surprising effects. These tensions and contradictions reflect the labor required to shoehorn one's experience into the unstable rhetorics of choice and intentionality.

Embracing Plan B

Another group of users acknowledge that elective single motherhood was in fact their Plan B. These users, however, characterize their process of embracing Plan B differently than those who, in their responses to Emma Johnson, emphasize their angst and sadness. Instead, they explain how relinquishing "the dream" and embracing Plan B transformed them in unexpected and overwhelmingly positive ways. Jennifer W.'s post from June 12, 2011, "On Moving from Thinking to Trying," received twenty-four comments. Jennifer W. does not seek to persuade herself or others to pursue single motherhood. She does attempt to articulate the hurdles she overcame to make the transition from being what SMCs call a "thinker," a woman considering single motherhood by choice, to a "tryer," a woman actively pursuing motherhood. She writes about the jumble of emotions she is experiencing, including feelings of excitement and anticipation, but also fears that she will not get pregnant, that others will judge her negatively, and that she will not be able to handle the stresses of single motherhood. She also writes about her grief: "[I'm] grieving the loss of my chance at the 'traditional' nuclear family—this one is so tough for me." The responses to Jennifer W.'s post reveal how rhetorical sharing moves thinking, decisions about, and evaluations of single motherhood. Users learn about others' experiences, bolster those who need support, feel inspired, and deliberate about their choices, celebrating some and critiquing others.

There is a pattern in these threads. Most begin with empathic statements that discursively construct the supportive relationships that users seek. Users establish solidarity and community, and their comments generate their own momentum. The effect of their rhetorical sharing is cumulative. Each instance of sharing builds on other users' narratives of psychic labor. On June 12, Mary writes in response to Jennifer W.: "I am at the cross-roads right now! This echoes my thoughts exactly." On June 12, Sarah exclaims similarly, "That is exactly how I am feeling! . . . for now, I'm just happy knowing I'm not crazy." Writing on June 12 as well, Tracy says, "I could have written this. Thank you. :-" Margo Grace writes on June 12, "I hear you!" On June 13, Lily writes, "God Bless all you courageous women and thank you for sharing your stories." On June 13, Anon writes, "I am going through this process too, and I too could have written exactly what you said." On June 16, Sam writes, "Thank you for posting this. You took the words write out of my mouth (keyboard?)" Tara writes on June 17, "WOW, reading your [Jennifer's] post was like I was reading my own story." On June 21, Andrea writes, "Thank you for sharing your thoughts and worries, so I know I am not totally off track. Good luck." On June 22, Jennifer W. responds to the torrent of praise and gratitude: "I am so touched that my words resonated with all of you! Even more, I am so thankful that I have a found a community of smart, caring women who understand what I'm going through and who can truly relate to me right now in a way my friends and family cannot." Jennifer W.'s response names how the

SMC blog creates the conditions for users to conceive and possibly pursue life paths considered unorthodox, unacceptable, or indeed unimaginable by their face-to-face community.

Even Jennifer W.'s follow-up comment does not stem the tidal wave of responses. Rachel's appreciation for the community of the *SMC* blog leaps off the screen in her June 28 comment, which suggests how participating on the blog diminishes her loneliness and feelings of isolation: "Oh my goodness, I would so love to sit down with all of you! The past 6 months have been the most emotional, difficult and lonely of my life—reading this post has made me feel enormously better . . . Walking this path can feel so agonizingly lonely, and I'm grateful to have found this blog . . . At every step of the way, with all these huge decisions I have to make on my own I feel simultaneously small and overwhelmed and then giddy with the knowledge that I really can take control of making my most important dream come true . . . Anyhow, glad to have found all of you!" On July 7, Marsha discusses her own experience with a known donor to acknowledge and address Rachel's specific concerns: "Rachel, your story sounds like mine . . . I went forward with a donor and I thank the stars every day that I didn't have a baby with him. Now I have a 15 month old son who is ALL mine." A different Jennifer contributes to the chorus of voices on the thread on August 11 and introduces another frequent topos on the *SMC* blog: Will I ever have a romantic life again if I have a child on my own? Jennifer writes: "Gosh—I hear every woman on here loud and clear. Maybe I need to hear more success stories of women who conceived on their own and still found a great guy after the child was born? Hang in there everyone. We'll all get through this." In this lengthy thread, we witness the formation of "rhetorical selves," made possible by rhetorical sharing on the *SMC* blog. Users do not seek to persuade themselves or one another to "move from thinking to trying," as doing so would violate the ethos of the blog's community. However, their identities and imaginaries do emerge and evolve in response to their collective and dialogic reflections. The support they offer each other contributes to their fashioning their identity as single mothers and gives some the confidence to take their first steps toward that goal.

Transformation

Whereas the rhetorical sharing of the users who responded to Emma Johnson's query emphasize the deliberate, well-reasoned, and often angst-ridden decision making that *precedes* SMCs' pursuit of single motherhood, that of the users to whom I turn now focus on the transformation that occurs *after* making the decision to become a single mother—that is, to the woman that elective single motherhood creates. Their rhetorical sharing helps them to understand the transformative effects of single motherhood. These users argue that transformation—the conversion to elective single motherhood—warrants the label SMC. Richard H. Dees argues that conversions, a form of transformation, consist of two phases: first, that of self-discovery, the search for what one finds important, and second, that of self-invention, as one builds a life premised on those values.[33] Rhetorical sharing on the *SMC* blog supports both phases. In writing on the blog, many users identify their values and then envision and articulate a life path guided by them. These users celebrate their newfound sense of agency and confidence, which they attribute to their pursuit of single motherhood. Theirs is a rhetoric of discovery and becoming that rhetorical sharing on the blog fosters and reinforces.

Dierdre Fishel's experience, about which she writes in an April 10, 2011, essay, exemplifies this transformation. In it, Fishel acknowledges society's perception of single motherhood as a Plan B, an undesirable deviation from the normal and ostensibly ideal family form, a framework with which, as Janine's post demonstrates, even the most confident SMC must contend. Fishel writes, "Perhaps society will eventually evolve to the point where being a single parent is seen by everyone as just a choice and not a departure." After making this point, however, Fishel shifts her focus away from society to the individual and explains the origins of her "heightened sense of personal freedom": "I'm different now and not just because I'm a mother. I'm different because I'm a single mother—by choice—and this journey has changed me." Here the rhetoric of choice and intentionality recedes and is replaced by a meditation on the choice's outcomes. Fishel takes pains to distinguish the transformation that results when a single woman chooses motherhood from that which occurs when a partnered woman becomes a mother. For her, the difference lies in the SMC's embrace of a nonnormative identity and life path, an embrace that liberates her. Fishel explains, "It isn't just having children alone that is empowering. It's the embracing doing it alone (whether at the beginning or somewhere along the trip) that can be life changing . . . What's different now is that I no longer hold out for refuge in a 'normal life.' I no longer want it to be different both because I went out on a limb to do something irrevocable, and because I know there is nothing second-rate about our family." Fishel acknowledges that she cannot reverse her "irrevocable" decision, a tacit admission that she is invested in considering the choice a wise one. But she also insists that the very experience of doing nonnormative family confirms her sense of the rightness of her path. She proceeds to describe how being an SMC changes her conduct in every area of her life: "It used to be hard for me to tell strangers, but that embarrassment has been replaced by a powerful sense of energy and pride. And this 'coming out' has freed me to live the life I really want—on many levels . . . This feeling of comfort, this trust in my own instincts has pervaded every area of my life." Fishel concludes by repeating that the power lies in owning the choice, no matter the outcome: "Making the choice in and of itself can be a transformative experience—whether you wind up having children biologically, through adoption or even in the case of one friend of mine—not having children at all . . . Women owning their desire, controlling their destiny (reproductive and otherwise) has rarely been supported throughout history. That we can do it now is something I think is worth celebrating." Fishel does not describe herself as feminist or elective single motherhood as a feminist act. However, she situates decisions around motherhood, including the one to remain childfree, in a feminist framework that relies on psychological understandings of empowerment and choice.

Rhetorics of freedom and normalcy, undergirded by the joy of acting upon maternal desire, appear in many of the responses to Fishel's essay. These users explain how Fishel's words affect their understanding of themselves and their families and the life-changing effects of these perspectival shifts. Some claim that they find themselves freed from the pressure to assimilate and opt instead to embrace their difference. For example, on April 11, 2011, Val explains how Fishel's essay compelled her to acknowledge and address her own resistance to seeing her family as "alternative." She writes, "The most eye opening was that I had not come to terms with the fact that I did have an alternative family. Now, looking at it from that perspective *frees* me to embrace my choice, and my althernative [*sic*] family" (my italics). Susan Charlotte's April 11, 2011, comment echoes Val's. She responds particularly to the line in Fishel's essay, which she quotes verbatim, about "no longer hold[ing] out for refuge in a 'normal life.'" She exclaims: "This resonated so deeply with me . . . This is exactly how I feel. And it feels wonderful to let go of worn out illusions of 'normal.' Currently pregnant, I feel *free* for the first time since my bio clock went 'ding' 11 years ago."[34] Val and Susan credit Fisher's essay with liberating them from internalized notions of the ideal family and with helping them to shed norms and assumptions that positioned them and their families as deficient or deviant. Tande's April 18 comment shows how Fisher's essay allows her to proceed despite her fears: "I have re-read this blog several times. I have decided to become a single mother and am planning to start treatment soon. As the time gets closer, the fear and apprehension gets stronger. Thanks for this article and for the comments that affirm what I am feeling is normal."[35]

The rhetoric of freedom is contagious. Users' comments gain momentum and take on a life of their own. Bethany responds powerfully to Fishel's rhetoric of freedom: "Your point about how '*freeing*' this choice is really hit the mark with me" (April 11, 2011).[36] After describing feeling "trapped into a life" she did not want, she goes on to writes about the dramatic turn her life took when she decided to become an SMC: "When I decided to become an SMC, it was like the clouds have parted." On April 15, 2011, Dora contributes with exuberance to the chorus of freedom rhetorics and riffs on the notion of "alternative." She exclaims: "YES! Successfully becoming a single mother by choice has been emotionally *freeing*. And yes, I embrace having an alternative family. We are 3x the alternative. Single mom, older mom (I was 46 when my daughter was born), and donor embryo family." Dora seems to shout, "I am different, and I embrace that difference." As evidenced by their comments, Fishel's affirmative legitimizing gives these users license, indeed encourages them, to acknowledge and celebrate the ways that ESM families fall outside of normative ideals, rather than feeling pressured to demonstrate their similarity to heterosexual two-parent families. In articulating their differences, these users discover what they find significant and valuable about their experience as SMCs, including their contagious maternal desire. In sharing their experiences with one another, they confirm the rightness of their life choices and of their identity as SMCs.

Users' rhetorical sharing in response to Fishel's essay also calls attention to the transformative power of language and naming. On April 13, 2011, Maria thanks Fishel for articulating what she feels and knows but could not express: "Thank you for helping me to realize what I couldn't really put into words." Maria implies here the causal relationship between articulation and understanding: her realization is the result of Fishel's articulation. In a different thread on August 26, 2012, Joanne H uses the metaphor of "rebirth" to describe the transformation she experienced after deciding to pursue motherhood as a single woman. She writes, "As difficult as my trying to conceive phase has been so far . . . the rebirth I first felt when I committed to becoming an SMC has remained . . . What seemed at times to be one of the darkest moments of my life, letting go of a life plan I had held close since childhood, may yet yield more hope than I ever would have imagined. There are so many side benefits when you give yourself what you truly want." One user characterizes Joanne H as "letting go" of her dream. Joanne H, in fact, reconceives and rearticulates her dream—another variation of definitional work. She always "truly" wanted to become a mother; it is simply that the "life plan" she assumed would lead to motherhood looks different than she had imagined it would. She is a reborn as a woman capable of envisioning herself and her life path differently. Users' responses to Joanne H's rhetorical sharing affirm her transformation and express their identification with her experience. Jenn comments on August 27, "I really could not have said this any better myself–you perfectly summed up everything I've been feeling on this topic!" On August 29, Tonya writes, "Thank you so much for sharing yourself. I can so relate to 'letting go' of the dream." On September 12, Lynne responds to Tonya: "Me too, Tonya."

Digital Consciousness Raising

In the twenty-first century, feminist meaning making and consciousness raising still happen via face-to-face encounters. However, online platforms, like the *SMC* blog, play an increasingly important role in this work by allowing strangers to engage in rhetorical sharing. Users' rhetorical sharing is a form of legitimizing, one that is directed internally toward themselves as well as toward other users of the *SMC* blog—women, like themselves, who are considering becoming or already are SMC. The blog reveals a complex, multivocal, and diverse picture of elective single motherhood as seen from within and as expressed by the women who are doing it. It constitutes a "collective rhetoric" among strangers, one characterized most powerfully not by consensus about the meaning or significance of Single Motherhood by Choice but rather by the nature and effects of users' engagement with one another.[37] Users' identity as SMCs is performative, iterative, and realized through their rhetorical sharing. As heretofore strangers post on the *SMC* blog, they identify and affirm their core values and commitments and posit various visions and narrative frames with which to explain, define, and constitute themselves as SMCs. Their rhetorical sharing underscores the notion that the "self" is "a rhetorical form—[one] that exists only in its continual aesthetic creation, in its indefinite becoming" and that this "becoming" happens not only with and through known others but also with and through interactions with strangers.[38]

The intimacy and subjectivity of rhetorical sharing among strangers on the *SMC* blog enable rhetorical becoming, underscoring Grabill and Pigg's conclusion that "thinking together in ways that [are] deeply personal may be one of the most important affordances of online interactions."[39] Mommyblogging, this analysis suggests then, is not merely "a private, meaning-making ritual which is open to public view."[40] Rather, it can be agonistic in the most generative sense, creating virtual spaces in which users' rhetorical sharing supports their private meaning making but also generates questions, creates knowledge and, alters the perspectives of others. Writing in a dialogic blog cultivates the questioning, negotiating, and, at times, awakening to a new way of viewing and being in the world that some theorists identify as features of feminist consciousness. Feminist thought seems to have shaped some *SMC* blog users' understanding of their identity and experiences, and, in some instances, has led them to identify explicitly as feminists. Regardless of their self-identification as feminists, the deliberations about the ethics, definition, and significance of elective single motherhood on the blog echo and extend theoretical debates about the existence and significance of gender difference as well as the goals of feminism itself (i.e., equality—sameness—or difference). Many of the users also engage enduring feminist concerns, such as the politics of separating motherhood from marriage, but they situate themselves and those concerns in the dynamic sociopolitical context of the early twenty-first century. This chapter thus complicates depictions of ESM as "reluctant revolutionaries" or "unwilling warriors," and, in so doing, demonstrates the contribution that careful analysis of ESM legitimizing can make to twenty-first-century rhetorical feminist theory.[41]

CHAPTER 3

CONTESTING THE SINGLE MOTHER BY CHOICE CONSTRUCT IN MEMOIR

> [Murphy Brown's] triumphant stance for lifestyle choices did not shape my idea of motherhood.
>
> —Nefertiti Austin, *Motherhood So White*

> They called it "Plan B." . . . Their stories depressed me.
>
> —Robin Silbergleid, *Texas Girl*

> The collective "we" is what I heard, and is why becoming a single mother has been nothing like what I imagined or feared . . . It was always "we" even though "we" never referred to the all-in-one husband and father.
>
> —Rachel Lehmann-Haupt, *DIY Mom: A Solo Parenting Adventure*

> I felt as if I was letting go of romantic love and the white picket fence and life in the normal lane—thin, married, with children.
>
> —Alexandra Soiseth, *Choosing You*

By the early aughts, Murphy Brown mothers had moved out of the margins of public consciousness. In addition to the publication of the guidebooks discussed in chapter 1 and media coverage in major news outlets, a spate of romantic comedies featured ESMs, who, as consistent with the genre, get married at the end of the movie, in several cases to the biological father of the child the protagonist conceived as an ESM.[1] Some ESMs chafed against these popular culture representations, which echoed the SMC construct's constraints and exclusions. Others identified with that same construct's assumptions that single motherhood is Plan B and expressed their yearning to adhere to the nuclear norm of family promulgated by proponents of family values. This era also witnessed the publication of a spate of life-writing by ESMs themselves. This chapter traces the evolution of and contestation around the ESM construct as it is adopted and reimagined by four memoirists, who represent a range of engagement with both the ESM image and the "assumed norm" of motherhood—white, married, heterosexual, middle-class, and able-bodied.[2]

These memoirists harness the affordances of the genre of memoir to make the ESM identity and construct their own. Each engages in legitimizing rhetorics of choice, desire, and intentionality, though their relationship to these rhetorics, as well as their aims in marshalling them, distinguish their efforts. Their memoirs illuminate deeply engrained assumptions about "legitimate" mothers and family forms, whether by revealing the fault lines and cracks in the logics undergirding these assumptions or by showing those same assumptions' stronghold on their imaginary. The memoir genre provides an apt vehicle for their engagement and legitimizing. While guidebooks are didactic and attempt to provide broadly universal advice about what or how to do something, often flattening and generalizing experience in the process, memoirs are typically expressive, individualized, and idiosyncratic. Though some readers use memoirs as guidebooks to a certain lifestyle or way of being, a memoir's primary aim is to explain the memoirist's subjective experience of their evolution from one "I" to another "I." The memoir chronicles and explains how that different person came to be. That explanation details, in part, the memoirist's negotiation of societal expectations and norms, the ones to which they adhere, those they resist, and those with which they ambivalently engage. Memoirs underscore that norms are complicated: they enable and constitute as much as they constrain and restrain. As feminist philosopher Marjorie Jolles suggests, "We are better suited to imagine normalization not as something to be escaped, but to be maneuvered around, through, and with."[3] Some memoirists seek to understand the origins of social norms, including the norm of motherhood, and to determine their relationship to, or stance toward, them. Others resist or avoid this kind of reckoning. The genre, then, is both a window onto norms and a vehicle through which this engagement—be it a form of repetition, critique, or novel uptake—can take place. Interrogation of these ESM memoirs illuminates maternal and familial norms and also clarifies the dynamics of the legitimacy continuum, which results in the veneration of some mothers and the excoriation of others, as well as attitudes that fall between those extremes. Because the assumptions and strategies of these memoirists' legitimizing elucidate broader questions of maternal and familial legitimacy, they are worthy of analysis.

As chapter 1 demonstrates, the conservative SMC construct established by the 1990s guidebooks legitimizes single mothers who attempt, to the extent possible, to adhere to dominant norms of good motherhood and neoliberal family values, and, implicitly, stigmatizes single mothers who fail to do so. The SMC construct serves to maintain exclusive discourses of maternal legitimacy, rooted in historically differential treatment of mothers based on their social location, while also capitalizing on contemporary discourses of "choice," which establish a hierarchy of "good" and "bad" choosers. Only single mothers who do not threaten the normative ideal of the nuclear family, despite their creation of nonnormative families, and who make "good" choices, like SMCs, can join the sanctioned circle of legitimate motherhood. Lying at the negative end of the legitimacy continuum, the SMC construct thus conserves and reinforces maternal hierarchies. Nefertiti Austin, Rachel Lehmann-Haupt, and Robin Silbergleid leverage the genre of memoir to engage in affirmative legitimizing that pushes against the constraints and exclusions of the SMC identity. Their legitimizing rhetorics expand conceptions of maternal and familial legibility and legitimacy. In contrast, Alexandra Soiseth, author of *Choosing You*, remains locked in dominant norms, and, consequently, struggles to demonstrate her worthiness as a mother, even by the standards established by the SMC construct. Her legitimizing falls squarely on the negative end of the legitimacy continuum and thus shores up dominant—and exclusionary—maternal and familial norms.

It is unproductive to impugn legitimizing that appears to bolster and reinforce patriarchal norms of race, gender, and parenthood. I aim instead to be what Amy Robillard calls an "adequate rhetorical witness" to these ESM memoirists, one who "will listen without judging, who will read without impugning, who will respond ethically to the crafted, narrated experiences of those whose stories we have not yet heard."[4] I am inspired by the work of feminist rhetorician Charlotte Hogg, who credits historian Brenda E. Brasher with modeling a scholarly approach that "understand[s] the deliberate choices that motivate the women in her study even if it seems to her audience that these choices work against their own interests."[5] I am also guided by feminist rhetoricians Royster and Kirsch's "ethics of hope and care," which they describe as follows: "Even if and when we find ourselves disagreeing in the end with [rhetors'] values, ideologies, or beliefs, we still look and listen carefully and caringly, contemplate our perceptions, and speculate about the promise, potential, and realities of these rhetors' lives and work."[6]

Memoir as Legitimacy Tool

Memoir is an apt vehicle through which to complicate both the generalized SMC construct and dominant norms of motherhood and family. Memoirs are personal, subjective, and idiosyncratic, even when, as is often the case with political memoirs and *testimonios*, the memoirist's personal experience is meant to represent a collective experience or identity. Rather than promising to provide a comprehensive account of the facts of the writer's life, as do autobiographies, memoirs focus on the writer's self and identity and often zero in on a particular moment or specific period of time. As critic Thomas Larson observes, they emphasize "the *who* over the *what*."[7] The topic and subject of memoir are the same: the self, selfhood, and the rendering intelligible of subjective and phenomenological experience. In this sense, memoirs are a technology of the self, for in writing, memoirists construct and enact themselves. No matter the memoirist's aim in sharing their personal experience, that experience indexes the social. As rhetorician Amy Robillard notes, "Personal experience is more than evidence and it is more than personal."[8] Memoirs enact the relationship between the self and world, revealing how the memoirists' relations with others, norms, and societal expectations constitute self and identity. According to Larson, "In memoir, how we have lived with ourselves teeter-totters with how we have lived with others—not only people, but cultures, ideas, politics, religions, history, and more."[9] Some memoirists critically reflect on the relationship between self and world, using the memoir not only to reveal but also to resist the influences and pressures that have shaped them, but are not immutable. Critic Leigh Gilmore explains, "While giving an account of oneself will always already be shaped by a given set of historical circumstances, such accounting *might* also consist of a deep questioning of such shaping, sometimes with the intent of transforming or transgressing norms."[10] I value the ESM memoirs that engage with maternal norms in this way, rather than uncritically or docilely acquiescing to them.

Memoirists seek to understand, explain, and, ultimately, legitimize who they are to themselves and to their readers. As such, all memoirs fall along the legitimacy continuum. A memoirist's legitimizing is propelled both from within, by an internal impulse to understand and then share their story, and from without, by forces beyond themselves that elicit their account.[11] The legitimizing of memoir is thus inherently relational, even when the primary Other in the relation is oneself; I can legitimize something to myself, as if I consisted of two or more selves that are not in harmony. While some memoirists seek political identification and solidarity—to "enlist" and "conscript" readers to their stance, as critic Thomas Couser suggests—others aim to achieve something more subtle: witnessing, and perhaps understanding or sympathy for their position or perspective.[12] These latter memoirists' aims are psychological and phenomenological, not explicitly political. The memoirist may seek only to explain themselves, their experiences, and their perspective, not to compel readers to identify with them. What matters, then, is that readers acknowledge and comprehend the memoirist, not necessarily that they admire, approve, or agree with them. This acknowledgement and comprehension are the legitimacy some memoirists seek, one that entails respect, as in due regard: a literal true seeing. ESM memoirists want readers to see them *as they see themselves*, not to place them in ill-fitting maternal frameworks or the straitjacket of the ESM construct. At a fundamental level, their efforts to achieve legitimacy are efforts to be legible.

Given that they write as mothers about motherhood, the work of ESM memoirists falls within the subgenre of the "momoir:" "a site for self-representation of the mother as she negotiates her multiple roles and how her roles are interpolated by the other aspects of her subjectivity."[13] Nancy Reddy observes, "What [momoirs] have in common is their commitment to capturing the joys and challenges of life with small children in an unvarnished and unglamorous manner." They help to construct a "shared narrative about mothering practice."[14] In large part, demographic shifts fueled the proliferation of the momoir. According to Andrea O'Reilly, third-wave "women, who were thinking and writing about other feminist issues in the 1980s and '90s, turned their attention to motherhood as they became mothers themselves."[15] Ideological shifts, however, also played a role. Stephanie Wilkinson and Jennifer Niesslein, editors of *Brain, Child*, speculate on feminism's influence, suggesting that "one less documented way that today's women's sense of entitlement has played out is in publishing. If football coaches and fishing enthusiasts could pen a book about their experiences, why not mothers?"[16] In a related vein, maternal theorist Andrea O'Reilly points to the effects of the "new momism," which suggests that mothering is, indeed that it *should* be, an identity and activity that gives mothers' lives meaning and pleasure.[17] O'Reilly argues that while "new momism" made motherhood "so important and central to women that, of course, they can and must discuss it," it has also had unintended consequences, as it "naturalizes and normalizes the very patriarchal conditions of motherhood that feminists, including the motherhood memoir writers themselves, seek to dismantle."[18]

The prototypical author of the momoir is a white, married, middle-class, heterosexual cisgender woman for whom motherhood is expected and lauded. Despite the particularity of this social location, many momoirists assume the universality of their maternal experience.[19] Because the typical momoirist assumes her maternal legitimacy, the desire or right to *become* a mother is typically not the focus of her momoir; her focus is instead on her experience of motherhood. Her tone is confessional, and her concerns are the (ostensibly) private and contained issues of home and family. Critic Nancy Reddy identifies a recurring motif in the typical momoir—"I don't know what I'm doing, and mothering isn't fun!"—that indexes this focus and concerns as well as the privileges that enables them.[20] She critiques this stance and analyzes why race and class privilege make some readers of the momoir more susceptible to it: "The very pose—*there are no experts here*—that I found so appealing is one that's likely inaccessible to women without the privilege that sustains these writers. The new dominant narrative of motherhood—women feeling like they are allowed to say about motherhood *this is hard and sometimes I'm bad at it and sometimes I don't like it*—is inextricably intertwined with race and class."[21] Only a mother secure in her legal and sociocultural legitimacy can express insecurities about how well she mothers. Mothers who are most vulnerable to state intervention stand to be penalized, or even lose custody of their children, if their mothering is deemed too deviant from middle-class norms. When the focus of a typical momoir widens beyond the exclusively domestic, it often turns to "work-life balance" issues. Many momoirs situate themselves within the "media-manufactured 'mommy wars'" between working and stay-at-home mothers.[22] Finally, momoirs typically present "childrearing solely as a private and non-political undertaking, with no social or political import," paying scant, if any, attention to the inextricable ties between the private realm and public life.[23]

ESM momoirists disrupt the ostensibly "shared [maternal] narrative" of the prototypical momoir and the expected ethos and stance of the momoirist.[24] As single women, they alter the standard subject position of the momoirist—a married or partnered cisgender woman—by recounting the maternal experience of women for whom motherhood was neither expected nor lauded. By focusing primarily on the imaginings and desires that precede their becoming mothers and on their attempts to become mothers, they further expand the scope of the momoir, which typically focuses on the daily experience of mothering. Additionally, paid work and professional identity figure centrally and (mostly) unapologetically in ESM momoirs, unsurprisingly, given that ESMs are, by force, at least in most cases, both the breadwinner and caregiver for their children. While many ESMs enjoy race, class, and citizenship privileges that protect them from the threat that their children will be taken away from them, they still risk social censure for "whining" about maternal challenges; after all, they did "choose" motherhood and opted to bring their children into a family form that many consider unacceptable. Finally, some ESM momoirs not only analyze but also celebrate the sociopolitical significance of their motherhood. As the following analysis reveals, Nefertiti Austin's, Robin Silbergleid's, and Rachel Lehmann-Haupt's affirmative legitimizing particularizes maternal norms and queers gendered assumptions, thereby revealing memoir's "poetic" and "world-making" potential, whereas Alexandra Soiseth's negative legitimizing upholds and reinforces the "assumed norm" of motherhood and mothering.[25]

Nefertiti Austin's *Motherhood So White*

Nefertiti Austin's *Motherhood So White* tackles not just the marital/partnered bias of representations of motherhood and family but also their whiteness.

Austin's affirmative legitimizing amplifies the SMC construct to include Black single mothers, especially those who adopt domestically, a process about which she addresses misinformation and provides guidance. Austin's critical racial consciousness inflects her rhetorics of choice, desire, and intentionality. In *Motherhood So White,* these rhetorics are not bulwarks of neoliberalism but rather tools to raise readers' consciousness about their assumptions around race and motherhood. Through her inclusion of sociological analysis and history, Austin expands the scope of the memoir beyond the reflective analysis of personal experience, and, more particular to the momoir, beyond the myopically domestic, thus underscoring the inextricable relationship of the "who" of the memoirist and the "what" of their social context.[26] Austin's vulnerability and self-reflection bestow depth and texture to her affirmative stance.

It is no accident that Austin's title, *Motherhood So White,* highlights race, not relationship status, though her memoir focuses on her experience as a single Black mother. Austin aims to counter racially monolithic representations of motherhood as white and to redress the concomitant absence of diverse and complex representations of Black motherhood. She explains, "As a writer, I was fighting against white privilege's erasure of Black parenting perspectives and insistence that the word *mother* automatically meant *white.*"[27] Austin recounts that she spent years looking for a publisher of her memoir, repeatedly hearing a version of, "Black mom narratives are too marginal to sell."[28] Deeshaw Philyaw unpacks the racist logic underlying publishers' decision making: "Publishers perpetuate the mythology that your face and my face are not the marketable faces of American motherhood, that Black women's motherhood journeys are 'fringe,' lacking in broad appeal, and therefore, not worth the investment."[29] Mothers of color get that message. Some thus may not bother writing a memoir, because they assume that it is unlikely to be published. As Filipina memoirist Angela Garbes observes, "many writers [of color] don't pursue writing about their journeys with pregnancy and motherhood because they don't believe they'll be given a chance. I know I was one of them."[30]

At the same time, Philyaw contends, "the widening of the motherhood memoir canon requires shifts in *supply* as well as demand."[31] The very notion that one could or should write a memoir indexes privilege. To write a momoir, mothers must believe that "mothering is worthy of expression and representation in art."[32] Indeed, it is that sentiment that compels mothers to write. Some women writers of color make the point that they simply *do* motherhood and mothering along with everything else in their lives. "It's what we do, what we've always done."[33] Yvonne Bynoe echoes Allen-Mercado: "For Black women, writing and telling our stories is not a priority, and if it is, the writing is not about motherhood, or anything personal, or family-oriented. We would rather talk topics like family on a macro level."[34] Deeshaw Philyaw concludes, "So if Black women haven't beaten down publishers' doors with manuscripts about mothering or about pulling second shifts, it's probably because this is what we've always done, without fanfare." Black writer Kim McClarin offers another explanation of the lack of "fanfare": "For my mother, having children was a fact, not a vocation; a duty, not a source of personal enrichment and not particularly fun."[35] For a mother to write about mothering, she must consider it to be something other than a "fact" and a "duty;" motherhood must instead be an identity and mothering an activity that merit reflection and a degree of "fanfare." She must feel that her individual experience and story are worthy of telling.[36] Some mothers do not experience a "sense of entitlement" to write about mothering and motherhood in the individualistic, emotionally raw, and candid manner that characterizes most momoirs.[37] In asserting her right to write a momoir on her terms and by doggedly pursuing a book deal, Austin counters not only the bias of publishers against Black mothers but also the thinking within the Black community that deprioritizes the telling of personal maternal narratives for Black women specifically.

Throughout *Motherhood So White*, Austin insists on the significance of race to maternal experience. She asserts, "Black mothers lived in a different America from white mothers."[38] Austin attributes her heightened awareness of racialized motherhood to her becoming a mother herself: "In my new skin as mother of a Black boy, I had to think through how we would navigate a world set up to challenge his very existence."[39] She begins a letter she wrote to her son, August, with an admission—"Up until now, my views on race and gender were academic"—and goes on to explain how she came to embrace "my conflicted intersectional feminism."[40] That intersectional feminist lens helps her to identify and name the problem—the dearth of representations of and literature for Black single women considering domestic adoption—and thus the exigence for *Motherhood So White*. In bookstores aimed at the general (read: white) public, she found books depicting transracial international adoptions, but "nothing that mirrored August's experience of being a Black American child adopted by a Black American mother."[41] In Black bookstores, "few [books] used the word *adoption*, showed nonrelative caregivers as main characters, or discussed Black people adopting Black children."[42] Austin asks rhetorically, "Did I not exist?"[43] Her frustration with this vacuum of resources motivated her to write *Motherhood So White*: "I spent a long time looking for representation in parenting, and this book is in your hands because one woman seeking to be [a mother] was looking for answers."[44]

Austin aims to carve a place for herself in maternal discourses, both white and Black, that do not recognize, let alone celebrate, her motherhood and that fail to reconcile the various facets of her maternal identity and experience. She offers readers a lens through which to understand kinship and family that is grounded both in her experience as a Black woman and in Black history. She identifies her decision to adopt domestically via the foster system as the primary cause of her unrecognizability, given that it is an atypical route to motherhood in both white and Black communities, though for different reasons. Most white people in the United States, including ESMs, opt to adopt transnationally. Austin explains: "I was an outlier in the white community for adopting a child domestically."[45] Black people, in contrast, do "Black adoptions," which occur outside of formal systems and institutions. "We [Black people] typically adopted relatives," writes Austin. "Having a connection, even a tenuous one, was culturally more acceptable than blindly accepting a child we knew nothing about."[46] Later, she states bluntly, "Adopting a child I did not know was breaking code. White people did shit like that."[47] Austin draws on her personal experience to explain "Black adoption," recounting how her grandparents adopted her and her brother, Kareem, when their parents could no longer take care of them. In the chapter titled "My Adoption So Black," she contextualizes her personal experience of Black adoption within African American history, starting with slavery and the cultural practices that this history engendered, including that of extra-kin family and child-rearing.

At the same time, Austin seeks to counter the misinformation and prejudices that characterize the Black community's attitudes toward formal adoption processes and about Black single mothers. After observing that "single Black mothers were marginalized on both [Black and white] sides," she claims her kinship with Black foster mothers, whom she describes as "generous citizens, called to help children in need:" "I was now one of these single Black women caring for a nonrelative."[48] Naming them "*sheroes*" and explicitly countering the myth of the "welfare queen," Austin expounds, "Far from the Black welfare queen, these primarily single women took on a responsibility that most coupled Blacks or whites with means and education would never embark upon."[49] Austin describes her own brother Kareem's resistance to her decision to adopt via the foster system as a case in point: "Kareem's reaction wasn't unexpected. Not only did white people believe that nonsense the media spread about kids in the foster system, Black people did too."[50] At the same time, Austin aims to dismantle the stereotype of the "strong Black woman": "I was tired of fulfilling the cultural expectation that unmarried, single mothers who were gainfully employed were *strong Black women*, defined as not needing or wanting a man."[51] While claiming her confidence and strength, Austin acknowledges the challenges of single parenting. "It probably appeared to the outside world that August and I were satisfied as a duo," she writes. "The truth, however, was more complicated. I could manage August by myself but felt the sting of my solo status when I was overwhelmed."[52] In memoir, Austin can simultaneously showcase her competence as a Black adoptive mother and also reveal her vulnerabilities.

Austin's primary audience are those "single, non-rich Black women," who, like her, find themselves at the interstices of different maternal experiences and who are stigmatized for considering (or already being) mothers as single women and un- or misrepresented in popular culture.[53] These women share the "concerns about exes, financing single motherhood, and feeling emotionally overwhelmed" addressed by white-authored guidebooks. [54] Austin insists, however, that a trio of factors influence the deliberations that precede her target readers' decision to become, as well as their experience being, solo mothers—namely, "Race, economics, and culture ratcheted up how and why we chose solo parenting."[55] Austin pinpoints the racial privilege that underlies dominant constructions of "choice" motherhood: "These mainstream images of white, single motherhood celebrated *oops* pregnancies, surrogates, sperm banks and stepmoms, and empowered white women to choose their own path to parenthood."[56] Though Austin declares that she personally felt "empowered to go where I pleased and take any route to parenthood I saw fit," she acknowledges that her primary readership does not easily identify with the SMC construct, which assumes a white woman subject unencumbered by racialized and racist baggage.[57] Austin mines her own experience to articulate the particular challenges faced by Black single women considering motherhood, writing, "I needed specific advice on how to handle the social and emotional consequences of becoming a single mother in a country where the term *single mother* was code for *Black welfare mother*."[58] *Motherhood So White* offers that "specific advice" from Austin as well as from other Black adoptive mothers whose stories she includes in the final chapter, "Stories of Parenting So Black."

Austin's affirmative legitimizing makes *Motherhood So White* a manifesto in addition to a memoir and guidebook. Austin redefines what constitutes legible and legitimate motherhood and, through her encouragement to her target readership, vivifies what could be, in the voice of a different writer, a postfeminist cliché: "Do what feels right *to you* and block out the cultural noise and expectations of how a single Black woman becomes a mother."[59] When issued by Austin, a conscious and critical Black writer to Black readers, this antinormative triumphalist injunction to just "do you" reads not as postfeminist posturing that willfully ignores the power of norms and normativity but rather as an empowered directive to live one's own story in spite of norms and expectations that threaten to hamper and constrain. *Motherhood*

So White thus resignifies rhetorics of choice, desire, and intentionality, thereby demonstrating their emancipatory potential.

Robin Silbergleid's *Texas Girl*

Robin Silbergleid's *Texas Girl* deploys the expected candor of the memoir genre to tackle the assumption that single women pursue motherhood with regret and sadness and to unveil the heterosexism that underlies discourses of motherhood and family. Rather than donning the stance of an apologetic, defensive, or lonely single mother in need of a man to make her family complete, Silbergleid presents herself as a whole woman and as a wholly capable mother. She defies the expectation to explain and justify her maternal decision making. As she states, "If I knew what I wanted, why should I risk losing it just because it made some people squeamish to think about women raising kids without husbands?"[60] *Texas Girl* does not detail Silbergleid's efforts to persuade herself that single motherhood is right for her. Instead, it recounts her realization that she would not adhere to normative ideals of motherhood or family (indeed, that she is uninterested in doing so) and, in most respects, recoils from those ideals. *Texas Girl* centers and celebrates Silbergleid's maternal experience, and, as importantly, her unequivocal and uncomplicated embrace of her maternal desire. Silbergleid demands acknowledgment of and respect for her decision to pursue single motherhood, rather than seeking to earn plaudits by explaining and justifying her maternal choices. In a word, she commands, rather than seeks, legitimacy. For Silbergleid, "adequate rhetorical witness" entails accepting the terms and (chosen) norms through which she lives her life, whether readers approve of them or not.[61] In detailing the ways in which her psychic life and maternal experience do not conform to expected and normative forms and timelines, *Texas Girl* offers readers alternative frameworks for understanding and inventing their own conceptions of motherhood and family. Her rhetorics of choice, desire, and intentionality thus further feminist aims by expanding readers' maternal imaginaries.

Silbergleid's maternal desire forms the backbone of her narrative. She asserts repeatedly and insistently that intentional single motherhood is her "first choice," both a plausible and desired Plan A.[62] Writing about her as-of-yet-unconceived daughter, she proclaims, "She would not be born of unprotected sex, by accident; no, my daughter would be chosen again and again and again. My first choice, and only."[63] Silbergleid shares that she has always desired motherhood, not marriage or a nuclear family. During a discussion with friends about their professional futures, she recalls thinking, "I just want to have a baby," markedly not *a husband and* a baby.[64] Her inverted syntax of the popular expression "how to find the man of your dreams" reflects her priorities. As she puts it, "the real issue" is "how to find the father of the baby of your dreams."[65] During a conversation about motherhood with an on-again, off-again boyfriend, with whom she had fantasized getting pregnant, she recalls thinking, "I didn't want to be married. And I certainly didn't want to be a stay-at-home mom."[66] For Silbergleid, desire is maternal, not romantic: "Not heated passion between man and woman, but the pure, basic need of a mother for a child."[67] She distinguishes herself from women who have internalized the assumed ideal timeline of partnership or marriage before baby: "Even women I'd chatted with online, women who were also thinking about becoming single moms, encouraged me to wait, date a little, keep single motherhood in mind as a backup plan; how could it possibly be my first choice?"[68] Counter to societal expectations, even those of her fellow ESMs, Silbergleid feels strongly—and tells her readers—that having a baby now, as a single woman, is her "first choice." After visiting Aimee, her best friend who is married and the mother of a newborn, she reflects, "I didn't have a husband. And most of the time I didn't consider this fact a problem but one of my better qualities . . . Visiting [Aimee] had only solidified my belief that having a child without all the nonsense of heterosexual partnership was the way to go."[69] Silbergleid's ideal is single motherhood: "If I could have everything I wanted, it would be Aimee and her baby in the downstairs apartment and me and my baby in the upstairs apartment . . . Where Rich [Aimee's husband] and Dr. Boy were in this fantasy I couldn't quite figure out."[70] Ultimately, Silbergleid concludes that, for her, men are not essential: "I didn't need Dr. Boy [her ex-boyfriend] to be happy, and I certainly didn't need him to have a baby."[71] Her attitude toward single motherhood is unabashedly proactive and affirmative.

Consistent with memoir's privileging of the personal as a primary source of evidence, Silbergleid draws on her own experiences and observations to question the presumed virtues of partnered parenthood and the nuclear family. Her analysis of her own feelings and experience, along with her critical observations of others, queer assumptions about the institution of motherhood and family, the meaning of intimacy, and the timeline of the life cycle. She makes strange what she deems "another galaxy, Hetero World," one in which marriage and men are the keys to contentment and in which there is a particular timeline for forming a family.[72] Of her friend Aimee, who has seemingly achieved the American dream—husband, baby, and single-family home—Silbergleid observes, "She had all the outward markers of happiness in American culture, and I'd never seen a person look so sad and out of place."[73] Silbergleid shows how the skepticism she faces about her pursuit of single motherhood at age twenty-nine stems from the belief that partnered parenthood is the ideal. A question lurks beneath the skepticism: why become a single mother when there is still time to meet a man? In a preliminary discussion about artificial insemination, even Silbergleid's reproductive endocrinologist harps on her age, saying, "You're so young."[74] Silbergleid parses the ageist and heterosexist subtext of comments like these and calls attention to their hold on the popular imaginary: "That was what everyone said when I told them I was thinking about having a baby. Some variation on you're so young, what if you meet a great guy? or why now? . . . these questions told me was how little my desires resembled those of other women my age, or how frightened most single women were of not finding a partner and how culturally expected marriage was."[75] By naming these fears and expectations, Silbergleid makes explicit and contestable what is often implicit and thus unassailable. Her sarcastic critique of *doxa* regarding the expected order of events—"everyone knew that dating was the first step toward having a baby, which was the only thing I ever really wanted"—underscores its stronghold on the popular imagination as well as its inaccuracy.[76] As *Texas Girl* demonstrates, dating is not necessarily the first step toward having a baby; it is one path among many. Of this conventional thinking, Silbergleid exclaims, "Now I could be done with all that. Thank goodness."[77] Her depiction of her experience of assisted reproductive technology also goes against the grain. Much of the writing about ART focuses on its strangeness and lack of humanity. Silbergleid casts the relations ART engenders in a new light. She describes her experience of a sonogram performed by a nurse with whom she has worked closely throughout her pregnancy: "It struck me as horribly intimate, more intimate than love or even sex. She knew my body better than anyone else in the world."[78] The intimacy she describes is caring, consensual, and, yes, reproductive. It is a form of queer intimacy, one not easily labeled, articulated, or validated by law. As she concludes, "We were two women who created a child together."[79]

Silbergleid challenges the deficit narrative of single motherhood, which positions her and her child as lacking and unhappy because a man does not figure centrally in their lives. Writing about her as-yet-not-conceived child, she asserts, "She would not be a child born of less, but a child born into plenty [of maternal desire, love, and attention]."[80] Silbergleid describes her birthing room as that "of a child who is wanted and adored, welcomed by a makeshift family of friends."[81] At the same time, Silbergleid decenters the "father question." When a relative asks about the identity of the father of her child-to-be, she shares her internal response to his question with her readers: "For me, the father was the least important part of the story, only necessary for about a split second when sperm met egg."[82] She celebrates her, quite literally, singular motherhood: "I was a woman who'd created her own fantasy—What could be better than that?"[83] She disidentifies with the real-life SMCs she meets, who see their motherhood as second best: "They called it 'Plan B.' . . . Their stories depressed me."[84] Aware of the conventional take on single motherhood, she claims, "There would be no boo-hooing for me."[85] Silbergleid presents single motherhood as an empowered and joyful choice, at least for her. "I realized how happy I was, how perfectly content to have this baby, my own child, my immaculate conception, wiggling around in my uterus."[86] Silbergleid's pleasure stems not only from her healthy pregnancy but also from her single status, which she marks by naming her baby her "immaculate conception." She reflects, "When it came down to it, I had no desire to share the pregnancy with anyone; this baby was all mine."[87] Finally, Silbergleid contests the assumption that to be single is to be lonely. She asserts, "Loneliness was [as] far away as another country. I felt grounded, connected to my friends and the world."[88] After the birth of her daughter, during which she was surrounded by friends, she reflects again on the disconnect between being single and being alone: "More than three years ago, I made the decision to become a single mother; today I am far from alone."[89] Silbergleid thus illustrates how elective single motherhood can generate extensive and deep connections, different from those in a nuclear family, but no lesser.

As Lauren Berlant observes, "Our accounts take shape in genres delivered to us as the proper way of thinking about affect and emotion."[90] Silbergleid resists the rom-com genres on offer to women-identified audiences and attempts in *Texas Girl* to imagine a genre of love and family that captures her distinctive maternal experience. Though she acknowledges her occasional vulnerability to the "made-for-TV movie on Lifetime Television for Women," she consciously and insistently distances herself from that genre's normalizing force. She describes the moment that she conceived the notion of becoming an ESM as "something beyond narrative, beyond the predictable life story of man plus woman equals baby . . . something marvelous."[91] She claims that hers is "a storybook ending after all," despite it not involving a husband or father to her child, and she imagines telling her daughter "the story of how she came to be . . . a story not of a man and a woman but a love story nonetheless."[92] In both statements, Silbergleid reinvents the genre of the love story, centering maternal rather than romantic love. In her revisioning, the birth of a child is the culmination and maximum expression of maternal desire, not of heterosexual romance. Contra the dominant narrative about lonely single mothers, she describes her maternal experience as "a Feminist utopia," though not in the literal sense of utopia as "no place," because she has in fact achieved what for her is a perfect maternal existence.[93] Silbergleid's imaginings in *Texas Girl* provoke readers to do the same: to imagine and then realize their own "Feminist utopia."[94]

Rachel Lehmann-Haupt's *DIY Mom: A Solo Parenting Adventure*

In contrast to Austin and Silbergleid, Rachel Lehmann-Haupt had to legitimize single motherhood to herself, as being an ESM was not her Plan A. Her short e-momoir, *DIY Mom*, showcases her internal legitimizing about and eventual embrace of elective single motherhood.[95] Lehmann-Haupt recounts how she allowed herself to stray from the path forged by dominant norms and heteronormative scripts, and, ultimately, how those experiences inspired her and facilitated her construction of a life that she had not originally envisioned. She shares the unexpected pleasures of being an ESM and the unanticipated boons of forming a non-nuclear family. Readers thus witness Lehmann-Haupt's evolution not only into motherhood but also into a woman who consciously "maneuvers around, through, and with" the norms that structure her imaginary.[96] Despite the title, then, *DIY Mom* is as much a memoir about the emergence of a new woman, one who finds her previous assumptions overturned and who crafts an identity that aligns with her new perspective, as it is a momoir about mothering and motherhood. Lehmann-Haupt's affirmative legitimizing demonstrates how a flexible and dynamic relationship to norms can facilitate heretofore unimagined, and, more importantly, pleasureful ways of being and living.

Lehmann-Haupt recounts grappling with the source of her maternal desires, finding herself unable to determine whether they were hers or what society told her she should want. She shares, "When I hit my 30s, I started to feel the ticking of not only my biological clock but even more urgently the social clock, which was telling me to find a husband. It seemed a lot of people in my social circles were coupling up and starting families, and I felt I should, too." Lehmann-Haupt's choice of the word "should" acknowledges the psychic pull of the normative life cycle. She struggled to disarticulate her personal desires from the mandates of the heteronormative timeline for marriage and children. Rather than disavowing the existence of norms or allowing them to control her imaginary uncritically, however, Lehmann-Haupt sought to understand their influence on her psychic life and to exert some agency "with and through" them.[97] She knew that single motherhood was not what she had originally envisioned. Ultimately, however, she determined that her desire for motherhood was strong enough, and enough hers, to act on, and she took the plunge: "I realized it was OK if I didn't do everything in the right order." At the end of *DIY Mom*, Lehmann-Haupt tells readers that she still wants to find a husband and father for her son, but that she no longer believes that this male figure is essential for a happy life or to the psychological health of her son: "I've accepted, as I expect Alexander to accept, that there are many kinds of families." At the same time, she notes, "I still crave a relationship with a man to share my life . . . We're just waiting to cross paths with him." Lehmann-Haupt's desire to meet Mr. Right feels positively charged, expressive of an affirmative personal desire for an intimate romantic connection, not of desperation to adhere to the "social clock."

Lehmann-Haupt discovers, and eagerly tells her readers, that being an ESM is personally transformative, and that the family she creates is satisfying and nourishing in ways that surprise her. After her first insemination, she reflects, "It was not the romantic dream I had imagined all my life of making a child with a man I loved, but having come to trust myself to move forward on my own toward my dream of motherhood felt in a way even more powerful." At this juncture, she did not know whether the insemination would culminate in a pregnancy. The empowerment to which she refers results from her decision to try to become pregnant as a single woman—to adopt the ESM identity—not from the realization of her efforts. Lehmann-Haupt explains how her experiences in pregnancy and motherhood compelled her to question the composition of a family unit and the primacy given to romantic love and marriage, its contemporary institutionalized expression. She states without qualifications or reservations that she, her baby, and her "tribe" are a family, that there is nothing less than or deficient about them: "In my new floating life in California, I had formed a different kind of family foundation to support me." Lehmann-Haupt's critical reflection on her experiences allow her to envision not only other ways of becoming a family but also other ways of doing family that are not reliant on the presence of particular (gendered) bodies and roles. She addresses the "linguistic inconceivability" of her ESM family by coining new terms:[98] "With each piece of advice or offer to help, these women took on a new kind of role. I started to call them my birth maids. Along with family and other friends, they formed a network of support and love that filled in for the husband I was missing." *DIY Mom* celebrates the family that Lehmann-Haupt creates and shows how her experiences as an ESM altered her maternal and familial imaginary.

Finally, writing *DIY Mom* gives Lehmann-Haupt the opportunity to reflect on the disjuncture between her experience of pregnancy as a single woman and the stereotypes about lonely single women. She notes with some surprise, "Despite my stalled love life, I didn't feel alone. As my belly grew, so did my network of support." She introduces the notion of the "collective 'we'" to counter the conflation of singleness and loneliness in discourses about single mothers: "The collective 'we' is what I heard, and is why becoming a single mother has been nothing like what I imagined or feared: lonely nights, no support, and experiencing every milestone alone. Taking this leap of faith without a partner has drawn a network that has gathered around me in numbers stronger than if I had conceived a child inside a traditional relationship and family. In the big and small moments of this new kind of passage, I've found love and connection in the intersecting hubs. Whether it was my best friends or distant acquaintances, it has never been just 'I,' but this collective 'we' . . . It was always 'we' even though 'we' never referred to the all-in-one husband and father." Here Lehmann-Haupt does not merely insist on the richness and viability of the family that she personally created. Instead she offers her experience as evidence of a broader claim suggested by Robin Silbergleid: pursuing a nonconventional path to motherhood can create more extensive connections than does motherhood in the context of a nuclear family. Readers of *DIY Mom* who open themselves to the unexpected and to the nonnormative might find themselves similarly surprised to be living their own "Feminist utopia."[99]

Alexandra Soiseth's *Choosing You: Deciding to Have a Baby on My Own* (2008)

Choosing You stands as the outlier in this cluster of ESM memoirs. Per the 1990s guidebooks, an SMC is aware that she must address the ostensible deficiencies of single-parent homes but is nevertheless confident about herself and her family's viability. Soiseth, in contrast, struggles to imagine motherhood outside of the "ideal," and that struggle leads to her feeling uncertain, insecure, and dissatisfied with herself and the family she creates. *Choosing You* reads like an extended, and, ultimately, failed exercise in self-persuasion in which Soiseth attempts to convince herself, first, that she deserves to be a mother, and second, that she wants to be a single one. Her strained efforts to legitimize herself serve to enhance the visibility of, reinforce the power of, and shore up the exclusive norms to which she cannot adhere but strongly desires to embody and inhabit. *Choosing You* demonstrates that a negative legitimizing strategy that remains firmly ensconced in the dominant paradigm cannot succeed, even on its own terms.

Soiseth might have titled her memoir *Legitimizing Me* instead of *Choosing You*, as it is first an account of her efforts to make herself a "normal" woman by losing weight, and only then, as a result, a woman worthy of motherhood. She informs readers, "I don't think I can overestimate how much losing all that weight made it possible for me to do all I was doing to try to make this pregnancy thing happen. Or, even more profoundly, to think that I could do this at all: have a baby on my own, get pregnant, be pregnant alone, have the baby, and then raise it by myself."[100] Consistent with this assertion, the first few chapters of *Choosing You* read like a weight-loss memoir to the extent that the "you" in the title could plausibly refer to Soiseth's new body, not to the daughter she ends up having. Losing weight is at once the precursor, prerequisite, and signal achievement of Soiseth's overarching goal of normalcy, which also entail biological motherhood in the context of a monogamous heterosexual relationship: "Wouldn't that be cool, if I were ever thin enough to do that [run a marathon] again? It would be so normal. Normal, of course, would also include being married and having kids. Being someone who brushed her teeth every day without having to force herself to."[101] Soiseth fantasizes about losing weight and becoming the heroine of the romances she grew up reading, describing herself as "a normalcy-seeking romantic."[102] Once pregnant, Soiseth celebrates her self-transformation and emphasizes her compliance with middle-class standards of hygiene and house-keeping: "I am a new person now . . . A normal person who is having a baby, flosses her teeth every day, keeps her house clean."[103] Soiseth's "normalcy" requires discipline and hard work: "I am normal (perhaps even better than normal) . . . I am so close to being all that I ever wanted to be . . . I can have what I've always wanted, *because I have worked very hard*."[104] Soiseth's personal transformation is undeniably bodily and psychic; her attempts at normalcy enable her to envision herself as and then become a mother. As feminist philosopher Cressida Heyes avers, dieting can be "a complex intervention in identity rather than a straightforward act of conformity to a beauty ideal."[105] And yet, Soiseth's transformation binds her ever more tightly to an ideal that, despite her efforts, she cannot wholly inhabit and that places unsurpassable limits on her imaginary.

Uncritiqued racialized, classed, and heteronormative norms shape—and therefore constrain—Soiseth's vision of a full and joyful life. Though she expresses some discomfort about her desire for a blonde child, she admits, "I totally want one of those white-haired babies I can buy a Gap bunny suit for, one of those babies that looks exactly like my sister's babies."[106] When her best friend observes that this preference is going to narrow her search for a sperm donor and suggests its racialized subtext, Soiseth retorts, "I would like my baby to look like me . . . I just want the baby to look like my family . . . This is about family!"[107] Rom-com conventions and fairy tales structure Soiseth's imaginary, including her raced and classed notions of female beauty: "I could be beautiful and special and married to someone amazing and fabulous, and we would have spectacular kids together. I could be like the heroine of the romances I grew up reading: someone with white teeth and long blond hair."[108] Unsurprisingly, for Soiseth, family necessarily also includes a father. She admits to herself and to her readers that she never intended to be a single mother for long, and that she mourns her ongoing status as a single mother. "I knew the daddy issue would be a big deal for [Kaj], but I didn't know how hard it would be for me. I don't want her to be without a father, and rocking her here, I realize that part of my being able to go ahead and have her was thinking that she wouldn't be fatherless for very long, because I would find a man soon after she was born. Long before now certainly. Long before she would be aware of her fatherlessness. He and I would have a child together too. And she would know she was born with donor sperm, but she would have a father nevertheless."[109] A "fatherless" existence, as she characterizes it, is a deficit, one to be mourned and corrected. Because Soiseth is boxed into normative ideals of motherhood and family, she cannot legitimize her single mother family to herself, others, or even her daughter.

Soiseth knows that she cannot achieve "normalcy" as she defines it. As such, she experiences deep uncertainty about her worthiness as a woman, as a mother, indeed as a person. She is a woman at war with herself, unable to reconcile the woman she is becoming—a single mother—with deeply entrenched beliefs about a good life and good motherhood specifically. Her internal dialogue demonstrates how profoundly she has internalized stigmas surrounding single motherhood and non-nuclear families: "I guess I actually think deep-down that I don't deserve to be pregnant. I'm trying to fast-track myself somewhere I'm not supposed to go. If you can't get a man, you can't have a family. End of story."[110] In her negative framework, only women who can "get" a man merit motherhood. Soiseth believes that single motherhood further distances her from what she deems the "land of normal," writing, "I was living in the land of normal for a while. There was potential for love. I was running. Fit. Dating. Have sex. Now I am slip-sliding back into the person I have been most of my life. Outside. Different. Alone."[111] Even during her third trimester, she wonders, "It seemed like a good idea at the time [getting pregnant as a single woman], but I wonder if suddenly I haven't just cast myself out of normalcy forever. Have I perhaps institutionalized my aloneness?"[112] After giving birth to Kaj, as she struggles to lose the weight of pregnancy, she thinks, "I am struck, for some reason, by the idea that the price I have paid to have her, to go against convention, is being paid by my body. *That's silly*, I think. *You're being melodramatic*. But the idea persists."[113] Soiseth believes that she is being punished—bodily, to boot—for violating maternal norms that vaunt partnered motherhood. In contrast to Lehmann-Haupt, neither being a single mother nor writing *Choosing You* prompts Soiseth to examine her assumptions about maternal and familial legitimacy. To the contrary, they seem to deepen her acquiescence to and entrenchment in norms to which she cannot adhere.

Soiseth's inability or unwillingness to think beyond "normal" likewise constrain her conceptions of family and intimacy. She attributes her reluctance to order sperm to her disappointment about losing the opportunity to experience heteronormative coupledom: "I felt as if I was letting go of romantic love and the white picket fence and life in the normal lane—thin, married, with children."[114] She eventually orders the sperm, but rather than feeling excitement during her insemination, she feels "very sad," for "it is technology, not love, making a baby."[115] In contrast to Silbergleid, who uses her experience of ART as a springboard for imagining queer intimacy and expanding our constrained maternal and familial imaginary, Soiseth remains locked in normative thinking about romance and reproduction. She uses the present tense to describe her grief: "I need to cry a little about my lost dream. I need to mourn the death of romance."[116] Soiseth accepts the vernacular definition of "alone" as uncoupled, thus disavowing the significance of her friendships. She writes, "With many friends, it's easy to ignore most of the time, but when I think about being old, the idea of being alone terrifies me."[117] Indeed, on the assumption that maintaining close friendships diminishes her chances of finding a husband, she seeks to avoid forming them: "Pat has become the very best friend I vowed I would not find as I was graduating with my MFA."[118] Rather than celebrating the intimacy that she and Pat share, Soiseth experiences regret over the depth of their friendship. In her hierarchy of affective relationships, romantic love remains at the top. At her birthing class, Soiseth's thoughts again turn to her singleness and her internalized assumptions about the relational and affective consequences of that status. In response to a prompt to list her fears about childbirth, she thinks, "What can I add, since I have no husband, no one who loves me in that way or who will be there experiencing the primal fear that [the teacher] is talking about? I feel stiff and uncomfortable. I want someone to love me so much, he is afraid I will die."[119] Later, Soiseth recalls that, at Kaj's birth, her sister felt compelled to leave the room out of worry and anxiety, suggesting that some people *do* love her "in that way."[120] And, yet, Soiseth's negative framework stubbornly casts single motherhood as lacking, precluding her from seriously reconsidering that framework's evaluative terms. The numerous examples of support and camaraderie that she recounts in *Choosing You* do not compel her to question her equation of "aloneness" with singledom.

Soiseth occasionally, but always equivocally, questions normative ideals and toys with alternative ways of evaluating her maternal and familial experience. She admits to having, forgetting, and then recapturing a "fleeting thought" from her baby shower: "*This is my family. This is the family I have made. Here are my people. This is my life. And what a wonderful life it is.*"[121] As Soiseth puts it, however, this "fleeting" thought did not take hold.[122] As her friends and sister help her prepare for Kaj's birth, she wonders, "Would this configuration be possible if I had a husband? I think not, and I am confused about how I feel, where that understanding fits in with my wanting to have a more traditional arrangement. It strikes me that maybe I don't want that so much after all."[123] Though here she momentarily questions her normative desires, her confusion, her hedging, and her qualifiers eclipse those questions. In one of her strongest, most affirmative statements about her "home-built" family, Soiseth asserts, Kaj "loves me and I love her, and between us we have all that it takes to be a family."[124] This assertion, however, seems more aspirational than assertive—a desired stance, not a statement. For Soiseth, single motherhood is a temporary status, a detour on her journey to life in the "normal lane."[125] She maintains her desire to construct a nuclear family as soon as the opportunity presents itself. Despite the seemingly affirmative subtitle of her memoir, *Deciding to Have a Baby on My Own*, "resigning" more aptly captures Soiseth's account of her process of becoming a single mother. She never relinquishes her definition, valuation, or desire for "normalcy." In the final lines of *Choosing You*, Soiseth still only begrudgingly embraces her nonnormative family, writing halfheartedly that she "can" and "may well" do a family on her own.[126] Noting one's capacity to do something is a far cry from celebrating that capacity: Soiseth can, but she does not want to do so.

Choosing You demonstrates that a legitimizing strategy that remains firmly ensconced in the dominant paradigm cannot succeed, even on its own terms. Negative legitimizing, which adheres to and upholds dominant norms, constrains more than it enables. Though it opens up certain fields of agency, the normalization process places limits on the self and psyche.[127] The power that compliance with norms confers is thus not synonymous with freedom. Soiseth is too deeply entrenched in the negative end of the legitimacy continuum to engage in critical reflection. Because she does not analyze the origins of her normative values or the way they structure her thinking, let alone imagine ways to "maneuver around, through, and with" them, she perpetuates them.[128] As Charlotte Hogg observes, "Studying those who embrace normative femininity through rhetorical practices allows us to interrogate more fully how such ideologies are not just subverted or challenged but disseminated, embraced, and perpetuated."[129] In the end, I read Soiseth's memoir as a cautionary tale.

Conclusions

These accounts of motherhood outside of the nuclear family are illuminating on many levels. Despite their different locations on the legitimacy continuum, Austin's, Silbergleid's, Lehmann-Haupt's, and Soiseth's momoirs expand the canon of this genre by centering the experience of single mothers. Their legitimizing reveals and enacts different affective, political, and rhetorical stances on elective single motherhood. Austin's and Silbergleid's external legitimizing are both unapologetic and particular, grounded in the specificity of their maternal location and experience. Austin contests norms that do not acknowledge, and therefore do not attend, to her distinctive maternal location, while Silbergleid recoils against a single mother construct—the SMC—that interpolates her into a subject position that violates her sense of self and does not recognize her unequivocal and uncomplicated maternal desire. Austin and Silbergleid expand the repertoire of single motherhood legitimizing through their insistence on being seen on their own terms—literally respected—as in given due regard. Lehmann-Haupt's and Soiseth's internal legitimizing—flexibility and receptiveness in the former, fixedness and rigidity in the latter—model different ways that single mothers legitimize single motherhood to themselves, providing texture and nuance to our understanding of intentionality and choice and to how rhetors turn those notions into tools of legitimacy.

In the introduction to this chapter, I committed to being an "adequate rhetorical witness," one who "will listen without judging, who will read without impugning."[130] In some respects, such witnessing is essential to coalitional work. Without it, we cannot see our similarities and differences and find both reasons and ways to work across them. Indeed "adequate rhetorical witness" is one way to describe the legitimacy that Austin and Silbergleid, in particular, seek. Witnesses, however, are not simply mirrors; life-writing acts on us readers just as it acts on the writer. In an article I coauthored with Jonathan Alexander, we observe, "Through their representation of memoirists' personal experiences, [memoirs] necessarily raise questions about individual agency and its relationship to both social constraints and opportunities . . . [They also] engage norms variously—consciously and unconsciously, defiantly and compliantly, playfully and subversively."[131] While Austin's, Silbergleid's, and Lehmann-Haupt's memoirs energize feminists' commitment to engage critically with normativity and to imagine ways of being and living that respect and celebrate difference, *Choosing You* testifies to the damaging effects of Soiseth's uncritical adherence to norms. Given that "life writing accomplishes rhetorical work," I feel compelled, perhaps ethically bound, to speculate about the effects of *Choosing You* on Soiseth and on her readers.[132] Rather than propelling Soiseth to critique racist and classist norms of beauty and family, writing *Choosing You* seems to have deepened her entrapment in normative thinking, leaving her further dissatisfied with herself and the family she created as a single mother. Readers like me might reasonably find *Choosing You* both painful to read and frustrating, because it strengthens and further entrenches norms that exclude and degrade those who do not adhere to them. In so doing, *Choosing You* potentially constrains the imaginary of its readers, both those who are considering elective single motherhood and those who already are ESMs.

I am left wondering how to reconcile the imperative to be an "adequate rhetorical witness" who "listen[s] without judging" with the simultaneous ethical imperative to take seriously the implications and effects of a rhetor's life-writing.[133] Reproductive justice activist and scholar Loretta J. Ross's cautionary statement about how to respond to the stories elicited by #MeToo offers a productive provocation to scholars engaged in the study of life-writing. She advises, "While you want to hold that story for another person, you have to be very, very careful what you do with it."[134] Through our scholarship and teaching, we "do" something with life-writing. Our scholarship shapes how our readers think about a text's rhetorical work, and it has the potential to influence what books faculty assign in their courses and the focus of their pedagogy. We are thus ethically beholden to be respectful, but still critical, witnesses of the life-writing we critique and teach. In some instances, as it has in my analysis of Soiseth's memoir, this critique might evolve into judgment.

CHAPTER 4

....

GUIDING IN THE AUGHTS

The Constrained Evolution of the Single Mother by Choice Identity

The world needs more kids who are raised by a loving person who actively chooses parenthood.

—Mikki Morrissette, *Choosing Single Motherhood*

I offer no apologies.

—Louise Sloan, *Knock Yourself Up—No Man? No Problem! A Tell-All Guide to Becoming a Single Mom*

When Louise Sloan and Mikki Morrissette published their guidebooks about single motherhood in 2007 and 2008, respectively, they faced far fewer rhetorical hurdles than Jené Stonesifer and Jane Mattes had in the 1990s. In the first decade of the second millennium, supermarket shoppers encountered the baby bumps and adoption stories of famous single mothers like Sheryl Crow, Angelina Jolie, and Meg Ryan, as they waited in checkout lines.[1] These white, wealthy single mothers rode the wave of the contemporary cultural obsession with motherhood. For the moment, motherhood was trendy, at least for women who met the class requirements. Though the demands of "good motherhood" were ever more numerous and intense, being single did not necessarily preclude middle-class mothers from achieving them, thanks in large part to the success of the LGBTQIA+ movement's efforts to redefine family beyond the nuclear ideal; the fruition of academic studies on the viability of so-called alternative family forms; and neoliberalism's support for the autonomous private family, however configured.[2] Still, while notions about viable families in the aughts were broader than they were in the 1990s, and the boundaries of legible and legitimate motherhood more expansive, they were not all-encompassing. Neoliberal axioms about choice and autonomy and the assumption that caretaking is a private responsibility still dominated thinking about maternal and familial legitimacy. The place of some single mothers within the hierarchy of motherhood had changed, but the hierarchy itself was still in place. While middle-class single women of any race could increasingly "choose" motherhood without censure, poor "dependent" women (still) could not. Mikki Morrissette's and Louise Sloan's guidebooks capitalize on these cultural shifts and showcase the new legitimizing strategies they enabled. At the same time, their guidebooks demonstrate the ongoing stronghold of neoliberalism on the cultural imaginary. As such, they illuminate not only the expansion, but also the limits, of maternal legitimizing in the twenty-first century.

Love Makes a Family

Though only roughly a decade separates the ESM guidebooks of the 1990s from those of the aughts, the public discourse around motherhood and family during those periods differs markedly. Cultural, legal, and scholarly advances provided fertile ground for ESM legitimizing in the aughts. Before turning to Sloan's and Morrissette's guidebooks, then, I zoom outward to paint the discursive and political landscape of family during this period. This picture centers LGBTQIA+ activism and legal victories, as they played a pivotal role in the cultural rhetorics of family from the latter decades of the twentieth century to the present day.

Caretaking prompted by the AIDS crisis changed the public's perception of the LGBTQIA+ community. Few could deny that the community's actions exemplified true "family values," even if the afflicted "families" looked different than Ozzie and Harriet's. As historian Linda Hirshman asserts, "The moral revolution was situated in the most contested arena of gay politics: family values."[3] While some deemed AIDS a punishment for so-called deviant lifestyles, many more noted the devotion shown by the LGBTQIA+ community toward those afflicted with AIDS.[4] Observers could not but acknowledge how friends and nonmarital romantic partners functioned as family. The failed public response to the AIDS crisis necessitated caretaking by lovers, partners, friends, and family. This highly visible caretaking, alongside the advocacy work of organizations like PFLAG to "restory" family, helped to instigate efforts to legalize gay marriage and expand family values to include LGBTQIA+-identified individuals.[5] As conservative writer Andrew Sullivan noted in his 1989 article "Here Comes the Groom," marriage equality "is not a denial of family values; It's an extension of them . . . merely ask[ing] that gays be allowed to join in."[6] Later in this same article, Sullivan asks provocatively, "Why not coax gays into traditional values?"[7] Some queer activists and scholars questioned the effort to claim, expand, and ultimately occupy family values. In addition to disputing the insinuation that gay relationships outside the carapace of marriage were typically "unfaithful, undeveloped, and insecure," these critics challenged the placement of monogamous, life-long commitment between two individuals at the peak of the relationship hierarchy.[8] In "How Gay Liberation Became a Family Values Movement," Aidan Rowe laments the narrowness of the "equality-through-assimilation" aims of the "inclusive" family values vision: "Within decades, we have gone from being a radical sexual liberation movement . . . to being little more than a movement beating at the door of family values ideology begging to be let in."[9] Rowe worries that the success of the new family values will further ensnare LGBTQIA+ in "the grip of bourgeois morality," and, ironically, "strengthen the institutions that keep our bodies and our hearts in chains."[10] Theorist Michael Warner likewise argues that the goal of normalcy (i.e., inclusion within a more expansive version of family values) traps queer people within existing frameworks and thus obscures the "world-making activity of queer life."[11] Like Rowe, he decries "the triumphalist narrative—according to which we have emerged from the long night of marginalization into the full glory of our rights, our acceptance, our integration, and our normalcy."[12] Warner celebrates the queer imaginary and the alternative ways of living that queer "counterpublics" imagine and enact.[13] Despite these critiques, the push to expand family values to include LGBTQIA+ people, rather than to reimagine structures of intimacy, took on steam. While the visibility and growing acceptance of LGBTQIA+-identified people provoked a backlash in some quarters, most evident in a spate of anti-gay initiatives throughout the 1990s, by the aughts, many people in the United States had come to see love and commitment, more than particular familial configurations and gender roles, as the defining features of a healthy family, a shift encapsulated by the slogan "Love makes a family."[14]

Indeed, the backlash to LGBTQIA+ rights and visibility served to catalyze the movement for LGBTQIA+ equality in law and discourse. The NGO Love Makes a Family was founded in 1992 to oppose an anti-gay ballot measure in Oregon. The name became a slogan and eventually a meme that encompassed a wide variety of "alternative" family formations. LGBTQIA+ people began to express publicly their ability and desire to form families consisting of long-term partnerships and children. The 1999 photographic essay collection *Love Makes a Family* celebrates this shift in visibility.[15] April Martin's jubilant remarks in the collection's afterword call attention to the heightened awareness of familial desire within the LGBTQIA+ community: "What dramatic changes the last few decades have seen! Gay, lesbian, bisexual, and transgender parents have become aware: Of ourselves. Of each other. Of our collective voice. Of our rich potential for parenting openly and proudly. Of the true definition of family. Of the majesty of love as it is revealed in the families we create."[16] Predictably, social conservatives challenged this notion of family. Indeed, one of the episodes in conservative Dennis Prager's *Same Sex Issues* series is titled "Love Is Not Enough," ironically demonstrating the slogan's rhetorical power and further entrenching its place in public discourse. Indeed, by most accounts, LGBTQIA+-identified people were winning the rhetorical and legal battle. As historian Lillian Faderman asserts, "Gays and lesbians, with a little help from their friends, had been transforming the rhetoric about who they were—rescuing their image from that of unsavory criminal to another member of the family, who must be treated as part of the American family, too."[17] *Obergefell v. Hodges*, the 2015 US Supreme Court decision that legalized gay marriage, demonstrated that most people in the United States no longer wanted to deny basic rights of family and belonging on the basis of an individual's gender identity or sexual orientation.

Of most significance to this study, LGBTQIA+-identified people's efforts to broaden the definition of family included some other so-called nonnormative families, which were also both increasingly visible and vilified by advocates of traditional family values. Kath Weston makes the links among these families explicit: "Nor have gay men and lesbians set about making their families in isolation. Their sisters make up a proportion of a growing number of single mothers; their parents have introduced them to the concept of blended families with each successive remarriage; their cousins struggle with the after-effects of divorce."[18] Psychotherapist April Martin lists the "basic presumptions" about what children ostensibly need, before characterizing those assumptions as simply "wrong": "They assumed that two was an optimal number of parents, that there should be one male and one female, that they should be biological creators of the children, and that they should be heterosexual."[19] By 2012 the "Modern Families" platform of the Family Equality Council, a nonprofit LGBTQIA+ advocacy group, could assert confidently, "We are a nation of blended and multi-generational families, adoptive and foster families, families headed by single parents, divorced parents, unmarried parents, same-sex couples, and more . . . We call for the full inclusion of all families." Their *Family Room* blog included multiple posts on the topic of "taking back family values." However, the new family values did not challenge the neoliberal underpinnings of the original family values rhetoric. Activists focused on the ways that sexual identity and familial configuration precluded recognition and respect for the diversity of US families, but not socioeconomic status. The Family Equality website showcases families with only one parent or two same-sex parents, but these families appear self-contained and financially autonomous. Family Equality's more inclusive version of family values would seem to draw the line at celebrating the loving family created by a queer mother who receives welfare.

Growing scholarly consensus about the viability of some so-called alternative families provided additional ballast to the "taking back [of] family values," though certain beliefs, especially concerning the risks of fatherless homes, still held sway.[20] In 2004 "the American Psychological Association (APA) and other health professional and scientific organizations adopted a policy resolution asserting that there is no scientific evidence that parenting effectiveness is related to parental sexual orientation."[21] Psychologist Peggy Drexler embraced the social and political importance of her research on what she calls "maverick moms." In *Raising Boys without Men* (2005), she addresses coupled lesbians and single women, straight or lesbian, who were considering motherhood: "The stories, voices, data, and findings here will reassure, hearten, and empower you . . . For women weighing their ticking biological clocks and their craving to nurture children, this book shows that you have reason to take that informed leap of faith."[22] Drexler concludes that "parenting is either good or deficient, not male or female . . . A good female parent will help a boy to develop his full potential as long as she values his manliness and encourages his growth, independence, and sense of adventure."[23] Susan Golombok, author of *Modern Families: Parents and Children in New Family Forms*, drew a related conclusion about one-parent versus two-parent homes: "There is no evidence to suggest that children who are raised by one parent differ from children who live with two parents with respect to gender identity or gender role behavior. Boys in single-parent families [of any gender] are just as masculine in terms of their identity and behavior, and girls are just as feminine, as are boys and girls from two-parent homes."[24] These scholars focus on the overwhelmingly typical psychosocial identity and development of children who grow up in queer and alternative families, admittedly with an uncritical eye about the meaning and stability of gender.

Despite the findings of these scholars, concerns about fatherlessness persisted. However, by the aughts, those who voiced them had shifted their focus, and their concerns reflected not only the "ongoing collaboration" but also the increasingly tight alliance of family values and neoliberalism.[25] Rather than shaming single mothers for their "fatherless" families, fatherhood advocates sought to rouse "deadbeat" dads to take on their paternal duties, namely the paying of child support. In January 2000 the Clinton administration launched the Responsible Fatherhood Initiative, which continued in various iterations through the administrations of George W. Bush and Barack Obama.[26] The well-being of children in single-mother households was the stated aim of these initiatives, but the economic cost of non-nuclear, especially fatherless, families was a just as powerful, although less overt, driving force behind them. These initiatives took on an increasingly racialized bent; according to Diane Weaver, "Most of the programming offered to fathers is geared toward men in urban, low socio-economic areas and men who are incarcerated. This essentially means that the targeted audience of the President's Fatherhood Initiative over the years has been the poor black male."[27] In this sense, the president's fatherhood initiative redirected the 1965 Moynihan Report's punitive gaze away from Black mothers onto Black (and brown) fathers. In 2010 then-President Barack Obama received praise from across the political spectrum for his Fatherhood and Mentoring initiative, which mushroomed into a variety of programs and grants under the rubric "Promoting Responsible Fatherhood and Strong Communities."[28]

By virtue of their whiteness and financial autonomy, and thanks to a decade of rhetorical efforts to mark their difference from poor, dependent single mothers, ESMs largely fell outside the purview of these fatherhood initiatives. Meanwhile, they reaped the benefits of the expansion of family values and the findings of psychologists, like Drexler and Golombok, about the well-being of children raised in "new" family forms. As the following analysis demonstrates, these shifts in the rhetorical landscape created openings for Mikki Morrissette's *Choosing Single Motherhood* and Louise Sloan's *Knock Yourself Up—No Man? No Problem! A Tell-All Guide to Becoming a Single Mom*, both of which seize the opportunity to expand notions of viable family configurations to include (some) single parent households. Neither Morrissette nor Sloan is tentative or apologetic about elective single motherhood, but they do legitimize in ways that reflect the affordances and constraints of their chosen subgenre of guidebook. Morrissette's more traditional "guide" is reasoned and dispassionate; it foregrounds elective single mothers' rationality and empirical decision making. Sloan's "girlfriends' guide" is assured, empathic, and inclusive; it emphasizes ESMs' feelings, intuitive decision making, and subjective and idiosyncratic thinking about and experience of single motherhood. Despite these differences in tone and strategy, however, both guidebooks envision and address a similarly situated woman-identified reader and demonstrate the persistent hold of neoliberal orthodoxies about self-sufficiency and economic autonomy on notions of ESM legitimacy.

Mikki Morrissette's 2008 *Choosing Single Motherhood*

I think and plan; therefore, I am legitimate. Mikki Morrissette makes the case that single motherhood is a viable familial configuration as long as the challenges it poses are addressed by "thinking" women, like her. The legitimacy of a single mother, and that of the family she forms, result from the putative wisdom of her parenting. Accordingly, *Choosing Single Motherhood* focuses on prospective and actual single mothers' deliberation about the legitimacy of their choice, not on their need to legitimize that choice to others.

Morrissette writes, "Women today tend to focus less on whether having a child will be seen as 'legitimate' for her and the child, and more on whether the decision itself is a legitimate one."[29] Consistent with the rhetorical aims of the genre, the characterizations in *Choosing Single Motherhood* of the typical Choice Mom are as much proscriptive as they are descriptive. If readers do not yet have the confident and rational attitude Morrissette attributes to the typical CM, *Choosing Single Motherhood* will help them to cultivate it. To that end, Morrissette aims to enlighten and support the thoughtful and diligent CM she envisions. She states clearly, "My goal is to offer an honest and realistic picture of what the lifestyle is and is not, so that all Choice Kids are raised by mothers who consciously, and continuously prepare for the challenge."[30] Morrissette ventriloquizes the questions a prospective mother should pose of herself: "Will I have the strength and energy to be a good mother? Do I have the financial, emotional, and support resources to pull it off?"[31] Her questions are those of an ideal neoliberal subject—self-reliant, rational, and responsible—concerned primarily about her ability to self-govern according to internalized norms of good motherhood. Though not presented as such, this performance is itself a form of legitimizing, demonstrating how seriously, conscientiously, and purposefully the prospective mother takes the decision to mother as a single woman: Look at the thoughtful questions I'm posing of myself! See, I am worthy of motherhood, because I am a "thinking woman"! Social class and a particular subjectivity make possible this mode of self-governance: "Strength" and "energy" are code for "Do you have the material resources and gumption to do this?" This diction is action-oriented, suggesting the importance of the CM's perception of her own agency, which is not synonymous with her access to material resources. The CM sees herself as a go-getter, as sitting in the driver's seat of her life, and as being entitled to get or do what she desires and works to achieve.

Morrissette repeatedly notes the centrality of choice, both as a principle and ideology, in her worldview. She tells her readers, "I am a huge believer in protecting the principle of Choice in its myriad forms."[32] Morrissette coined the label "Choice Mom" to describe the single mother she addresses. In *Retrospective: Eighteen Years As a Choice Mom*, Morrissette explains that the label CM appropriately and consciously highlights the mother's intentionality, rather than her marital or relationship status: "I coined the term 'Choice Mom' as an alternative to 'single mother by choice' because I believed the emphasis should be on women choosing to be mothers—being single is the happenstance."[33] This coining is also a form of branding in which the Choice Mom and Choice Kid are trademarked and recognizable categories in the marketplace. While intentionality and choice were also central to the SMC construct of the 1990s, the label CM distills their significance and reflects the intensification in the aughts of neoliberal values of rationalism, individual autonomy, and self-reliance. Because they adhere to these neoliberal norms, CMs are legitimate mothers. The language of choice also allows Morrissette to parry the charge that CMs are "selfish" for raising children without a father.[34] To the contrary, she asserts, "The world needs more kids who are raised by a loving person who actively *chooses* parenthood. That is, in fact, why I refer to it as *Choice* Motherhood. Those who make this *choice* are actively choosing to parent (and reading this book, among others, because they want to make a responsible decision and effort). It is not a *choice* that is made lightly."[35] Morrissette's explanation underscores CMs' conscientiousness and maturity—reflected in their "choice" to become mothers—and implies that these characteristics in the mother mitigate the potential damage wrought by the absence of a father in the families they create. To emphasize further the significance of "choice," Morrissette refers to "Choice households" and to "Choice Kids," and she labels the section of *Choosing Single Motherhood* in which she addresses different paths to motherhood "Choosing the Method."[36] Though Morrissette refers to single motherhood as a "challenge," thereby acceding to the *doxa* that partnered parenthood is easier, she employs the language of hard work and self-improvement to distinguish CMs from less conscientious mothers, single or not, and to underscore their status as hard-working, responsible, and empowered neoliberal subjects. "Choice"—of motherhood itself and of a particularly conscientious and performative approach to mothering—encapsulates the ethos of a legitimate mother.

However, Morrissette restricts the choice of parenthood to those who are economically and psychologically stable, be they single or married: "A single woman who is unable to provide a secure environment—who cannot earn an income, find quality childcare, maintain relationships with a healthy network of supportive people and offer authoritative parenting—is not Choice Mother material. Period. Married couples who cannot provide the same have no business becoming parents either."[37] Morrissette describes the "ideal" family in similarly neoliberal terms. The "ideal" is dependent not on the number of parents, but rather on the existence of a parent who is not "too overwhelmed to provide the affectionate and disciplined style of parenting that is required" and who is able "to maintain the emotional and financial resources in order to be the authoritative parent every child needs."[38] In other words, as long as the parent is a responsible adult and good parent according to middle-class standards of parenting (i.e., "affectionate and disciplined" and with plentiful access to resources), a single mother family is one of many, equally viable familial configurations. Morrissette's example of single mothers who are shattering the stereotype is telling. She notes that "the image of single motherhood expanded from that of welfare-dependent teenagers to include strong, empowered women such as . . . Angelina Jolie, Meg Ryan, and Sheryl Crow."[39] Jolie, Ryan, and Crow are "empowered" women by virtue of their fame, wealth, and whiteness. They dodge the stigma of their single status by capitalizing on their status and the privileges it confers. Though Morrissette's target readers are not necessarily famous, rich, or even white women, her attribution of the shift in the image to the motherhood of women like these reinforces the raced and classed dimensions of the ESM construct and reifies divisions within the category of single mother: older white professionals versus teenage women of color and welfare-dependent versus self-supporting. In short, she implies that the "disapproval and scorn" for some single mothers has diminished due to public recognition that not all single mothers are cut from the same cloth. That is, CMs are qualitatively different from the vilified and racialized "welfare queen." Morrissette directs her readers to adhere to neoliberal norms of being and mothering because doing so will further their efforts to legitimize themselves, but she also suggests that these norms are righteous. Adherence to them is thus not only rhetorically strategic but also morally imperative.

In contrast to the first generation of ESMs, Morrissette presents herself as a woman who was never interested in conforming to conventional gender roles and trajectories, not as a woman who was pushed by circumstances to make an unconventional maternal choice. She does not apologize for or explain away her disinterest in domesticity, recalling that "I tended to be a tomboy, with no daydreams of marriage and children and domestic life."[40] Morrissette breezily dispatches the news of the end of her seven-year marriage in two sentences before moving on to discuss her "new dream, the one that had started growing in me about becoming a single mom."[41] Readers then learn about her daughter, Sophie, and her son, Dylan, born five years apart. Her ethos stands in stark contrast to that of Jane Mattes, author of the 1994 *Single Mothers by Choice*, who writes that she had nightmares of being stoned for being a single mother.[42] Morrissette expresses neither regrets nor compunctions about her family configuration. Though she refers to the first generation of ESMs respectfully as "the pioneers of the 1980s," she distinguishes them from the 2000s generation: "When Mattes chose to become the unmarried mother to her son, the decision was a much lonelier one to make. It was more subject to disapproval and scorn than it is today."[43] Morrissette attributes her comfort and confidence to the expansion of the family values umbrella. She concludes, "Untraditional households are simply more acceptable [now]."[44] With "simply," she implies, but does not name or evaluate, the changes that make some "untraditional households" more "acceptable": the interlocking expansion of family values and the neoliberal turn in which maternal legitimacy is predicated and dependent on financial autonomy.

Morrissette's deliberate rhetorical choices construct her ethos as an unbiased "thinking woman." They also model for her readers how they can construct their ethos as thinking CMs. Morrissette uses a question—"Is It Fair to the Child?"—to title the section containing the chapters "The Impact of a Single-Parent Home" and "Growing Up without a Father" and goes on to explain her rhetorical choice: "My intention was to give everyone a chance to hear both sides of the issue and make their own judgment. That is still the goal of the entire book."[45] In contrast to some single mother advocates who seek to paper over obvious differences between single-parent and dual-parent families, or to reject all of the evaluative conclusions about those differences, Morrissette acknowledges the advantages of a two-parent household, which she imagines as heterosexual. She writes, "I have no doubt that stable, loving two-parent homes—where both mother and father have a healthy emotional investment in their children—offer tremendous benefits."[46] She further concedes that no matter a CM's love and efforts, the lack of a second parental figure in Choice households creates a void: "There are some things a Choice Mom cannot provide for her child no matter how great she is as a parent. The most important of these, in my view, is the absence of a second person who is actively involved and emotionally present."[47] As concessions typically do, her admission of this deficit in CM households deflates and deflects at least some criticism. Morrissette moves on, though, to reframe the discussion: "Every family can be dysfunctional if we let it. And every child will grow up with 'issues,' whether we like it or not."[48] In other words, no familial situation is perfect or ideal. The issues of a "Choice Kid" may revolve around or stem from the absence of a second parent, but, Morrissette suggests, it is fallacious to assume that kids in two-parent families will not have any issues at all, or that children in one-parent homes will necessarily have more issues than their two-parent counterparts. Finally, she notes repeatedly that studies showing the negative effects of single motherhood focus on children from "disrupted" two-parent households, not from homes, like those of CMs, that are headed by a single parent from the start.[49] Furthermore, she points out, it is illogical to pathologize fatherlessness or any other "variable": "One or two variables—growing up poor, moving a lot as a kid, even losing a parent—does not take precedent over every other variable in life. We all grow up with influences and adjustments that help make us who we are."[50] Morrissette's rhetoric is consistently rational, reasonable, and empirical, consisting of research-driven responses to the questions and concerns typically voiced by critics of single mothers. *Choosing Single Motherhood* thus provides its readers with ready-to-order answers to the difficult questions they are likely to encounter as CMs.

In addition to providing her readers with specific talking points, Morrissette models the reasonable and assured stance she encourages CMs to adopt.

She relies on a rhetoric of logic and reason to show the weaknesses of arguments about the necessity of fathers. She acknowledges the obvious and indisputable truth that some advocates of single motherhood nevertheless downplay or disregard: "I make no claims that raising children without a father does not have an impact on their development."[51] She goes on, however, to recontextualize that claim by pointing that it is also true that *any* and *all* family structures affect the development of a child: the presence of siblings, grandparents, etc. To admit the significance of the presence (or not) of a father is thus not, in the end, acquiescing to much. Moreover, she points out the logical fallacy in many claims about fatherless homes: "It should not be assumed that the opposite result [that children are less confident, more easily frustrated, and better learners] is true when the home has no father—which is the conclusion most people leap to."[52] She acknowledges that studies demonstrate some gender-based differences in parents' communication style, play styles, comfort with risk-taking, and discipline. However, she challenges concerns about the gendered effects of fatherless homes, which she mockingly labels "boys and guns" and "girls and babies."[53] Morrissette points out that role models, including parental figures, are only one of many factors that influence children: "Children all have the potential to make bad choices with their lives—big and small—and it's a combination of genetics, environment, and individual emotional and mental health that plays into the end result, as well as values imparted by important role models."[54] In all cases, Morrissette points to the blind spots in the existing research, as the comparison of partnered parents to single mothers typically involves "fathers and children who grew up with less-involved fathers," rather than CM households that consist of one heavily involved female parent and a variety of other committed adult influences.[55] Throughout *Choosing Single Motherhood*, she writes with assurance, as befitting a rhetor who claims that a mother's legitimacy stems from *how* she mothers, not in *what* familial configuration she does so.

Morrissette's earnestness, equanimity, reasoned stances, skillful deployment of logic, and only occasional quiet championing of choice motherhood are subtle strategies of affirmative legitimizing. Morrissette observes neutrally that critics believe that biological fathers are uniquely able to meet children's various needs, while proponents of nonnuclear family structures "believe that the support of extended family and friends can—and should—play an important role in raising kids."[56] Without bashing the former position, she demonstrates her confidence in the latter, a stance she supports with psychological studies and first-person accounts of Choice Kids, as if to say, "These aren't my opinions; these are facts!" Even in her most overt instance of affirmative legitimizing, Morrissette proceeds cautiously. She gently refutes the notion that her children are at a disadvantage simply because they have one parent with whom to bond: "I do not consider that to be a 'bad' thing. It simply is the unique structure our family was founded on."[57] At this point, her stance is dispassionate, grounded in the claim that there are many equally viable familial configurations. She proceeds, however, to assert an advantage of a single-parent family like hers in language that is exploratory and nondecisive: "*Perhaps* because of our dynamic, Sophie and Dylan might be exposed to a wider network of loving relationships and diverse experiences than other kids will. Theirs will be an upbringing that I *believe* will bless them with unique gifts."[58] Here she hints that there are unique advantages to the one-parent configuration of CM families, making them not only different but also better, at least in certain respects.

In the final analysis, Morrissette expresses neither guilt nor misgivings about the single mother families she and other CMs create. The confidence of the CM distinguishes her from the tentative and defensive SMCs of the 1990s. However, in other respects, the two constructs are strikingly similar: Both the SMC and CM are presumedly white, self-sufficient, and solidly middle-class, demanding nothing from the state to support their private familial decisions and choices. Their legitimacy depends on the mother's adherence to norms of self-management and financial autonomy and is thus both steeped in and indebted to neoliberalism. While different in tone from the guidebooks of the 1990s, then, *Choosing Single Motherhood* reflects and sustains a neoliberal paradigm in which single parenthood is legitimate only for responsible, autonomous, and "thinking" women, like Morrissette and her readers, who adhere to its norms, which *Choosing Single Motherhood* guides them to do.

Louise Sloan's 2007 *Knock Yourself Up—No Man? No Problem! A Tell-All Guide to Becoming a Single Mom*

In contrast to the other writers of ESM guidebooks, Louise Sloan, a journalist, out lesbian, and self-described liberal who became a single mother at age forty-one, is enthusiastic and unapologetic about elective single motherhood. She states that the children of the women she interviewed to write *Knock Yourself Up* are "lucky," noting that "about the only thing we don't have to offer our kids was a guy named Dad."[59] Rather than seeking overtly to legitimize elective single motherhood, then, *Knock Yourself Up* aims instead to provide support to women already mothering as single women and to those who are considering doing so.[60] Sloan contrasts *Knock Yourself Up* to what she respectfully describes as Jane Mattes's and Mikki Morrissette's "excellent how-to books on choosing single motherhood, [which are] based on sound psychology and reams of research."[61] She explains, "Though I brought in a few experts to elucidate some of the thornier issues, *Knock Yourself Up* is generally light on research and heavy on anecdotes, covering both the serious and the silly." Sloan's description of *Knock Yourself Up* conveys her confidence: she does not feel obliged to defend the choice to parent as a single woman by showcasing her own maturity and wisdom or by referencing the studies of ostensible experts. Her assuredness is a form of backdoor affirmative legitimizing: in recognizing and treating ESMs as a growing and distinctive community of mothers, one in need of support and only a couple paragraphs of justification and defense, Sloan legitimizes them. At the same time, she directs her readers to adopt the confident stance that she models.

Sloan characterizes *Knock Yourself Up* as a "girlfriends' guide," which she defines as "a lively support group in text form, offering a diversity of perspectives."[62] Girlfriends' guides are a gendered and neoliberal genre of self-care. They promise to offer the kind of emotional ballast provided by a group of close women-identified friends for readers undergoing challenging experiences, such as a divorce or the first year of motherhood. Girlfriends' guides acknowledge, and, in some instances, celebrate the difference that marks their readers but refrain from making evaluative claims about that difference: girlfriends are different by virtue of their experience, but not worse, bad, good, or better because of it. The genre enables a kind of interiority and intimacy that the practical orientation of more traditional guidebooks precludes. Girlfriends' guides' candid airing of a diversity of perspectives helps to normalize the range and depth of emotions that readers might experience and to reduce the stigma of common, yet often still taboo, experiences and feelings. In this regard, they serve rhetorical, in addition to psychological, ends. Their affect, language, and tone are gendered feminine, as the code of homophobic masculinity discourages men from referring to their friends as "boyfriends" and from indulging in the emotional vulnerability typical of the genre. Girlfriends' guides are neoliberal in the sense that they address their readers as agentic individuals who can, with emotional support, survive, learn from, and, ultimately, thrive in the circumstances in which they find themselves. The genre empowers, or, from another perspective, places the burden on, individual readers to do the work to feel and do differently and better, rather than inviting them to challenge the historical and political structures as well as the legal and institutional systems that create those circumstances, define the "choices" within them, and pose obstacles to changing them.

In accordance with the genre, Sloan's ethos is that of a girlfriend among girlfriends. She uses her angst-ridden journey to single motherhood to build that ethos, presenting herself as a girlfriend who is honest about the challenges of single motherhood but ultimately content and proud. Her account of her movement through and beyond this angst supports the neoliberal belief that growth, improvement, and happy outcomes are possible, if one works hard enough to attain them. Sloan is candid about the fact that being a single mother was not her Plan A: "I had to be dragged into it kicking and screaming by my biological clock."[63] She describes herself as "definitely the marrying kind" and shares her "lesbian version of the white picket-fence dream," which simultaneously reinforces and pokes fun at the notion of the two-parent family as the ideal: "I wanted there to be *three* parents: two mommies and a noncustodial dad."[64] While Sloan acknowledges that research demonstrates the viability of "alternative families"—"Sure, everything I'd ever read about alternative families with donor dads indicated that the kids do just fine"—her dismissive tone makes the point that this research, though reassuring, does not assuage her disappointment about forming this particular form of an "alternative family."[65] She *knew* that her child would "do just fine," but she tells readers that she still *felt* worried. Notable here is that Sloan does not present herself as wholly in control and rational and thus worthy of and ready for motherhood. Throughout *Knock Yourself Up*, she exposes her vulnerabilities and thus makes herself relatable to her readers. In the following example, she leads with the zinger: her age. The short sentences that follow read like a series of data points, except for the pathos of single motherhood being the "inverse of [her] dream": "Age forty-one. Single. Anonymous donor sperm. At the doctor's office. The inverse of my dream, but my bio clock was sounding more like a car alarm."[66] Though Sloan expresses disappointment about her deviation from the familial path she had imagined, she does not express shame. She recounts with humor and chagrin the "grueling" process of getting pregnant through alternative insemination in a section titled "The Artificial Insemination Grind": "My son, Scott, was the result of lucky try number fourteen."[67] Of most significance, however, at the end of *Knock Yourself Up* Sloan emphasizes her current emotional state. Her description of her feelings about being Scott's mother are the clearest and most unassailable examples of her affirmative stance. Sloan writes of the ESMs she interviewed and with whom she identifies: "*Happy, relaxed, content* are the kinds of words they use. And I am."[68]

Sloan strengthens her "girlfriend" ethos by acknowledging the relevance of an ESM's social location to her internal and external experience of legitimacy. She makes aspects of her background—"conservative Southern Republican"—rhetorically salient, referring to them as evidence that ESMs can experience legitimacy even in a conservative family like hers.[69] As evidence, she shares the email she received from the ninety-one-year-old matriarch of her family in response to her announcement that she was single and pregnant: "Congratulations!. . . . What a brave thing to do."[70] Though she does later in *Knock Yourself Up*, Sloan does not acknowledge the significance of her whiteness in this particular section. A conservative Southern Republican family of color would likely have particular concerns about single motherhood in response to racist and racialized assumptions about motherhood and family. To underscore her point that most families of ESMs will be supportive, regardless of their social locations, Sloan notes that of the ESMs she interviewed, "most are surprised to find their families more receptive to [their single motherhood] than they expected . . . Turns out, Toto, that times have really changed: even Kansas isn't in Kansas anymore."[71] Sloan also draws on her experience as an "out" lesbian to empathize with the challenges of "coming out" as an ESM, noting that "'coming out' isn't always so easy."[72] Her analysis helps girlfriends who identify as "mainstream" to understand and articulate that being perceived as different is uncomfortable: "It's hard to adjust to being considered 'alternative,' especially if what you'd been aiming for was a *Leave it to Beaver* kind of normalcy."[73] There is power in naming the desire for normalcy, the legitimacy that normalcy can bestow, and the psychic consequences of deviating from the normal. Doing so reduces normalcy's hold on the imaginary, as norms that go unnamed maintain their ability to distinguish the normative from the deviant and to provoke compliance, to build self-esteem, and/or to shame.

At the same time, Sloan explores how what is considered "normal," and, consequently, an ESM's relationship to norms and "normalcy," hinges on her social location, particularly race. In contrast to the unstated, but assumed, whiteness of the ESM construct in other guidebooks, Sloan, as a white woman, names the ways that race affects an ESM's experience and others' perceptions of her. She writes, "For most of the middle-class white women I spoke to, having a baby solo, whether by choice or by accident, was virtually unheard of in their communities."[74] As outliers to their community, these middle-class white ESMs feel compelled to explain and justify their status. In contrast, Sloan acknowledges that Black ESMs face the stereotype of the "ubiquitous single Black mother."[75] She gives voice to a range of Black ESM perspectives on the effects of this stereotype. Alice told her, "I don't want to be thought of as a stereotypical careless single mother."[76] Others told Sloan about the misrecognition of their *elective* single mother status in the Black community, leading Charlene to want to exclaim that Black women "*do* do this. And you need to know that you have a choice."[77] Still others noted how single motherhood reinforced their Black identity and sense of belonging to the Black community: single motherhood "lets you be part of a club . . . once I had my child, I became a 'real' Black woman."[78] Sloan's voicing of a range of experiences and attention to the effects of social location give heft and depth to *Knock Yourself Up*. She does not assume similitude of ESM experience. Her recognition of difference increases the potential for *Knock Yourself Up* to appeal to a diverse readership.

Sloan similarly recognizes ESMs' diverse perspectives on family. She emphasizes that most ESM are, citing scholar Rosanna Hertz, "reluctant revolutionaries" for whom elective single motherhood was not "Plan A."[79] She writes, "Having a child alone is not most women's childhood dream, and becoming a single mom is, for most women, a mother of a compromise."[80] To be clear, though, Sloan does not imply that an ESM's legitimacy turns on her longing for, and thus her implicit validation, of the nuclear norm. She simply aims to depict the emotional landscape of the majority of ESMs, herself included, fairly and accurately. Her affirmative legitimizing, however, admits the perspectives of ESMs who do not feel regret about their single motherhood and whose ideas about family "may seem unusual or even offensive."[81] Of these "who actually embrace the revolution are absolutely thrilled to be living in an age where the traditions are more easily bypassed."[82] She further suggests that these revolutionaries "may just be the canaries in the coal mine of a society that's still having a lot of trouble figuring out how romantic love and family life can work with equality of the sexes."[83] She cites two ESMs on why being a single mother is better for mothers and children: Melle "not only loves being a single mother, she thinks it's preferable. 'For me,' [Melle] says, 'raising children and being with a man have to be two separate things. Marriage really does not create the environment for child rearing.'"[84] Sloan concludes, seemingly a little surprised herself, "Some do feel that one good parent can be even better than two."[85] In "The Pluses of Parenting Solo," Sloan recounts that mothers "talked about the unexpected ways that single motherhood is better, and easier. You've got total responsibility, to be sure, but you've also got total control and freedom."[86] In articulating these potential advantages of single motherhood, *Knock Yourself Up* pushes against conventional thinking about maternal and familial legitimacy.

Because Sloan is confident that ESMs are legitimate mothers, and the ESMs she interviews convey the same self-assuredness, she devotes little time and attention to the "concerns" about them.[87] Building on the work of LGBTQIA+ activists, Sloan appropriates and resignifies "family values" to include single parent families, offering a concise list of what she deems "Single Parent Family Values." She briefly lists her "apparently controversial assumptions. Single moms can be great moms. When raised in a safe, loving environment with their basic emotional and physical needs met, kids turn out OK. Being raised by a good single mom is a lot better than being brought up inside a bad marriage. Love makes a family."[88] Instead of devoting multiple chapters to backing up what, she implies, should *not* be "controversial assumptions," she notes breezily that there is a "fair amount of research to back [them] up."[89] In a circumlocution that partially undermines itself, she acknowledges that the father issue is "not exactly a nonissue."[90] Nevertheless, she maintains that a woman can both value fathers and men and decide to have a child on her own. As she states succinctly, the two are not mutually exclusive: "Most of us value fatherhood. And men."[91] Sloan argues that it is in fact ESMs' valuing of men as human beings, and of the institution of marriage, that leads to their pursuit of single motherhood: "Many have made the decision to bear a child out of wedlock because they respect marriage too much to enter into it lightly for reasons of social and procreational expedience."[92] She turns on its head the notion that intentional single mothers mock, hate, or otherwise disparage men and fathers: "Far from seeing men as unnecessary, these are women who, I'd argue, really value men and see them as equals, partners, lovers, soul mates—not as turkey basters attached to a paycheck."[93] Finally, Sloan devotes not a word to the theological and ideological concerns of critics about fatherless homes. In the chapter entitled "The Daddy Question," she states, "Research consistently indicates that most kids of anonymous donor insemination grow up happy and secure in families without a father present," and then proceeds to give voice to various single mothers' approaches to building strong father-free families.[94] Combining sincerity with humor, she bats away the "concerns" of skeptics and critics as if they were flies at a picnic. Sloan's statement aptly captures her confidence about the viability of ESM families: "I address concerns, but I offer no apologies."[95] In contrast to Morrissette's thorough and well-considered responses to skeptics, Sloan models breeziness, an attitude befitting her judgment of the merits of their concerns.

Sloan's unabashedly affirmative legitimizing distinguishes *Knock Yourself Up* from the other guidebooks to elective single motherhood. And, yet, the ESM Sloan envisions and addresses, and whose legitimacy she assumes, is, like the SMC and the CM, clearly middle-class and a faithful adherent to the neoliberal paradigm of self-sufficient motherhood. Neoliberal buzz words, reminiscent of Morrissette's rhetoric in *Choosing Single Motherhood*, pepper what Sloan describes as her grounding assumption: "[I] start with the idea that a *mature* single woman with *adequate* resources having a baby *thoughtfully* on her own is an OK thing to do."[96] Sloan further notes that "without certain educational, financial, and community resources, raising kids alone can be a lot harder."[97] Admittedly, Sloan denounces the progressive neoliberal notion that only people with resources should be allowed to become parents. She writes, "There are some who basically position child rearing as a middle-class privilege, something that's OK only if you have a certain amount of money. That's not right."[98] She also notes that "resources," while helpful, are not indispensable for successful mothering: "With enough determination and community support, their [not adequately resourced] kids can do fine, too."[99] Nevertheless, Sloan does distinguish the "new set of single moms . . . educated adult women, usually over thirty, who want to have kids and have the resources to do it alone" of *Knock Yourself Up* from the single teen and divorced moms who give single motherhood "a bad rap," though she adds, as an aside, a critique of the blame-the-mother paradigm: "I could suggest that blaming [the suffering of children] on the moms alone is not the way to go."[100] Ultimately, while not as central to her ethos or to her rhetoric as they are to the other ESM guidebooks, neoliberal tenets undergird Sloan's conception of legitimate single motherhood. Her affirmative legitimizing lies on the bedrock of neoliberalism and implicitly enacts its attendant exclusions. Though Sloan "offer[s] no apologies," she does so only for the neoliberal middle-class single mother that *Knock Yourself Up* envisions and addresses.[101]

Conclusions

Analysis of *Choosing Single Motherhood* and *Knock Yourself Up* demonstrates the challenge, perhaps the impossibility, of legitimizing outside of dominant, even while more expansive, maternal and familial frameworks. Mikki Morrissette and Louise Sloan capitalize on and contribute to the movement for a new, more inclusive family values by demonstrating the viability of ESM families. However, they do not, perhaps cannot, critique the entwinement of family values—both old and new—with neoliberalism. To the contrary, their legitimizing further entrenches the neoliberal underpinnings of earlier ESM constructs in an effort to build support for ESMs' inclusion in the family values tent. In so doing, though in different ways, *Choosing Single Motherhood* and *Knock Yourself Up* shore up the long-standing alliance of family values and neoliberalism. Nor do Morrissette and Sloan use elective single motherhood as a springboard for a radical revisioning of family and intimacy. While they occasionally speculate about the advantages of single-mother homes, both are constrained by the inherent conservatism of family values, a discourse that serves their legitimizing aims but also places limits on their imaginary. Morrissette's and Sloan's affirmative legitimizing situates ESM in the "land of [a new] normal," one that now includes more diverse families but that continues to exclude many others.[102] Moreover, the "new" familial norm their guidebooks envision is still tethered to a concept of family as (primarily) a reproductive unit, a concept that disregards "other modes of relating, belonging, caring, and so on."[103] Paradoxically, then, though Morrissette and Sloan direct their readers to do family in a novel way, their guidebooks direct their readers—potential ESMs—to think narrowly. Ultimately, Morrissette's and Sloan's legitimizing threatens not only to deepen divisions among single mothers and thus hinder coalitional work but also to squash ESMs' use of their maternal experience to reimagine the meaning, form, and purpose of family itself.

CONCLUSION

Beyond Legitimacy

Maternal identities, experiences, and constructs are powerful rhetorical resources that can further or undermine feminist agendas; support or destabilize rhetors' standing; and create or limit opportunities for individuals and communities. As Lindal Buchanan writes, "Monitoring [motherhood's] cultural meanings, rhetorical operations, and political implications for women is, therefore, critical."[1] This study's analysis of the contours, registers, and limits of elective single mother legitimizing, which both position and are leveraged by rhetors in different social locations who bear distinctive maternal histories, contributes to this goal. ESM legitimizing reveals dominant thinking about and norms of motherhood and family, while also showing how ESM rhetors seize openings and opportunities to negotiate and resist those norms. In these concluding pages, I draw on John Schilb's notion of "rhetorical refusals" to demonstrate the limits of legitimizing, even the negotiations and resistance revealed in this study, and to make the case for ESMs to move beyond legitimizing by adopting what I call an *assumptive maternal stance*.[2] I argue, further, that elective single motherhood must align with reproductive justice (RJ), "a theoretical paradigm shift and a model for activist organizing" that builds on and applies Black feminist theory to reproductive politics.[3] RJ provides guardrails against the possibility of an assumptive maternal stance becoming a simplistic and exclusionary version of postfeminist woman power. Together, Schilb's "rhetorical refusals" and RJ help to articulate the rationale and potential of an assumptive maternal stance that is not only inclusive and empowered but also attentive to historic and current injustices that differently position maternal rhetors, ESMs among them.

The Constraints of Legitimacy

The ESM construct is dynamic. As this study demonstrates, ESMs continuously revision the labels they use to describe themselves and that shape others' understandings of them. They represent what Jenna Vinson calls an "embodied exigence": "an ongoing rhetorical campaign—a movement to change something that is 'other than it should be'—*for which those who represent it are made to answer.*"[4] Single and other stigmatized mothers who are "made to answer" for their situation, like the teen mothers at the center of Vinson's study, can capitalize on that stigmatizing attention and redeploy it to serve their own rhetorical ends. Their rhetorical efforts underscore Vinson's claim that "this [stigmatizing] recognition can function as a means of resistance, providing a way for marginalized subjects to speak back to social practices and norms."[5] Most ESMs respond to the demand "to answer" for their embodied exigence with labels, like Single Mother by Choice and Choice Mom, that emphasize their "choice" to become mothers. In so doing, these ESMs capitalize on their ability and privilege to choose without acknowledging the deleterious effects of their rhetoric on the mothers their labels exclude.

Not all ESMs take this rhetorical path, however. In her 2016 *Huffington Post* article, self-identified "black queer single mother" Nicole C. Mason aims to demonstrate that it is possible to resignify the label from within and redeploy the stigmatizing attention toward progressive ends.[6] Mason explains that she claims the label of SMC, because doing so "disrupts dominant narratives about motherhood and about who can be mothers on their own terms."[7] Her act of definitional activism contests the dominant construction of the SMC as white, heterosexual, and, middle-class, and, in so doing, amplifies the label's representational purview. Mason explains that she also claims the SMC label to contest the racism that devalues Black lives and non-nuclear family structures: "Identifying as a single mother by choice is a political and defiant act of asserting my bodily integrity and reproductive choice in a society that doesn't value black motherhood and most certainly black single motherhood."[8] After noting that she is not "distancing myself from other single mothers (read: poor black single mothers)," Mason asserts, "We are all in this motherhood boat together."[9] With this statement, Mason acknowledges the divisive effects of the SMC label and claims her coalitional intentions.

This study's analysis of ESM legitimizing suggests, however, that the various ESM labels (SMC and CM) inevitably enact distance, division, and judgement. Ultimately, they work against the formation of what Chávez and Griffin describe as "coalitional subjectivities": seeing one's own "oppression and privilege as inextricably bound to others."[10] Stated bluntly, the act of legitimizing, no matter the rhetor's intentions, creates or reinforces categories: the legitimate and the illegitimate. Moreover, legitimizing, no matter how expansive and inclusive, remains tethered to dominant norms and frameworks. Even when that relationship is oppositional, in contesting or rejecting dominant norms and frameworks, the legitimizer remains in relation to, and thereby, at least partially, defined by them. That is, the act of legitimizing ensnares the legitimizer in a dynamic the terms of which are inevitably limiting and often disadvantageous. Jené Stonesifer's *When Baby Makes Two*, Jane Mattes's *Single Mother by Choice*, and Alexandra Soiseth's *Choosing You* demonstrate the stranglehold of the intertwined discourses of family values and neoliberalism on ESMs' external legitimizing. As users of the *SMC* blog legitimize themselves to themselves and to other users through their rhetorical sharing, they negotiate their ambivalence about their deviation from maternal and familial norms. In so doing, some of them contrast themselves favorably to other, ostensibly less mindful and responsible single mothers, thereby creating a hierarchy within the category of single mother that celebrates some mothers—those who are intentional and choice-driven—while disparaging others. Even Silbergleid's and Sloan's affirmative legitimizing in their memoir and girlfriend's guide, respectively, articulates itself through a rejection—subversive in Silbergleid's case, playful in Sloan's—of traditional family values. Throughout, neoliberal values of personal responsibility and self-reliance maintain their strict hold on ESM rhetors' notions of legitimate single motherhood. Of the texts in this study, Nefertiti Austin's *Motherhood So White* is the exception. Though Austin explains how being an adoptive Black mother deviates from idealized maternal and familial norms in both Black and white communities, she does not compare herself or her maternal experience to those norms. Instead, her narrative centers her distinctive maternal journey and grounds it in her experience as an adopted Black person, as a student of Black history, and now as a proud single adoptive Black mother. Externalities, including prejudices against Black mothers, adoptive mothers, single mothers, and Black adoptive single mothers especially, pose challenges both logistical and psychological, but Austin resists allowing them to structure the narrative she presents of her thinking, mindset, and decisions. Women considering nonnormative paths to motherhood might follow the example that Austin sets as they consider their options, determine their path, and construct their maternal identity.

Assumptive Maternal Stance as Rhetorical Refusal

There is rhetorical power in doing the unexpected and in refusing to do the expected. An assumptive stance toward maternal legitimacy does both. Given that legitimacy matters practically and legally, and also emotionally and psychically in terms of acceptance, approval, and inclusion, to assume one's legitimacy and thus to refuse to seek it—to assert oneself as beyond legitimacy—is powerful. John Schilb's notion of "rhetorical refusals," which he defines as "an act of speaking or writing in which the rhetor pointedly refuses to do what the audience considers rhetorically normal," illuminates the rhetorical operations of an assumptive stance.[11] Rhetorical refusals can affect power relations. For, in many instances, entering a rhetorical framework that is built on socially and/or politically consequential hierarchies accedes to "power relations [rhetors] should probe and perhaps resist."[12] In refusing to enter and engage, "consciously or unconsciously, often the refusers contest hierarchies that would otherwise govern their utterances."[13]

In the case of ESMs, the dominant framework of maternal and familial legitimacy is steeped in prejudices about single mothers that place them in an uphill rhetorical battle. Cultural logics hold that single mothers struggle emotionally, financially, and logistically; that they do not consistently or authoritatively discipline their children; and, that their children long for a second parent, specifically, a male role model. ESMs that enter this framework are immediately and inevitably on the defensive, compelled to demonstrate that these cultural logics either should not or do not apply to them. Either stance—*should not* or *do not*—structures, and thus constrains, a single mother's self-presentation and the narrative about her motherhood that she tells herself and others. This dominant framework encourages comparisons and rankings, leading to the construction of maternal hierarchies. Not legitimizing has the potential to alter the rhetorical dynamics maternal rhetors face by changing the framework itself. Drawing on sociologist Erving Goffman's work on "breaking frame," Schilb explains the power of refusals: "Through what I am calling rhetorical refusals, writers and speakers deliberately challenge the frame that their audience brings to the occasion."[14] The social and political hierarchies that structure audiences' frames are undeniably stubborn, persistent, and powerful. Challenging them presents the opportunity to construct alternative frames through which rhetors can interpret, evaluate, and act. Rhetorical refusals thus have the potential to be critically generative and "go on to create *new norms* through the spectacle that often results from the dissonance between audience expectations and a particular refusal's failure to meet them."[15]

I thus propose that ESMs and other mothers who find themselves outside dominant maternal and familial norms adopt an assumptive stance, one that assumes their maternal legitimacy and thus entails a less charged relationship to their maternal difference, thereby enabling a mode of engagement that gestures beyond legitimizing. An assumptive stance has the potential to interrupt, perhaps even preclude, the construction of the maternal hierarchies that situate some mothers on the lowest and most disparaged ranks. An assumptive stance could encourage mothers who fall outside of normative maternal frameworks to place themselves, both unapologetically and nondefensively, at the center of their identity constructs and narratives. It could thereby foster the expression of a diversity of maternal histories, experiences, and perspectives, and, at the same time, by reducing these maternal rhetors' sense that they are on the defensive, discourage comparisons that lead to the creation of labels that laud some mothers while excluding, disrespecting, and disparaging others. Given the effects of racism, classism, heterosexism, ageism, and ableism on maternal identities, experiences, and constructs, maternal rhetors must develop critical awareness of the privileges inherent to their social location and of the blind spots that social location produces, so that their assumption of maternal legitimacy does not enact violence but instead contributes to coalitional maternal narratives and activism. To that end, an assumptive maternal stance would necessarily entail a commitment to "*performative disidentification*," everyday discursive attempts at resisting full interpellation into dominant norms of particular subject positions" and the privileges those subject positions bestow.[16]

To be clear, an assumptive maternal stance is aspirational, not wholly realizable. We are social and socially situated beings who gauge our relationship to norms and normative frameworks so as to understand ourselves, our social location, and the options and decisions available to us. Moreover, narrative identity systems make only some identities available to us and legible to others, no matter our self-perception and intentions.[17] Moving wholly beyond legitimizing, comparative thinking, and normative frameworks is thus neither possible nor necessarily desirable. Mothers can, however, aim to inhabit an assumptive maternal stance and, with repetition and conscious practice, make that stance more ingrained and habitual. The goal is not blindness to maternal difference but rather a thoughtful and productive engagement with that difference. Tensions, conflicts, and callouts are inevitable and productive, but they must proceed from, at a minimum, recognition and respect, and, in their ideal expression, a sense of shared purpose. The goal is a "sort of incommensurable communion . . . through which we can think beyond the register of the individual and see ourselves networked in larger discourses of belonging."[18] In short, discursively and materially, mothers must stop stepping or rolling on and over. We must see, hold, and support one another—be cognizant and appreciative of our differences and yet be interested in and committed to the pursuit of our common goals as mothers.

Why Reproductive Justice?

Reproductive justice brings a historical perspective on reproductive injustices, a critical perspective on reproductive rights, and a commitment to activism that counter the neoliberal underpinnings of the "choice" rhetorics favored by most of the ESM texts in this study and that enrich thinking about an assumptive stance. Like the most powerful rhetorical refusals, an RJ-guided assumptive stance would alter the power relations between would-be maternal legitimizers and dominant neoliberal norms of maternal and familial legitimacy but would not entail excluding or trampling over some mothers in the process of lifting others. Assumptive maternal rhetors can both learn from and be inspired by the attitude of RJ theorists: an indifference to their difference, a centering of themselves, and an assumption of their legitimacy. RJ activist and theorist Loretta Ross explains, "Reproductive justice theorists prefer to become our own subjects, without permission and without apology. We are decentering those alienating realities and putting ourselves in the center of the lens. As well as being different, we are indifferent."[19] Indifference, however, is not synonymous with inattention. Reproductive justice interrogates the factors that determine maternal legitimacy and that allow some mothers to legitimize themselves more easily, in addition to identifying the differential effects of the stigma around single motherhood on mothers' self-perception and rhetoric about themselves. Ross avers, "We understand how differences matter, and how we can [and must] account for power inequities to achieve our vision for justice."[20] RJ is thus committed to understanding how practices, ideologies, and, institutions have and continue to shape maternal experience and affect broader contexts of "physical, reproductive, and cultural safety."[21] As rhetorical critic Kathleen de Onís explains, RJ thus provides a "broad social justice frame" that lends itself to "the ever-increasing number of present-day concerns implicating health and well-being."[22]

Reproductive justice proposes a set of "*new norms*" through which to conceptualize maternal and familial legitimacy and to enact reproductive justice.[23] Twelve Black women initially conceptualized RJ at a 1994 conference sponsored by the Illinois Pro-Choice Alliance.[24] These RJ originators argued that the conference proposals "inadequately addressed the range of intersectional reproductive health concerns in the African American community" and set themselves the task of articulating a framework that would do better.[25] To that end, "RJ centers the lives of communities of color instead of the middle-class white people on both sides of the abortion divide."[26] In the two and half decades since, the work of theorizing and activating RJ has happened primarily through SisterSong, "the only national membership organization that works exclusively around RJ," though organizational and political activism around RJ has exploded in the last five years.[27] Today, RJ is "an expansive and multilayered approach to the fight for reproductive freedom for all people" that uses a human rights framework premised on "three interconnected human rights values: the right *not to have children* using safe birth control, abortion, or abstinence; the right *to have children* under the conditions we choose; and the right *to parent the children we have* in safe and healthy environments."[28] In asserting that birthing and parenting are human rights, and thus foundational and incontrovertible, RJ performs a "rhetorical refusal," disavowing the legitimacy of the question of maternal legitimacy itself.[29]

Reproductive justice also highlights the ways that white supremacist and neoliberal ideologies structure conceptions of and activism around reproductive justice rights in the late twentieth and early twenty-first centuries.[30] RJ counters neoliberal motherhood specifically by shifting the focus away from individual mothers and toward the systems, institutions, and policies that structure maternal choices, experiences, and opportunities. For this reason, the following two criteria, among others, are essential to RJ work: that it "makes the link between the individual to the community" and that it "addresses government and corporate responsibility."[31] These two criteria situate mothers and maternal experience in material, sociocultural, historical, and institutional contexts, thereby refuting the fantasy of the private, self-reliant, and autonomous mother who lies at the heart of the neoliberal imaginary.

Analysis of social location, understood as the intersectional influences of identity factors, such as race, class, religion, class, gender identity, and, sexual orientation, and status related to immigration and disability, is also integral to an RJ approach. This attention to difference among maternal identities and experiences is not a means of legitimizing but rather a step toward coalitional work predicated on understanding and appreciation. RJ "addresses the essentialism of gender-specific accounts that neglect how differences shape people's material realities, leaving undiscovered reproductive vulnerabilities shaped by white supremacy and neoliberalism."[32] Among these "reproductive vulnerabilities" is the very possibility of choosing motherhood (or not) and the individual neoliberal subject who is imagined to be in the position to make that choice. While some "choice" rhetorics can encompass a broad social justice vision,[33] the neoliberal assumption that only those who are economically autonomous can and deserve to exercise reproductive agency still underlies most "choice" rhetorics. As Andrea Smith explains, "Pro-choice argues that women should have freedom to make choices rather than [that they] possess inherent rights to their bodies regardless of their class standing."[34] That is, most neoliberal informed "choice" rhetorics assume the bodily integrity and material standing of the women they envision, rather than addressing the fact that many women, under neoliberalism, have neither access to a broad range of choices in any area of their lives, including reproduction, nor the agency to act on those choices. For these reasons, RJ problematizes *choice* itself. Rather than taking choice for granted, it investigates the constraints on reproductive choices and analyzes the ways that individual and institutional choices—discursive, material, and political—limit the reproductive options and choices for some women, while expanding that range for others.

RJ insists on a different set of key terms. Instead of choice, RJ emphasizes *access*: "Reproductive justice links reproductive rights with the social, political and economic inequalities that affect a woman's ability to *access* reproductive health care services. Core components of reproductive justice include equal *access* to safe abortion, affordable contraceptives and comprehensive sex education, as well as freedom from sexual violence."[35] RJ thus combats neoliberal assumptions by shifting the focus from individual mothers' personal decisions, for which they are seen as wholly responsible, to the cultural, sociopolitical, and institutional structures that enable some women to become mothers and then to mother in societally approved ways, while making it impossible for many others to do either. Intensive mothering, the maternal ideology of postfeminist neoliberalism, is held up as the gold-standard in educated middle-class circles,[36] and, as the preceding chapters demonstrate, some ESMs legitimize themselves by demonstrating their adherence to it. Intensive mothering assumes a private, autonomous mother, though, in practice, the intensive mother often outsources the intensive maternal work to others.[37] RJ-inspired analysis, specifically its insistence on linking "the individual to the community," both illuminates the neoliberal tenets that underlie intensive mothering and calls attention to the ways that neoliberal-informed policies and institutions preclude most mothers from mothering according to its dictates.[38] In lieu of proscriptive maternal dictates directed at individual mothers, RJ dedicates itself, as the name indicates, to *justice*—to enacting systemic changes that make a broader range of choices and access to those choices available to more people. Monica Simpson, current executive director of SisterSong, declares, "It's about liberation . . . and it's about dismantling systems of oppression that make our lives hard in this country but also that make it impossible for us to have the access and the choices that we want to have."[39]

Looking Ahead

In adopting an assumptive maternal stance and aligning themselves with the RJ movement, ESMs could cease to legitimize themselves, thereby marking a departure from even the most affirmative ESM legitimizing analyzed in this study. ESM who adopt an RJ-informed assumptive maternal stance could cultivate a reflective and analytical stance toward the differential effects of the stigma around single motherhood on their own and other mothers' self-perception and rhetorics. While eschewing the quest for maternal legitimacy would not actively dismantle neoliberal and white supremacist ideologies, it could undermine their stronghold through the refusal to endorse them. Furthermore, an assumptive maternal stance would provide ESMs with a perspective from which to examine the demand to legitimize and to determine whether to respond to that demand. It would enable them to critique, and perhaps reject, the kinds of rhetorical positioning that divide and pit mothers against one another. ESMs could then opt not to distinguish themselves from other mothers on the basis of their elective motherhood. This heightened consciousness about how our social location and ideological context shape the choices available to us, as well as our very ability to choose, is valuable, as we can share this critical perspective through the intimate pedagogy of our relationships and have it inform our political engagement. I feel comfortable identifying as an ESM, when I can explain that I do so within an RJ-informed framework. More often than not, however, I find myself identifying as simply a mother among mothers, because I've found that each woman's maternal experience is unique and reflective of so much more than her relationship status. Indeed, Loretta Ross notes that "supporters [of RJ] devote time and energy to understand their experiences through their own lens . . . offering little purchase for claims of exclusion."[40] In this sense, reflective centering of one's experience fosters an inclusive environment.

An assumptive maternal stance, envisioned and enacted as I have proposed here, has the potential to direct the attention of maternal rhetors who stand outside normative frameworks beyond the quest for legitimacy and to harness those legitimizing energies in the service of inclusive maternal activism instead. It could encourage and enable maternal rhetors to demand recognition and acknowledgment on terms they establish and determine meaningful. It could create space for narratives about different points of entry to and experiences of motherhood. By attending to the reciprocal and dynamic relations of privilege and oppression, it could support the development of "coalitional subjectivities,"[41] inspired by what Karma Chávez describes as a "differential vision." She writes, "A differential vision reflects an impure orientation . . . [it] can aid in creating, and perhaps sustaining, coalitional subjectivities and coalitions of resistance with both those who share the vision and those who may share only particular goals. This is because differential visions are multifaceted in how they present politics, and they also provide numerous opportunities for people to see their issues as inextricably connected."[42]

Finally, an assumptive maternal stance could foster utopian imaginings about and new language to describe motherhood, kinship, and family. Directing one's gaze, energy, and intentions beyond maternal legitimacy would be empowering and liberating. Ultimately, it would allow maternal rhetors to harness their energy and time toward the work that bonds and motivates us: that of mothering.

NOTES

INTRODUCTION

1. I use the umbrella term "elective single mother" to describe single women who pursue motherhood, rather than "Single Mother by Choice" or "Choice Mom," because I want to avoid the judgment, exclusions, and ideological cargo of the word "choice."

2. Rosanna Hertz, *Single by Chance, Mothers by Choice* (Oxford, UK: Oxford University Press, 2006), 19.

3. Hertz, *Single by Chance*, xvii.

4. Hertz, 15.

5. Jane Bock, "Doing the Right Thing? Single Mothers by Choice and the Struggle for Legitimacy," *Gender and Society* 14, no. 1 (February 2000): 70.

6. Susanna Graham, "Choosing Single Motherhood: Single Women Negotiating the Nuclear Family Ideal," in *Families beyond the Nuclear Ideal*, ed. Daniela Cutas and Sarah Chan (London: Bloomsbury, 2012), 97.

7. Graham, "Choosing Single Motherhood," 101.

8. Hertz, *Single by Chance*, 141; Bock, "Doing the Right Thing?" 70; *Aristotle: A Theory of Civic Discourse*, trans. George A. Kennedy (New York: Oxford University Press, 1991), 36.

9. Joan W. Scott, "The Evidence of Experience," *Critical Inquiry* 17, no. 4 (Summer 1991): 797.

10. For more on the relationship of articulation and aspiration, see Agnes Callard's *Aspiration: The Agency of Becoming* (New York: Oxford University Press, 2018).

11. Susan B. Boyd et al., *Autonomous Motherhood? A Socio-Legal Study of Choice and Constraint* (Toronto: University of Toronto Press, 2015), 26.

12. Vivian May, *Pursuing Intersectionality, Unsettling Dominant Imaginaries* (New York: Routledge, 2015), 23.

13. Loretta J. Ross, "Conceptualizing Reproductive Justice Theory: A Manifesto for Activism," in *Radical Reproductive Justice: Foundation, Theory, Practice, Critique*, ed. Loretta J. Ross et al. (New York: Feminist Press, 2017), 184.

14. As journalist Rebecca Traister astutely observes, "it has long been the replicative behaviors or perspectives of *white* women—and not the original shifts pioneered by poor women and women of color—that make people sit up and take notice and that sometimes become discernible as liberation." See Traister, *All the Single Ladies: Unmarried Women and the Rise of an Independent Nation* (New York: Simon and Schuster, 2016), 191.

15. Loretta J. Ross and Rickie Solinger, *Reproductive Justice: An Introduction* (Oakland: University of California Press, 2017), 3.

16. Elizabeth C. Britt, *Conceiving Normalcy: Rhetoric, Law, and the Double Binds of Infertility* (Tuscaloosa: University of Alabama Press, 2001), 11.

17. Legal scholars Boyd et al. and Twila Perry, along with cultural critic Jane Juffer, likewise argue that ESMs' adherence to liberal notions of autonomy reinforces troubling divisions among single mothers. See Boyd et al., *Autonomous Motherhood?* and Twila L.

Perry, "Symposium, Family Values, Race, Feminism and Public Policy," *Santa Clara Law Review* 36 (1996): 345–74.

18. Michael Warner, "Introduction: Fear of a Queer Planet," *Social Text*, no. 29 (1991): 16.

19. Lauren Berlant and Jay Prosser, "Intimate Publics: A Conversation," *Biography* 34, no. 1 (Winter 2011): 182.

20. Berlant and Prosser, "Intimate Publics," 181.

21. Marjorie Jolles, "Between Embodied Subjects and Objects: Narrative Somaesthetics," *Hypatia* 27, no. 2 (Spring 2012): 305.

22. Britt, *Conceiving Normalcy*, 14.

23. Michael Warner, *The Trouble with Normal: Sex, Politics, and the Ethics of Queer Life* (Cambridge, MA: Harvard University Press, 2000), 116.

24. Mary Bernstein and Renate Reimann, "Queer Families and the Politics of Visibility," in *Queer Families, Queer Politics: Challenging Culture and the State*, ed. Mary Bernstein and Renate Reimann (New York: Columbia University Press, 2001), 3.

25. J. Jack Halberstam, *Gaga Feminism: Sex, Gender, and the End of Normal* (Boston: Beacon Press, 2012), 313.

26. Halberstam, *Gaga Feminism*, 317.

27. Dana Cloud, "Queer Theory and 'Family Values:' Capitalism's Utopias of Self-Invention," in *Marxism, Queer Theory, Gender* (Syracuse, NY: Red Factory, 2001), 72.

28. Some ESMs have intercourse with the sole purpose of becoming pregnant, but the majority pursue motherhood through other means (e.g., intrauterine insemination, in vitro fertilization, and/or adoption). See Laura Mamo, *Queering Reproduction: Achieving Pregnancy in the Age of Technoscience* (Durham, NC: Duke University Press, 2007), 5.

29. Kath Weston, introduction to *Love Makes a Family: Portraits of Lesbian, Gay, Bisexual, and Transgender Parents and Their Families*, ed. Peggy Gillespie (Amherst: University of Massachusetts Press, 1999), 3–11. See also Weston, *Families We Choose: Lesbians, Gays, and Kinship (Between Men—Between Women)* (New York: Columbia University Press, 1997).

30. Elizabeth Freeman, "Queer Belongings: Kinship Theory and Queer Theory," in *A Companion to Lesbian, Gay, Bisexual, Transgender, and Queer Studies*, ed. George E. Haggerty and Molly McGarry (Hoboken, NJ: John Wiley and Sons, 2007), 297.

31. Robert O. Self, *All in the Family: The Realignment of American Democracy since the 1960s* (New York: Hill and Wang, 2012), 8.

32. Melinda Cooper, *Family Values: Between Neoliberalism and the New Social Conservatism* (Brooklyn, NY: Zone Books, 2017), 9.

33. Stephanie Coontz, *The Way We Never Were: American Families and the Nostalgia Trap* (New York: Basic Books, 1992), 24.

34. Coontz, *The Way We Never Were*, 28, 24.

35. Coontz, 27.

36. See Coontz, 29–30, for statistics on poverty in the 1950s.

37. Coontz, 30.

38. Coontz, 29.

39. Bernstein and Rainmann, *Queer Families*, 2.

40. See Linda Nicholson's "The Myth of the Traditional Family," in *Feminism and Families*, ed. Hilde Lindemann Nelson (New York: Routledge, 1997), 27–42.

41. Patricia Hill Collins, "It's All in the Family: Intersections of Gender, Race, and Nation," *Hypatia* 13, no. 3 (Summer 1998): 63.

42. Jyl J. Josephson and Cynthia Burack, "The Political Ideology of the Neo-Traditional Family," *Journal of Political Ideologies* 3, no. 2 (June 1998): 227.

43. Seth Dowland, "'Family Values' and the Formation of a Christian Right Agenda," *Church History* 78, no. 3 (September 2009): 607.

44. Cooper, *Family Values*, 9.

45. Cooper, 9.

46. Gillian Anderson and Joseph G. Moore, "'Doing It All . . . and Making It Look Easy!': Yummy Mummies, Mompreneurs and the North American Neoliberal Crisis of the Home," in *Mothering in the Age of Neoliberalism*, ed. Melinda Vandenbeld Giles (Bradford, ON: Demeter Press, 2014), 96.

47. "Elevat[ing] . . . market forces . . .": Celia Winkler, "Redefining Single Motherhood: The 1990s Child Support Discourse and the Dismantling of the U.S. Welfare State," in Giles, *Mothering in the Age of Neoliberalism*, 256. For Brown, see Wendy Brown, "Neo-Liberalism and the End of Liberal Democracy," *Theory and Event* 7, 1 (January 2003): para. 7 (emphasis in original).

48. Family values is an "ideograph." According to Dana L. Cloud, ideographs are "powerful tools of political language [that] provide an analytical link between rhetoric—understood as situated, pragmatic, instrumental, and strategic discourse—on the one hand, and ideology—the structures or systems of ideas within which individual pragmatic speech acts take place and by which they are constrained—on the other." Ideographs are "abstract, easily-recognized, and evoke near-universal and rapid identification within a culture." They are the most "commonplace and hallowed terms in rhetorical discourse." See "The Rhetoric of Family Values: Scapegoating, Utopia, and the Privatization of Social Responsibility," *Western Journal of Communication* 62, no. 4 (June 2009): 389.

49. Dowland, "'Family Values'," 607, 609.

50. Moral Majority, "Family Manifesto," Jerry Falwell Library website, 1988. It was not until 2015 that the Supreme Court legalized gay marriage in *Obergefell v. Hodges*.

51. Advocates of traditional "family values" rightly intuited that same-sex parents would "undo gender by refusing the relationality through which dichotomous gender is defined." See Mamo, *Queering Reproduction*, 6.

52. Cheshire Calhoun, *Feminism, the Family, and the Politics of the Closet: Lesbian and Gay Displacement* (Oxford, UK: Oxford University Press, 2003), 137.

53. David Popenhoe, "The Controversial Truth: Two-Parent Families Are Better," *New York Times*, December 26, 1992.

54. Patricia Hill Collins, *Black Feminist Thought: Knowledge, Consciousness, and the Politics of Empowerment*, rev. tenth anniversary ed. (New York: Routledge, 2000); Coontz, *The Way We Never Were*. See also Collins, "All in the Family."

55. Cloud, "Queer Theory," 388.

56. Barbara Dafoe Whitehead, "Dan Quayle Was Right," *Atlantic*, April 1993.

57. Judith Stacey, *In the Name of the Family* (Boston: Beacon Press, 1996), 4.

58. Bill Clinton quoted in Michael Kranish, "In the Bully Pulpit, Preaching Values," *Boston Globe*, December 10, 1993.

59. David Popenhoe, *War Over the Family* (New Brunswick, NJ: Transaction Publishers, 2005), 254.

60. Cooper, *Family Values*, 9.

61. Laura Briggs, *How All Politics Became Reproductive Politics: From Welfare Reform to Foreclosure to Trump* (Oakland: University of California Press, 2018), 55.

62. Cooper, *Family Values*, 21.

63. Briggs, *How All Politics Became Reproductive Politics*, 13.

64. Laura Curran and Laura Abrams, "Making Men into Dads: Fatherhood, the State, and Welfare Reform," *Gender and Society* 14, no. 5 (October 2000): 662–78; Michael Enku

Ide et al., "Emerging Adult Sons and Their Fathers: Race and Construction of Masculinity," *Gender and Society* 32, no. 1 (February 2018): 5–33; Jennifer Randles, "'Manning Up' to Be a Good Father: Hybrid Fatherhood, Masculinity, and U.S. Responsible Fatherhood Policy," *Gender and Society* 32, no. 4 (August 2018): 516–39.

65. Moral Majority, "Family Manifesto."

66. David Blankenhorn, *Fatherless America: Confronting Our Most Urgent Social Problem* (New York: BasicBooks, 1995), 26.

67. Blankenhorn, *Fatherless America*, 25.

68. Moral Majority, "Family Manifesto."

69. Blankenhorn, *Fatherless America*, 173.

70. John Fiske, *Media Matters: Everyday Culture and Political Change* (Minneapolis: University of Minnesota Press, 1994), 29.

71. Kara W. Swanson, *Banking on the Body: The Market in Blood, Milk, and Sperm in Modern America* (Cambridge, MA: Harvard University Press, 2014), 201.

72. Swanson, *Banking on the Body*, 226.

73. Swanson, *Banking on the Body*, 230.

74. For "most doctors refused to inseminate any unmarried woman," see Swanson, *Banking on the Body*, 227. In the 1930s, Dr. Frances Seymour inseminated unmarried "businesswomen" who met the same criteria she required of her married patients: "a minimum IQ of 120" in the prospective mother as well as a commitment to secure an educational insurance policy for the prospective child. Grant S. Beardsley, "Artificial Cross Insemination," *Western Journal of Surgery, Obstetrics and Gynecology* 48 (February 1940): 94, quoted in Swanson, *Banking on the Body*, 205.

75. Swanson, *Banking on the Body*, 209.

76. See Swanson, 202–9; also, Margaret Marsh and Wanda Ronner, *The Empty Cradle: Infertility in America from Colonial Times to the Present* (Baltimore: Johns Hopkins University Press, 1996), 161–67.

77. Swanson, *Banking on the Body*, 210.

78. Swanson, 227.

79. Swanson, 232.

80. Marsh and Ronner, *Empty Cradle*, 236–37.

81. Marsh and Ronner, 195.

82. Susan Faludi, *Backlash: The Undeclared War against American Women*, 15th anniversary ed. (New York: Three Rivers Press, 2006).

83. Faludi, *Backlash*.

84. Sharon Hays, *The Cultural Contradictions of Motherhood* (New Haven: Yale University Press, 1996), 6; Susan Douglas and Meredith Michaels, *The Mommy Myth: The Idealization of Motherhood and How It Has Undermined All Woman* (New York: Free Press, 2004), 4; Andrea O'Reilly, "We Need to Talk about Patriarchal Motherhood: Essentialization, Naturalization, and Idealization in Lionel Shriver's *We Need to Talk about Kevin*," *Journal of the Motherhood Initiative for Research and Community Involvement* 7, no. 1 (Spring/Summer 2016): 65; D. Lynn O'Brien Hallstein, "Introduction to Mothering Rhetorics," *Women's Studies in Communication* 40, no. 1 (2017): 4.

85. Cloud, "Queer Theory," 400.

86. Shanara Rose Reid-Brinkley, "Mammies and Matriarchs: Feminine Style and Signifyin(g) in Carol Moselet Braun's 2003–2004 Campaign for the Presidency," in *Standing in the Intersection: Feminist Voices, Feminist Practices in Communication Studies*, ed. Karma R. Chávez and Cindy L. Griffin (Albany: SUNY Press, 2012), 46.

87. Winkler, *Redefining Single Motherhood*, 256.

88. [D.] Lynn O'Brien Hallstein, *Bikini Ready Moms* (Albany: SUNY, 2015), 36.

89. Hallstein, *Bikini Ready Moms*, 35.

90. See chapter 1 in this book for a history of the demonizing of women of color who receive public assistance.

91. Self, *All in the Family*, 10.

92. Pew Research Center, "The Decline of Marriage and Rise of New Families," *Social and Demographic Trends*, November 18, 2010.

93. Kay Hymowitz et al., "The Great Crossover," in *Knot Yet: The Benefits and Costs of Delayed Marriage in America*, report produced by the National Marriage Project at the University of Virginia, the National Campaign to Prevent Teen and Unplanned Pregnancy, and the Relate Institute, 17–19.

94. Chapter 4 in this book explains how LGBTQIA+ activists' efforts led to the expansion of family values.

95. Susan Golombok, *Modern Families: Parents and Children in New Family Form* (Cambridge, UK: Cambridge University Press, 2015), 3.

96. Jessica Bennett, "Meet the Groundbreaking New Second Family," *New York Times*, January 17, 2021.

97. McClain defines the diversity approach as one that "recognizes and supports pathways to parenthood in addition to heterosexual procreation within marriage and does not restrict parental rights and responsibilities to biological parents." This approach not only assumes that diverse family forms are a fact but goes further, emphasizing their "function" over their "form." See Linda C. McClain, "A Diversity Approach to Parenthood in Family Life and Family Law," in *What Is Parenthood? Contemporary Debates about the Family*, ed. Linda C. McClain and Daniel Cere (New York: New York University Press, 2013), 42, 49.

98. Self, *All in the Family*, 331.

99. Erik Klinenberg, *Going Solo: The Extraordinary Rise and Surprising Appeal of Living Alone* (New York: Penguin Books, 2013), 6.

100. Klinenberg, *Going Solo*, 212.

101. Bella DePaulo, *Singled Out: How Singles Are Stereotyped, Stigmatized, and Ignored, and Still Live Happily Ever After* (New York: St. Martin's, 2007), 259.

102. Tracy Henke, "The Choice to Be Childfree: An Increasing Factor in the U.S. Population Growth," Negative Population Growth, August 25, 2014. Negative Population Growth (NPG) states that its "goal is to slow, halt, and eventually reverse U.S. population growth until America reaches an optimum level—a population size where our nation is self-sustaining with its own resources and we do not destroy our environment." NPG proposes to achieve this not only though limiting birthrates but also by sharply curtailing immigration into America.

103. Amy Blackstone, *Childfree by Choice: The Movement Redefining Family and Creating a New Age of Independence* (New York: Dutton, 2019), x.

104. Joel Kotkin, *The Rise of Post-Familialism: Humanity's Future?* (Singapore: Civil Service College, 2012), 9.

105. Adrienne Rich, "Motherhood in Bondage (1976)," in *On Lies, Secrets, and Silence: Selected Prose 1966–1978* (New York: W. W. Norton, 1979), 196.

106. Rich Morin, "Disapprove of Single Mothers," Pew Research Center, January 6, 2011.

107. Jodi Vandenberg-Daves, *Modern Motherhood: An American History* (New Brunswick, NJ: Rutgers University Press, 2014), 250.

108. Mikki Morrissette, *Choosing Single Motherhood: The Thinking Woman's Guide* (Boston: Houghton Mifflin, 2008), 2. Two years earlier, Morrissette had self-published

this book under the same title (*Choosing Single Motherhood: The Thinking Woman's Guide* [Minneapolis: Be-Mondo Publishing, 2006]), but the 2008 edition is the one cited in this book.

109. Critics of liberalism, both traditional and "neo," as well as critics of "choice feminism," point to the ways these ideologies mask differences in women's personal, professional, and political lives, all of which affect the choices available to them. They also critique these ideologies' tendency to divide women into categories of "good" and "bad" choosers. Among others, see Celeste Michelle Condit's *Decoding Abortion Rhetoric: Communicating Social Change* (Champaign: University of Illinois Press, 1990); Michaele L. Ferguson's "Choice Feminism and the Fear of Politics" in *Perspectives on Politics* 8, no. 1 (March 2010): 247–53; Sara Hayden and D. Lynn O'Brien Hallstein's *Contemplating Maternity in an Era of Choice: Explorations into Discourses of Reproduction* (Lanham, MD: Lexington Books, 2010); Nancy J. Hirschmann's "Choosing Betrayal," *Perspectives on Politics* 8, no. 1 (March 2010): 271–78; Ross and Solinger, *Reproductive Justice*; and Rickie Solinger's *Wake Up Little Susie: Single Pregnancy and Race before Roe v. Wade* (New York: Routledge, 1992) and *Beggars and Choosers: How the Politics of Choice Shapes Adoption, Abortion, and Welfare in the United States* (New York: Hill and Wang, 2002).

110. Solinger, *Beggars and Choosers*, 199–200.

111. Kathryn Edin and Maria J. Kefalas, *Promises I Can Keep: Why Poor Women Put Motherhood before Marriage* (Oakland: University of California Press, 2011), 212. In "Outcast Mothers and Surrogates: Racism and Reproductive Politics in the Nineties," Angela Davis writes, "Is it really so hard to grasp why so many young women would choose motherhood? Isn't this path toward adulthood still thrust upon them by the old but persisting ideological constructions of femaleness? Doesn't motherhood still equal adult womanhood in the popular imagination? Don't the new reproductive technologies further develop this equation of womanhood and motherhood? I would venture to say that many young women make conscious decisions to bear children in order to convince themselves that they are alive and creative human beings" (in *American Feminist Thought at Century's End: A Reader*, ed. Linda S. Kauffman [Cambridge, MA: Blackwell, 1993], 362).

112. Edin and Kefalas, *Promises I Can Keep*, 6.

113. Edin and Kefalas, 185.

114. Coontz, *The Way We Never Were*, 252.

115. The character Murphy Brown actually became pregnant unintentionally and then decided to have the baby. Nevertheless, her story so powerfully conforms to the stereotype of women who put motherhood on hold for career advancement that Angela's (mis) interpretation makes sense. Murphy Brown personifies the planning that white professional women can engage in. Edin and Kefalas, *Promises I Can Keep*, 208.

116. Edin and Kefalas, 208.

117. Britt, *Conceiving Normalcy*, 6.

118. Maria Lugones, "From within Germinative Stasis: Creating Active Subjectivity, Resistant Agency," in *Entremundos/Among Worlds: New Perspectives on Gloria Anzaldúa*, ed. AnaLouise Keating (New York: Palgrave Macmillan, 2005), 86.

119. Janet M. Atwill, *Rhetoric Reclaimed: Aristotle and the Liberal Arts Tradition* (Ithaca, NY: Cornell University Press, 2009), 206.

120. Jacqueline Jones Royster and Gesa E. Kirsch, *Feminist Rhetorical Practices: New Horizons for Rhetoric, Composition, and Literacy Studies* (Carbondale: Southern Illinois University Press, 2012), 145.

121. May, *Pursuing Intersectionality*, 12.

122. May, *Pursuing Intersectionality*, 12; Adrienne Rich, *Of Woman Born: Motherhood*

as Experience and Institution, 2nd ed. (New York: W.W. Norton, 1986), 13, italics in the original.

123. Hallstein, "Introduction to Mothering Rhetorics," 2.

124. Lindal Buchanan, *Rhetorics of Motherhood* (Carbondale: Southern Illinois University Press, 2013), 23.

125. Star Medzerian Vanguri, ed., *Rhetorics of Names and Naming* (New York: Routledge, 2018), 2.

126. Cindy L. Griffin and Karma Chávez, "Introduction: Standing at the Intersections of Feminisms, Intersectionality, and Communication Studies," in Chávez and Griffin, *Standing in the Intersection*, 17.

127. Buchanan, *Rhetorics of Motherhood*, 21. I join other rhetoricians in this code-cracking work, beginning with Julie M. Thompson, whose trail-blazing *Mommy Queerest: Contemporary Rhetorics of Lesbian Maternal Identity* focused on the rhetorical construction of a particular kind of mother—lesbian mothers—and the "competing and sometimes contradictory characterizations of lesbianism and motherhood [that] trap lesbian mothers in a web of illegitimate subject positions" (Amherst: University of Massachusetts Press, 2002), 8. More recently, the essays in Heather Hundley and Sara Hayden's *Mediated Moms: Contemporary Challenges to the Motherhood Myth* further query constructions of particular kinds of mothers by analyzing how "varied, often contradictory depictions of mothers begin to crack open the good/bad mother dichotomy" (New York: Peter Lang, 2015), 11. Contributors to the edited collection *The Motherhood Business: Consumption, Communication, and Privilege* (ed. Anne Teresa Demo, Jennifer L. Borda, and Charlotte Kroløkke) analyze how different kinds of mothers leverage different forms of capital expenditures—economic, cultural, social, and emotional—"to justify privilege and confer advantage" (Tuscaloosa: University of Alabama Press, 2015), 20. Jenna Vinson's *Embodying the Problem: The Persuasive Power of the Teen Mother* investigates "how young pregnant and mothering women seize the opportunity engendered by the public attention to the so-called teenage pregnancy problem to speak back to those who confront them in public and to write counter-narratives of pregnancy and motherhood—stories that explicitly resist the statistics, experts, and assumptions that dehumanize 'them' as a supposedly coherent category of problem people" (New Brunswick, NJ: Rutgers University Press 2017), ix.

128. By "culturally white," I mean that the ESM protagonists of these feature films embody the resourced ideal of whiteness, such that even ethnic difference is subsumed by class privilege. The label "SMC," in particular, perpetuates identification with middle class white womanhood and draws on the cultural capital contained therein.

129. Several documentaries also represent elective single motherhood. See Beth Cramer's *Plan B: Single Women Choosing Motherhood* (New York City: Brave Films, 2009); Katz and Rudavsky's *And Baby Makes Two* (New York City: First Run Features, 1999); and Shannon O'Rourke's *Maybe Baby* (Beacon, NY: New Day Films, 2007). See here also Katherine Mack, "Do Two a Family Make: Hollywood Engages Intentional Single Motherhood," in *Motherhood and Single-Lone Parenting: A Twenty-First Century Perspective*, ed. Maki Motapanyane (Bradford: Demeter Press, 2016), 53–71, and Robin Silbergleid, "'Oh Baby!' Representations of Single Mothers in American Popular Culture," *Americana: The Journal of American Popular Culture* 1, no. 2 (Fall 2020): n.p.

130. Hertz, *Single by Chance*, xvii.

131. Robin Jensen, *Infertility: Tracing the History of a Transformative Term* (University Park: Penn State University Press, 2016); Marika Siegel, *The Rhetoric of Pregnancy* (Chicago: University of Chicago Press, 2013); Vinson, *Embodying the Problem*; Kim Hensley Owens, *Writing Childbirth: Women's Rhetorical Agency in Labor and Online* (Carbondale:

Southern Illinois University Press, 2015); Heather Brook Adams, *Enduring Shame: A Recent History of Unwed Pregnancy and Righteous Reproduction* (Columbia: University of South Carolina Press, 2022); Demo, Borda, and Kroløkke, *Motherhood Business*; [D.] Lynn O'Brien Hallstein, *Bikini-Ready Moms: Celebrity Profiles, Motherhood, and the Body* (Albany: State University of New York Press, 2015); Hudley and Hayden, *Mediated Moms*; and Natalie Fixmer-Oraiz, *Homeland Maternity: US Security Culture and the New Reproductive Regime* (Champaign: University of Illinois Press, 2019).

132. Buchanan, *Rhetorics of Motherhood*, 23.

133. Kathleen Blake Yancey, *Writing in the 21st Century*, report, National Council of Teachers of English, February 2009; see also Doug Hesse and Kathleen Blake Yancey, "Permission to Write," *Writing on the Edge* 25, no. 1 (Fall 2014): 13–29.

134. Youngjoo Yi and Tuba Angay-Crowder, "Self-Sponsored Writing," *TESOL Encyclopedia of English Language Learning*, January 18, 2018, 2; Youngjoo Yi and A. Hirvela, "Technology and 'Self-Sponsored' Writing: A Case Study of a Korean-American Adolescent," *Computers and Composition* 27, no. 2 (June 2010): 97.

135. Rachel Lehmann-Haupt, *DIY Mom: A Solo Parenting Adventure* (Bronx: She Writes Press, 2013) (eBook); Nina Davenport, *First Comes Love* (Baby Pictures, 2012).

136. Hallstein, "Introduction to Mothering Rhetorics," 2.

137. Rich, *Of Woman Born*, 13; Hallstein, "Introduction to Mothering Rhetorics," 2.

138. Carolyn Miller, "Genre as Social Action," *Quarterly Journal of Speech*, 70 (1984): 165.

139. See Micki McGee, *Self-Help, Inc.: Makeover Culture in American Life* (Oxford, UK: Oxford University Press, 2005), 11.

140. Anis S. Bawarshi and Mary Jo Reiff, *Genre: An Introduction to Theory, History, Research, and Pedagogy* (West Lafayette, IN: Parlor Press, 2010), 4.

141. Aristotle, *On Rhetoric*, 121.

142. Michael Halloran, "Aristotle's Concept of Ethos, or If Not His, Somebody Else's." *Rhetoric Review* 1, no. 1 (September 1982): 60.

143. Nedra Reynolds observes how, "considering the social construction of *ethos* . . . shifts its implications of responsibility from the individual to a negotiation or mediation between the rhetor and the community." Reynolds, "Ethos as Location: New Sites for Understanding Discursive Authority," *Rhetoric Review* 11, no. 2 (Spring 1993): 327–38.

144. William Benoit, "On Aristotle's Example," *Philosophy and Rhetoric* 20, no. 4 (1987): 264.

145. Krista Ratcliffe, "In Search of the Unstated: The Enthymeme and/of Whiteness," *JAC* 27, nos. 1/2 (2007): 282.

146. Lisa Flores, "Between Abundance and Marginalization: The Imperative of Racial Rhetorical Criticism," *Review of Communication* 16, no. 1 (January 2016): 17.

147. Kimberlé Crenshaw, "Demarginalizing the Intersection of Race and Sex: A Black Feminist Critique of Antidiscrimination Doctrine, Feminist Theory and Antiracist Politics," *University of Chicago Legal Forum* 1, no. 8 (1989): 149.

148. Sumi Cho, Kimberlé Williams Crenshaw, and Leslie McCall, "Toward a Field of Intersectionality Studies," *Signs* 38, no. 4 (Summer 2013): 795.

149. Anna Carasthatis, *Intersectionality: Origins, Contestations, Horizons* (Lincoln: University of Nebraska Press, 2016), 307.

150. May, *Pursuing Intersectionality*, 4, viii.

151. DePaulo, *Singled Out*, 13.

152. Kate Bolick, "All the Single Ladies," *Atlantic*, November 2011.

153. Claire Cain Miller, "The Divorce Surge Is Over, But the Myth Lives On," *New York Times*, December 2, 2014.

154. Traister, *All the Single Ladies*, 83.

155. Traister, *All the Single Ladies*, 108.

156. DePaulo, *Singled Out*, 186.

157. Barbara Kingsolver, *High Tide in Tucson: Essays from Now or Never* (New York: Harper, 1995).

158. Annette Lareau calls this form of parenting "concerted cultivation," which she defines as the efforts undertaken by middle-class parents to foster the development and talents of their children through organized activities. See Lareau, *Unequal Childhoods: Class, Race, and Family Life*, 2nd edition (Berkeley: University of California Press: 2011), 2.

159. Nicholson, "Myth of the Traditional Family," 37.

160. Asha Bandele, "Woman Up," in *One Big Happy Family*, ed. Rebecca Walker (New York: Riverhead Books, 2009), 21–22.

161. Traister, *All the Single Ladies*, 209.

162. Andrew Solomon, *Far from the Tree: Parents, Children, and the Search for Identity* (New York: Scribner, 2012), 1 (my emphasis).

163. Solomon, *Far from the Tree*, 686.

CHAPTER 1

Epigraph. Jené Stonesifer, *When Baby Makes Two: Single Mothers by Change or by Choice* (Los Angeles: Lowell House, 1994), 188.

Epigraph. Jane Mattes, *Single Mothers by Choice: A Guidebook for Single Women Who Are Considering or Have Chosen Motherhood* (New York: Three Rivers Press, 1994), xxi

1. Dan Quayle, "Address to the Commonwealth Club of California," May 19, 1992. Found on the Dan Quayle website.

2. Quayle, "Address to the Commonwealth Club of California."

3. Patricia Hill Collins, *Black Feminist Thought: Knowledge, Consciousness, and the Politics of Empowerment*, rev. tenth anniversary ed. (New York: Routledge, 2000), 154–55 (my italics).

4. See Charles Murray's "The Coming White Underclass," *Wall Street Journal*, October 29, 1993. The Southern Poverty Law Center classifies Murray as someone who uses "racist pseudoscience and misleading statistics to argue that social inequality is caused by the genetic inferiority of the black and Latino communities, women and the poor." See the Southern Poverty Law Center website, Extremist Files database, "Charles Murray" entry (under Individual Profiles).

5. Marian Wright Edelman, "Colorado College Baccalaureate Address," Colorado Springs, May 16, 1999, Iowa State University, Archive of Women's Political Communication.

6. Dorothy Roberts, *Killing the Black Body: Race, Reproduction, and the Meaning of Liberty* (New York: Vintage Books, 1997), 17.

7. Sara McLanahan and Christopher Jencks, "Was Moynihan Right? What Happens to Children of Unmarried Mothers," *EducationNext* 15, no. 2 (Spring 2015): 14–20.

8. Factoring in the mothers' intentionality complicates the picture. "In the five years before 1988, 5.5% of first births were intended births to unpartnered mothers; in the early 2000s, the corresponding figure was 6.2%, although levels were slightly higher in the 1990s." See Sarah R. Hayford and Karen Benjamin Guzzo, "The Single Motherhood by Choice Myth," *Contexts* 14, no. 4 (Fall 2015): 70–72.

9. In contrast, a combination of racism and historical ignorance led some to claim that an intractable "culture of poverty" led to the high number of African American and Latinx unmarried mothers: "The belief that there is something about the lives and choices of Black and Latina poor women that lead them to perpetuate poverty across generations . . . has a

long genealogy in liberal sciences and policy." See Laura Briggs, *How All Politics Became Reproductive Politics: From Welfare Reform to Foreclosure to Trump* (Oakland: University of California Press, 2018, 53.

10. Star Medzerian Vanguri, ed., *Rhetorics of Names and Naming* (New York: Routledge, 2018.

11. Jane Mattes, *Single Mothers by Choice: A Guidebook for Single Women Who Are Considering or Have Chosen Motherhood* (New York: Three Rivers Press, 1994), xxi.

12. According to Scott Coltrane (citing Letty Cottin Pogrebin's *Family Politics: Love and Family on an Intimate Frontier* [New York: McGraw-Hill, 1983]), "The idea that all women should be mothers and that they should gain intense satisfaction from it has been characterized as compulsory motherhood (Pogrebin, 1983). According to this view, a woman's ultimate purpose is to be a mother, and everything else she does is secondary." See Coltrane, *Gender and Families* (Thousand Oaks, CA: Pine Forge Press, 1998), 90.

13. Natalie Fixmer-Oraiz, *Homeland Maternity: US Security Culture and the New Reproductive Regime* (Urbana: University of Illinois Press, 2019), 25. See also Angela Davis's intersectional analysis of compulsory motherhood in "Outcast Mothers and Surrogates: Racism and Reproductive Politics in the Nineties," in *American Feminist Thought at Century's End: A Reader*, ed. Linda S. Kauffman [Cambridge, MA: Blackwell, 1993].

14. This specter has a long history. Since the first slave ships arrived on the shores of the United States, Black women's reproduction has been controlled, regulated, and made to serve social objectives not of their design. In *Killing the Black Body*, Dorothy Roberts demonstrates how Black people in the United States have experienced "systemic, institutionalized denial" of their reproductive freedom (4). Compulsory motherhood for enslaved Black women (and men) was literal: they were considered and treated as "breeders" (see *Killing the Black Body* chapter 1, "Reproduction in Bondage"). Enslaved women bore children, some conceived through rape, and then had to mother those children in the constrained circumstances of slavery, knowing that their children could be taken from them at any point. In this sense, "black women in bondage were systematically denied the rights of motherhood" (Roberts, 33). When chattel slavery ended in the United States, Black people's reproduction was discouraged. "For several decades, peaking in the 1970s, government-sponsored family-planning programs not only encouraged Black women to use birth-control but coerced them into being sterilized" (56). These historic practices and policies, and the popular support they received, suggested that Black lives did not matter, or only mattered when they served white interests. As Roberts concludes, "a lurid mythology of Black mothers' unfitness, along with a science devoting to proving Black biological inferiority, cast Black childbearing as a dangerous activity" (21). In sum, "black motherhood has borne the weight of centuries of disgrace manufactured in both popular culture and academic circles." See also Elaine Tyler May, *Barren in the Promised Land: Childless Americans and the Pursuit of Happiness* (New York: BasicBooks, 1995), 54.

15. In the early years of the US republic, "republican motherhood" held these women responsible for bearing children who would serve the nation and for "raising sons and disciplining husbands to be virtuous citizens of the republic" (Linda K. Kerber, "The Republican Mother," in *Women's America: Refocusing the Past*, ed. Linda K. Kerber and Jane Sherron De Hart, 6th ed. [New York: Oxford University Press, 2004], 126). "By 1800 . . . republican motherhood shaded into religiously infused moral motherhood" (Jodi Vandenberg-Daves, *Modern Motherhood: An American History* [New Brunswick, NJ: Rutgers University Press, 2014], 19). The nineteenth century was the heyday of "True Womanhood," which held middle-class white women to "four cardinal virtues—piety, purity,

submissiveness, and domesticity" (Barbara Welter, "The Cult of True Womanhood: 1820–1860," in *The American Family in Social-Historical Perspective*, ed. Michael Gordon [New York: St. Martin's, 1973], 225), an ideological framework that worked in tandem with the mandates of pronatalism to bear children, to rear them according to societal dictates, and to enjoy mothering them. The twentieth century witnessed the rise of the eugenics movement in which "all the tools and theories of reproductive engineering would be marshaled to enable and encourage the 'best stock' [northern European] to procreate" (May, *Barren in the Promised Land*, 59). Despite the efforts of the eugenicists and pronatalist campaigns, however, "with few material incentives and virtually no public policies that eased the burden of parents, the crusade for positive eugenics failed" (*Barren in the Promised Land*, 92): "The rate of childlessness [reached] an all-time high in the 1920s and 1930s" (*Barren in the Promised Land*, 87).

16. Pronatalism did not extend to all white women in the United States. Negative eugenicists sought to curb the reproduction of immigrants from certain European countries as well as the "feebleminded," a category based largely on class and sexual behavior. The case of Carrie Buck, a poor white seventeen-year-old who became pregnant through rape and was sent to a state institution where she was sterilized in 1927, provided legal ballast for these efforts. In *Buck v. Bell*, the Supreme Court ruled that compulsory sterilization of "the manifestly unfit" did not violate the due process clause of the Fourteenth Amendment. Following World War II and the taint of Nazism on compulsory sterilization, eugenicists came to emphasize "voluntary" sterilization instead, "but the principle of 'consent' remained grounded in eugenic ideas, rather than in the concept of individual reproductive choice." Moreover, the line between consent and compulsion was often blurry at best. In many instances, the only way a woman could be released from a state institution was if she consented to sterilization. Furthermore, in the postwar period, the federal government covered the costs of sterilization, but not of abortion or contraception. Beginning in the 1960s, sterilization campaigns shifted their emphasis from the "feebleminded" to low-income women of color. See May, *Barren in the Promised Land*, 119, 112, 120; Anna Stubblefield, "'Beyond the Pale': Tainted Whiteness, Cognitive Disability, and Eugenic Sterilization," *Hypatia* 22, no. 2 (Spring 2007): 162–81; and Linda Villarosa, "The Long Shadow of Eugenics in America," *New York Times Magazine*, June 12, 2022.

17. May, *Barren in the Promised Land*, 129.

18. *Barren in the Promised Land*, 128.

19. *Barren in the Promised Land*, 127.

20. Rickie Solinger, *Wake Up Little Susie: Single Pregnancy and Race before Roe v. Wade* (New York: Routledge, 1992), 16–17.

21. May, *Barren in the Promised Land*, 153.

22. Solinger, *Wake Up Little Susie*, 20–21.

23. Solinger, *Wake Up Little Susie*, 3.

24. "Race-specific policies and practices regarding unwed mothers emerged and were institutionalized in the 1940s . . . It was at this point that public and professional attitudes about *who was a mother* emerged as racially variable" (Solinger, *Wake Up Little Susie*, 24).

25. *Wake Up Little Susie*, 57.

26. Solinger notes, "Many black community leaders continued to consider the Crittenton association an exclusionary white organization throughout the postwar era." Further, she writes, "By the time that the white homes began to accept blacks . . . the fit was particularly infelicitous. In the 1950s, these homes had become deeply enthusiastic promoters of the postwar adoption mandate for illegitimate babies, while black unwed mothers traditionally kept their babies" (*Wake Up Little Susie*, 74–75).

27. For a detailed history of Black mothers and maternity homes, see chapter 2 in Solinger's *Wake Up Little Susie*.

28. "In 1958 only 9 percent of all adoptions were of nonwhite babies." See Solinger, *Wake Up Little Susie*, 57. In *Black Feminist Thought*, Patricia Hill Collins describes how African American communities care collectively for children, arguing that "their approach to mothering represent[s] one of many real-world counterexamples to the ideal of a private nuclear family" (38–39).

29. Solinger, *Wake Up Little Susie*, 28.

30. *Wake Up Little Susie*, 25.

31. Roberts, *Killing the Black Body*, 17, 292.

32. Fixmer-Oraiz, *Homeland Maternity*, 10. See also Jessica Enoch, "Survival Stories: Feminist Historiographic Approaches to Chicana Rhetorics of Sterilization Abuse," *Rhetoric Society Quarterly* 35, no. 3 (Summer 2005): 5–30.

33. Solinger, *Wake Up Little Susie*, 14.

34. *Wake Up Little Susie*, 24.

35. Heather Brook Adams, "Rhetorics of Unwed Motherhood and Shame," *Women's Studies in Communication*, 40, no. 1 (2016): 96.

36. Solinger, *Wake Up Little Susie*, 10.

37. *Wake Up Little Susie*, 16.

38. Adams, "Rhetorics of Unwed Motherhood and Shame," 105.

39. "Nearly 40 percent of *married* mothers of young children were working for pay in 1976 and a higher percentage of single mothers" (Rickie Solinger, *Beggars and Choosers: How the Politics of Choice Shapes Adoption, Abortion, and Welfare in the United States* (New York: Hill and Wang, 2002), 93). To be clear, the particular circumstances and social location of the mother, as well as the types and degree of societal support available to her, influence how *well* and how easily she can support her child and the costs, psychological and physical, that doing so entails.

40. Solinger, *Beggars and Choosers*, 94.

41. Mikki Morrissette chose the moniker "choice mom" to deemphasize marital status and instead emphasize the "choice" of motherhood.

42. Nefertiti Austin, *Motherhood So White: A Memoir of Race, Gender, and Parenting in America* (Naperville, IL: Sourcebooks, 2019), 117.

43. Solinger, *Beggars and Choosers*, 97. Solinger also notes, "By the mid 1980s, only about 7 percent of unwed mothers—still mostly white—placed their babies for adoption, and the administration made strenuous efforts to convince unmarried young women that mothers who chose adoption fared better than those who kept their babies" (*Beggars and Choosers*, 198).

44. Solinger, *Beggars and Choosers*, 220. She also writes, "'Choice' turned out to be a term and an idea that reflected and foreshadowed the commodification of reproduction and a new, hard set of financial qualifications for motherhood" (*Beggars and Choosers*, 35).

45. Solinger, *Beggars and Choosers*, 223. No one raises their children without assistance. The assistance some caregivers receive is simply more visible and marked than the assistance received by others.

46. Solinger, *Beggars and Choosers*, 99. Monica Simpson, executive director of SisterSong Women of Color Reproductive Justice Collective argues similarly that exercising "choice" is itself a privilege of having choices. See Simpson, "To Be Pro-Choice, You Must Have the Privilege of Having Choices," *New York Times*, April 11, 2022.

47. ADC was established in 1935, and, until the 1960s, primarily served white mothers. According to Roberts, "The welfare system systemically excluded Black people for most

of its history. The first maternalist welfare legislation was intended for white mothers only. Administrators either failed to establish welfare programs in locations with large Black populations or distributed benefits according to standards that disqualified Black mothers . . . Even ADC was created primarily for white mothers, who were not expected to work. Black mothers, who had always been in the paid labor force in far higher numbers than white mothers, were considered inappropriate clients of a system geared to unemployable women" (*Killing the Black Body*, 204, 206).

48. "Despite the fact that by 1960, a growing percentage of white unwed mothers and their children required such aid, and despite the fact that most black women with illegitimate children did not receive ADC, ADC was, in the public consciousness, a black-identified program," writes Solinger in *Wake Up Little Susie* (42). She continues, "The identification of ADC as a black program in the public mind created a racial dimension to welfare opposition that many found appealing but did not represent the reality of the ADC picture" (49). See also Jill Quadagno, *The Color of Welfare: How Racism Undermined the War on Poverty* (New York: Oxford University Press, 1994).

49. "By the mid-1960s, many politicians, taxpayers, and social analysts had become willing to locate the genesis of problems in the black community—and many problems that threatened the white community—in the wombs of black unwed mothers" (Solinger, *Wake Up Little Susie*, 18).

50. Roberts, *Killing the Black Body*, 207.

51. Solinger, *Wake Up Little Susie*, 53.

52. Wahneema Lumbiano, "Black Ladies, Welfare Queens, and State Minstrels: Ideological War by Narrative Means," in *Race-ing Justice, En-gendering Power: Essays on Anita Hill, Clarence Thomas, and the Construction of Social Reality*, ed. Toni Morrison (New York: Pantheon, 1992), 335.

53. Robert Asen, "Imagining in the Public Sphere," *Philosophy and Rhetoric* 35, no. 4 (2002): 347.

54. Lumbiano, "Black Ladies, Welfare Queens, and State Minstrels," 339.

55. Lindal Buchanan, *Rhetorics of Motherhood* (Carbondale: Southern Illinois University Press, 2013), 9.

56. "The presence of shame invokes the fear that an unwed mother's shame will (or has already) spread to those around her, making it not only *communicated* but also *communicable*" (my italics). See Heather Brook Adams, *Enduring Shame: A Recent History of Unwed Pregnancy and Righteous Reproduction* (Columbia: University of South Carolina Press, 2022), 50.

57. Natalie Fixmer-Oraiz, "Contemplating Homeland Maternity," *Women's Studies in Communication* 38, no. 2 (2015): 131.

58. Their publication coincided with the explosive growth of self-help literature in the first half of the 1990s: "The trade publication *American Bookseller* reports that self-help book sales rose by 96 percent in the five years between 1991 and 1996" (Micki McGee, *Self-Help, Inc.: Makeover Culture in American Life* (Oxford, UK: Oxford University Press, 2005), 11).

59. McGee, *Self-Help, Inc.*, 18.

60. McGee, 12.

61. McGee, 16.

62. The two subject positions are not mutually exclusive: a single woman considering motherhood could be skeptical of single motherhood herself and need persuading not only that she could handle mothering singly but that doing so would not damage her child-to-be.

63. The racial line separating single mothers was clearer: the differential treatment of

single mothers and their children in public discourse and policy in the postwar era simultaneously highlighted and reinforced their racial identity.

64. Though Stonesifer divides *When Baby Makes Two* into two sections, one targeted at "by chance" single mothers and the other at "by choice," her introduction groups them together, focusing only on the mothers' marital status at the time of birth: "The number of women who "gave birth outside of marriage in 1991 . . . has more than doubled since 1980" (Jené Stonesifer, *When Baby Makes Two: Single Mothers by Change or by Choice* [Los Angeles: Lowell House, 1994]), xiii.

65. Stonesifer, *When Baby Makes Two*, xiv.

66. *When Baby Makes Two*, 188.

67. *When Baby Makes Two*, xiv.

68. Ruth Frankenberg, *White Women, Race Matters: The Social Construction of Whiteness* (Minneapolis: University of Minnesota Press, 1993).

69. Stonesifer, *When Baby Makes Two*, 170.

70. *When Baby Makes Two*, 116.

71. *When Baby Makes Two*, 169–70.

72. Were Stonesifer writing twenty years later, she might have picked from a host of other "special challenges" that single mothers face. According to Mikki Morrissette's 2015 and 2016 "Choice Mom Survey Results," elective single mothers report stress around finance, adequate support networks for themselves and their children, and the process of becoming a mother (biological or adoptive). While some express concerns about the absence of a father in the families they create, this is not the most reported or seemingly dominant concern among this population of mothers in the aughts, and it may well not have been even when Stonesifer wrote her book. See Morrissette's 2015 and 2016 "Choice Mom Survey Results" on the Choice Moms website.

73. Stonesifer, *When Baby Makes Two*, 4.

74. Solinger, *Wake Up Little Suzie*, 85.

75. Stonesifer, *When Baby Makes Two*, 4.

76. *When Baby Makes Two*, xvii, xx.

77. *When Baby Makes Two*, 37.

78. *When Baby Makes Two*, 5–6.

79. *When Baby Makes Two*; 6–7.

80. Solinger, *Beggars and Choosers*, 220.

81. Stonesifer, *When Baby Makes Two*, 114.

82. *When Baby Makes Two*, 116, 117, 119.

83. *When Baby Makes Two*, 118.

84. Mattes, *Single Mothers by Choice*, 4. These descriptors—"single" as well as the phrase "parenting alone"—warrant further critique and interrogation. Mothers who are technically "single" (unmarried) and thus "parenting alone" recount the substantive role that others play in their lives, suggesting the need for a critique of language that relies on legal status—married or unmarried—or romantic status—partnered or unpartnered—to describe them and their families.

85. Mattes, *Single Mothers by Choice*, xviii.

86. *Single Mothers by Choice*, xix.

87. *Single Mothers by Choice*, xx.

88. *Single Mothers by Choice*, xxi.

89. *Single Mothers by Choice*, xxi.

90. *Single Mothers by Choice*, xxii.

91. *Single Mothers by Choice*, xxiii.

92. Emails from Gail Gonzalez (Random House representative). Subject lines were: "Single Mothers by Choice" and "Two Additional Questions." Received on August 14, 2019. Until the aughts and the publication of Mikki Morrissette's *Choosing Single Motherhood: The Thinking Woman's Guide* (Boston: Houghton Mifflin, 2008), and Louise Sloan's *Knock Yourself Up—No Man? No Problem! A Tell-All Guide to Becoming a Single Mom* (New York: Penguin, 2007), Mattes's guidebook dominated the market and Mattes herself was *the* public face of intentional single motherhood.

93. Mattes, *Single Mothers by Choice*, xvii.

94. *Single Mothers by Choice*, xvii.

95. *Single Mothers by Choice*, xvii–xviii.

96. This is not to suggest that *some* unmarried mothers of color at the time did not also seek to conform to normative family structures or that *all* white mothers did, nor that there were no pressures to conform to normative structures in communities of color and uniform pressures to do so among the white population. I refer here to dominant norms and expectations, which, by definition, flatten out the diversity within groups.

97. Mattes, *Single Mothers by Choice*, xxiii.

98. *Single Mothers by Choice*, 25.

99. *Single Mothers by Choice*, 5.

100. *Single Mothers by Choice*, 25.

101. *Single Mothers by Choice*, 25.

102. *Single Mothers by Choice*, 20, 125.

103. *Single Mothers by Choice*, 11.

104. *Single Mothers by Choice*, 4, 193 (my italics).

105. *Single Mothers by Choice*, 123.

106. *Single Mothers by Choice*, 159.

107. *Single Mothers by Choice*, 161.

108. *Single Mothers by Choice*, 162.

109. Laura Mamo, *Queering Reproduction: Achieving Pregnancy in the Age of Technoscience* (Durham, NC: Duke University Press, 2007), 5.

110. Mattes, *Single Mothers by Choice*, xxi (italics in original.)

111. Mattes, *Single Mothers by Choice*, x.

112. Mattes acknowledges the rhetorical power of the neoliberal tenets of the SMC identity in her comments about the medical profession's increasing receptivity to facilitating motherhood for single women: "The medical profession is fairly positive about *mature, responsible* single women trying to get pregnant by insemination." Mattes, *Single Mothers by Choice*, 29.

113. Mattes, *Single Mothers by Choice*, 21.

114. Relatedly, Mattes cites a study that directs attention to the negative psychological effects of instability, rather than of single parenthood itself (*Single Mothers by Choice*, 19). Since instability often results from precarity, this assertion likewise distinguishes economically autonomous SMCs from other single mothers.

115. Benita Miller, "Mothering while Poor: Utilizing the Reproductive Justice Framework to Build the Capacities of Young Mothers," in *Radical Reproductive Justice: Foundations, Theory, Practice, Critique* (New York: Feminist Press, 2017), 359.

116. Jane Juffer, *Single Mother: The Emergence of the Domestic Intellectual* (New York: NYU Press, 2006), 26.

117. Juffer, *Single Mother*, 212.

118. Loretta J. Ross and Rickie Solinger, *Reproductive Justice: An Introduction* (Oakland: University of California Press, 2017), 40.

CHAPTER 2

Epigraph. Anonymous, *Single Mothers by Choice* (blog hosted by the Single Mothers by Choice website), February 26, 2011

Epigraph. Ali, *Single Mothers by Choice* (blog hosted by the Single Mothers by Choice website), December 27, 2014

1. Jane Mattes, *Single Mothers by Choice: A Guidebook for Single Women Who Are Considering or Have Chosen Motherhood* (New York: Three Rivers Press, 1994).

2. Tasha N. Dubriwny, "Consciousness-Raising as a Collective Rhetoric: The Articulation of Experience in the Redstockings' Abortion Speak-Out of 1969," *Quarterly Journal of Speech* 91, no. 4 (2005): 418.

3. Michael Warner's theorization of publics and counterpublics influences my thinking here. The *SMC* blog is not a "pure" public as Warner defines it—an entity that "unites strangers through participation alone"—because users' interest and (potential) shared identity precedes and motivates their participation. However, the blog does constitute a counterpublic in that "a hierarchy [of motherhood] or stigma [against single motherhood] is the assumed background of practice"; it also constitutes a space "of circulation in which it is hoped that the poesis of scene making will be transformative [for users]" (*Publics and Counterpublics* [New York: Zone Books 2005], 75 and 121–22).

4. Bradford Vivian, "The Threshold of the Self," *Rhetoric and Philosophy* 33, no. 4 (2000): 312.

5. Dubriwny, "Consciousness-Raising."

6. May Friedman, *Mommyblogs and the Changing Face of Motherhood* (Toronto: University of Toronto Press, 2013), 9.

7. Laura Gurak et al., "Introduction: Weblogs, Rhetoric, Community, and Culture," in *Into the Blogosphere*, 2004, p. 2, retrieved from the University of Minnesota Digital Conservancy.

8. Friedman, *Mommyblogs*, 11.

9. Gurak et al., "Introduction," 2.

10. Judith Statman Tucker, "Small World: Maternal Blogging, Virtual Friendship, and the Computer-Mediated Self," in *Mothering and Blogging: The Radical Act of the Mommy-Blog*, ed. May Friedman and Shana L. Calixte (Toronto: Demeter Press, 2009), 9.

11. Jeffrey T. Grabill and Stacey Pigg, "Messy Rhetoric: Identity Performance as Rhetorical Agency in Online Public Forums," *Rhetoric Society Quarterly* 42, no. 2 (2012): 113.

12. Tucker, "Small World," 13.

13. Tucker, "Small World," 13.

14. Gurak et al., "Introduction," 1.

15. Carolyn R. Miller and Dawn Shepherd, "Blogging as Social Action: A Genre Analysis of the Weblog," *Into the Blogosphere*, 2004, p. 2, retrieved from the University of Minnesota Digital Conservancy.

16. Miller and Shepherd, "Blogging as Social Action," 12.

17. May Friedman and Shana L. Calixte, "Introduction," in Friedman and Calixte, *Mothering and Blogging*, 22.

18. Tucker, "Small World," 7.

19. Plato, *Gorgias*, trans. James A. Arieti and Roger M. Barrus (Newburyport, MA: Focus Publishing, 2007), 462d.

20. Tucker, "Small World," 7.

21. Vivian, "Threshold of the Self," 304.

22. Vivian, "Threshold of the Self," 311.

23. Vivian, "Threshold of the Self," 316.

24. Friedman, *Mommyblogs*, 87.

25. Dubriwny, "Consciousness-Raising."

26. White SMCs may also not think of themselves as raced subjects.

27. Dawn Marie Dow suggests that there is in fact *no* common denominator among mothers: "Racial identity, class and gender work in tandem to produce a different set of default negotiations against which mothers must negotiate in their daily decisions" (*Mothering while Black: Boundaries and Burdens of Middle-Class Parenthood* [Oakland: University of California Press, 2019]), 6.

28. Grabill and Pigg, "Messy Rhetoric," 115.

29. See the *Single Mothers by Choice* blog.

30. Grabill and Pigg, "Messy Rhetoric," 102.

31. In the 1990s there was a surge of media attention and onslaught of warnings directed to women about their aging eggs. In some senses, then, intentional single motherhood is also a constrained choice, a response to this rhetorically cultivated sense of urgency around women's biological clock.

32. Sandra Lee Bartky, "Toward a Phenomenology of Feminist Consciousness," *Social Theory and Practice* 3, no. 4 (Fall 1975): 404.

33. Richard H. Dees, "Moral Conversions," *Philosophy and Phenomenological Research* 56, no. 3 (September 1996): 536.

34. My italics.

35. It is interesting to note how the meaning of normalcy varies in these users' rhetorical sharing: in one instance, it is oppressive, as in normative notions of family; in another, being "normal" is comforting, offering a sense of alignment and belonging in a community.

36. My italics.

37. Dubriwny, "Consciousness-Raising."

38. Vivian, "Threshold of the Self," 304.

39. Grabill and Pigg, "Messy Rhetoric," 115.

40. Tucker, "Small World," 16.

41. Rosanna Hertz, *Single by Chance, Mothers by Choice* (Oxford, UK: Oxford University Press, 2006), 141; Jane Bock, "Doing the Right Thing? Single Mothers by Choice and the Struggle for Legitimacy," *Gender and Society* 14, no. 1 (February 2000): 70.

CHAPTER 3

Epigraph. Nefertiti Austin, *Motherhood So White: A Memoir of Race, Gender, and Parenting in America* (Naperville, IL: Sourcebooks, 2019), 115.

Epigraph. Robin Silbergleid, *Texas Girl* (Bradford, ON: Demeter Press, 2014), 99.

Epigraph. Rachel Lehmann-Haupt, *DIY Mom: A Solo Parenting Adventure* (Bronx: SheWrites Press, 2013) (eBook).

Epigraph. Alexandra Soiseth, *Choosing You: Deciding to Have a Baby on My Own* (Berkeley, CA: Seal Press, 2008), 129

1. By the aughts, popular culture brought elective single mothers into the spotlight. The protagonists of feature films mentioned previously (such as *Baby Mama*, *The Switch*, *Back-Up Plan*, and *The Single Moms Club*) reinforce the ESM construct developed in the 1990s guidebooks; they are rational choice-makers and full of agency, women who frame their life paths as a series of conscious decisions around career and family.

2. Dawn Marie Dow, *Mothering while Black: Boundaries and Burdens of Middle-Class Parenthood* (Oakland: University of California Press, 2019), 194. To be clear, the "*assumed norm*" is actually particular, as it describes only a small number of mothers. Nevertheless, this norm and its accompanying maternal ideology set a standard to which all mothers are expected to adhere.

3. Marjorie Jolles, "Between Embodied Subjects and Objects: Narrative Somaesthetics," *Hypatia* 27, no. 2 (Spring 2012): 305.

4. Amy E. Robillard, "Seeking Adequate Rhetorical Witness for Life Writing," *Rhetoric Society Quarterly* 49, no. 2 (2019): 185.

5. Charlotte Hogg, "Including Conservative Women's Rhetorics in an 'Ethics of Hope and Care,'" *Rhetoric Review* 34, no. 4 (2015): 402.

6. Hogg, "Conservative Women's Rhetorics."

7. Thomas Larson, *The Memoir and the Memoirist: Reading and Writing Personal Narrative* (Athens, OH: Swallow Press, 2007), 18.

8. Robillard, "Seeking Adequate Rhetorical Witness," 187.

9. Larson, *Memoir and the Memoirist*, 23.

10. Leigh Gilmore, *Tainted Witness: Why We Doubt What Women Say about Their Lives* (New York: Columbia University Press, 2017), 54 (emphasis in original).

11. "Coaxers" elicit life narratives. Sidonie Smith and Julia Watson, *Reading Autobiography: A Guide for Interpreting Life Narratives* (Minneapolis: University of Minnesota, 2010), 64.

12. G. Thomas Couser, *Memoir: An Introduction* (New York: Oxford University Press, 2012), 170.

13. Justine Dymond and Nicole Willey, "Introduction: Creating the Collection," in *Motherhood Memoirs: Mothers Creating/Writing Lives*, ed. Dymond and Willey (Bradford, ON: Demeter Press, 2013), 10.

14. Dymond and Willey, "Introduction," 15.

15. Andrea O'Reilly, "The Motherhood Memoir and the 'New Momism:' Biting the Hand That Feeds You," in *From the Personal to the Political: Toward a New Theory of Maternal Narrative*, ed. Andrea O'Reilly and Sylvia Caporale Bizzini (Selinsgrove, PA: Susquehanna University Press, 2009), 240.

16. Stephanie Wilkinson and Jennifer Niesslein, "Tales from the (Mother) Hood: Motherhood in Book Publishing," *Brain, Child*, Spring 2005, 5.

17. Susan Douglas and Meredith Michaels, *The Mommy Myth: The Idealization of Motherhood and How It Has Undermined All Woman* (New York: Free Press, 2004). On the one hand, "new momism" recognizes mothers and validates the work of mothering, which most women do in some form or another and which has historically not been considered as challenging or mentally taxing as other kinds of labor. On the other hand, "new momism" creates standards for good mothering that no actual mother can meet and suggests that the failure to meet those standards lies with the individual mother, not with the standards themselves or with the social context.

18. O'Reilly, "Motherhood Memoir," 244, 240.

19. In an essay about recent books about motherhood, critic Parul Sehgal observes, "So many of these books (almost all of them are by white, middle-class women) seem wary of, if not outright disinterested in, more deeply engaging with how race and class inflect the experience of motherhood." White memoirists' inattention to race is not surprising. A truism of whiteness studies is that "for white people, whiteness is the transcendental norm in terms of which they live their lives as persons." See George Yancy, *Look, a White! Philosophical Essays on Whiteness* (Philadelphia: Temple University Press, 2012), 7.

20. Nancy Reddy, "We Need to Talk about Whiteness in Motherhood Memoirs," Electric Literature, December 4, 2018.

21. Reddy, "We Need to Talk about Whiteness."

22. Douglas and Michaels, *Mommy Myth*.

23. Andrea O'Reilly, "We Need to Talk about Patriarchal Motherhood: Essentialization,

Naturalization, and Idealization in Lionel Shriver's We Need to Talk about Kevin," *Journal of the Motherhood Initiative for Research and Community Involvement* 7, no. 1 (Spring/Summer 2016): 65.

24. Dymond and Willey, "Introduction," 15.

25. Michael Warner, *Publics and Counterpublics* (New York: Zone Books, 2005), 114.

26. Larson, *Memoir and the Memoirist*, 18.

27. Nefertiti Austin, *Motherhood So White: A Memoir of Race, Gender, and Parenting in America* (Naperville, IL: Sourcebooks, 2019), 9.

28. Austin, *Motherhood So White*. See also Austin's on "Adoption's #PARENTING-SOWHITE Problem," *Mutha Magazine*, July 26, 2016.

29. Deeshaw Philyaw, "Ain't I a Mommy: Why Are so Few Motherhood Memoirs Penned by Women of Color?" *bitchmedia*, February 23, 2016.

30. Angela Garbes, "Why Are We Only Talking about 'Mom Books' by White Women?" *Cut*, November 1, 2018.

31. Philyaw, "Ain't I a Mommy," 221–2 (my italics).

32. Dymond and Willey, "Introduction," 17.

33. Tameka Allen-Mercado quoted in Philyaw, "Ain't I a Mommy," 221.

34. Yvonne Bynoe quoted in Philyaw, "Ain't I a Mommy," 221.

35. Kim McClarin, *Womanish: A Grown Black Woman Speaks on Love and Life* (New York: Ig, 2019), 156.

36. Relatedly, Black writers in the United States have historically felt compelled to use their writing to effect sociopolitical change, rather than to explore their interior lives and the richness of Black life. Memoirist Kiese Laymon writes, "I wondered what black writers weren't writing when we spent so much creative energy begging white folks to change." See Kiese Laymon, *Heavy: An American Memoir* (New York: Scribner, 2018), 144.

37. Wilkinson and Niesslein, "Tales from the (Mother) Hood," 5.

38. Austin, *Motherhood So White*, 9.

39. *Motherhood So White*, 5.

40. *Motherhood So White*, 143, 147.

41. *Motherhood So White*, 130.

42. *Motherhood So White*, 130.

43. *Motherhood So White*, 130.

44. *Motherhood So White*, 237.

45. *Motherhood So White*, 9.

46. *Motherhood So White*, 55.

47. *Motherhood So White*, 86.

48. *Motherhood So White*, 118, 211, 122.

49. *Motherhood So White*, 122.

50. *Motherhood So White*, 85.

51. *Motherhood So White*, 181.

52. *Motherhood So White*, 182.

53. *Motherhood So White*, 237.

54. *Motherhood So White*, 118.

55. *Motherhood So White*, 118.

56. *Motherhood So White*, 113.

57. *Motherhood So White*, 146.

58. *Motherhood So White*, 113.

59. *Motherhood So White*, 240.

60. Robin Silbergleid, *Texas Girl* (Bradford, ON: Demeter Press, 2014), 67.

61. Robillard, "Seeking Adequate Rhetorical Witness for Life Writing."
62. Silbergleid, *Texas Girl*, 66.
63. *Texas Girl*, 39.
64. *Texas Girl*, 3.
65. *Texas Girl*, 53.
66. *Texas Girl*, 3–4.
67. *Texas Girl*, 39–40.
68. *Texas Girl*, 66.
69. *Texas Girl*, 53.
70. *Texas Girl*, 15.
71. *Texas Girl*, 39–40.
72. *Texas Girl*, 14.
73. *Texas Girl*, 43.
74. *Texas Girl*, 66.
75. *Texas Girl*, 66.
76. *Texas Girl*, 154.
77. *Texas Girl*, 154.
78. *Texas Girl*, 112.
79. *Texas Girl*, 112.
80. *Texas Girl*, 39.
81. *Texas Girl*, 222.
82. *Texas Girl*, 171.
83. *Texas Girl*, 195.
84. *Texas Girl*, 99.
85. *Texas Girl*, 182.
86. *Texas Girl*, 165.
87. *Texas Girl*, 184.
88. *Texas Girl*, 194.
89. *Texas Girl*, 222.
90. Lauren Berlant and Jay Prosser, "Intimate Publics: A Conversation," *Biography* 34, no. 1 (Winter 2011): 185.
91. Silbergleid, *Texas Girl*, 3–4.
92. *Texas Girl*, 223–23.
93. *Texas Girl*, 182.
94. *Texas Girl*, 182.
95. Shebooks, the publisher of *DIY Mom*, describes itself as "an e-book publisher devoted to great writing by and for women. We publish memoir, fiction and journalism, and each of our books can be read in under two hours—perfect for a short plane ride or to relax before bed."
96. Jolles, "Between Embodied Subjects and Objects," 305.
97. Jolles, 305.
98. Elizabeth Freeman, "Queer Belongings: Kinship Theory and Queer Theory," in *A Companion to Lesbian, Gay, Bisexual, Transgender, and Queer Studies*, ed. George E. Haggerty and Molly McGarry (Hoboken, NJ: John Wiley and Sons, 2007).
99. Silbergleid, *Texas Girl*, 182.
100. Alexandra Soiseth, *Choosing You: Deciding to Have a Baby on My Own* (Berkeley, CA: Seal Press, 2008), 99.
101. Soiseth, *Choosing You*, 37.
102. *Choosing You*, 129.

103. *Choosing You*, 177.
104. *Choosing You*, 42; my italics.
105. Cressida Heyes, *Self-Transformations: Foucault, Ethics, and Normalized Bodies* (New York: Oxford University Press, 2007), 67.
106. Soiseth, *Choosing You*, 89.
107. *Choosing You*, 90.
108. *Choosing You*, 37.
109. *Choosing You*, 283.
110. *Choosing You*, 152.
111. *Choosing You*, 189.
112. *Choosing You*, 194.
113. *Choosing You*, 265 (original italics).
114. *Choosing You*, 129.
115. *Choosing You*, 120.
116. *Choosing You*, 109.
117. *Choosing You*, 69.
118. *Choosing You*, 88.
119. *Choosing You*, 189.
120. *Choosing You*, 189.
121. *Choosing You*, 200 (original italics).
122. *Choosing You*, 200.
123. *Choosing You*, 214.
124. *Choosing You*, 275.
125. *Choosing You*, 129.
126. *Choosing You*, 284.
127. For more, see Heyes, *Self-Transformations*.
128. Jolles, "Between Embodied Subjects," 305.
129. Hogg, "Conservative Women's Rhetorics," 404.
130. Robillard, "Seeking Adequate Rhetorical Witness for Life Writing," 185.
131. Katherine Mack and Jonathan Alexander, "The Ethics of Memoir: Ethos in Uptake," *Rhetoric Society Quarterly* 49, no. 1 (2019): 67.
132. Robillard, "Seeking Adequate Rhetorical Witness for Life Writing," 192.
133. Robillard, 185.
134. Loretta Ross quoted in Maggie Bullock, "The Abortion Doctor and His Accuser," *Atlantic*, March 2020.

CHAPTER 4

Epigraph. Mikki Morrissette, *Choosing Single Motherhood: The Thinking Woman's Guide* (Boston: Houghton Mifflin, 2008), 65.

Epigraph. Louise Sloan, *Knock Yourself Up—No Man? No Problem! A Tell-All Guide to Becoming a Single Mom* (New York: Penguin, 2007), xiii.

1. "14 Celebrities Who Adopted as Single Mothers," Ranker: Vote on Everything, October 13, 2018.
2. See Angela McRobbie, "Post-Feminism and Popular Culture," *Feminist Media Studies* 4, no. 3 (2004); Susan Douglas and Meredith Michaels, *The Mommy Myth: The Idealization of Motherhood and How It Has Undermined All Woman* (New York: Free Press, 2004).
3. Linda Hirshman, *Victory: The Triumphant Gay Revolution* (New York: HarperCollins, 2012), 184.
4. In 1983 Jerry Falwell claimed that "AIDS is not just God's punishment for homosexuals,

it is God's punishment for the society that tolerates homosexuals." See "Gay History—June 19, 1983: Founder of the Moral Majority Jerry Falwell: AIDS Is God's Punishment for Homosexuals," Back2Stonewall: LGBT News, Media and History, June 19, 2021.

5. PFLAG advocates for the inclusion of LGBTQI family members and for a redefinition of family in public discourse. PFLAG "restories" family, "talk[ing] of themselves as family and story[ing] themselves as successful families that produce happy, well-adjusted adult children." In K. L. Broad, Sarah L. Crawley, and Lara Foley, "Doing 'Real Family Values': The Interpretive Practice of Families in the GLBT Movement," *Sociological Quarterly* 45, no. 3 (Summer 2004): 516.

6. Andrew Sullivan, "Here Comes the Groom: A (Conservative) Case for Gay Marriage," *New Republic*, August 27, 1989. It should be noted that, like Charles A. Murray, Sullivan has expounded debunked theories linking IQ to race; see Ben Smith, "The Conservative Pundit with a Legacy From 1994," *New York Times*, August 31, 2020, B1. Simultaneously, Sullivan is sometimes listed as "the most influential political writer of his generation" (in Ross Douthat's words) and has bucked some conservative positions. Regarding the push to legalize gay marriage, Tyler Cowen calls Sullivan the "the dominant intellectual influence on this issue, from the late 1980s on, and that is from a time where other major civil liberties figures didn't give gay marriage much of a second thought, one way or the other, or they wished to run away from the issue" (Sullivan is himself openly gay). In 2007, Sullivan endorsed presidential candidate Barack Obama. Ross Douthat, "The Influence of Andrew Sullivan," *New York Times* (blog) July 2, 2013; Tyler Cowen, "Who Is the Most Influential Public Intellectual of the Last Twenty-Five Years?," *Marginal Revolution* (blog), June 27, 2013.

7. Sullivan, "Here Comes the Groom."

8. Sullivan.

9. Aidan Rowe, "Same-Sex Marriage: An Alternative Gay Liberation Viewpoint," *Redline* (blog), August 23, 2013.

10. Rowe, "Same-Sex Marriage: An Alternative Gay Liberation Viewpoint."

11. Michael Warner, *Publics and Counterpublics* (New York: Zone Books, 2005), 146.

12. Warner, *Publics and Counterpublics*, 146.

13. See Warner, 65–124.

14. Anti-gay initiatives were launched in Oregon and Colorado in 1992, Idaho in 1994, and Maine in 1995, 1998, 2000, and 2005. The Defense of Marriage Act was passed in 1996. Frank Rich referred to the "homophobic epidemic of '98" (*New York Times*, July 3, 1999).

15. As Kath Weston observes, "What made the 1980s and 1990s different was the way in which so many LGBT people laid claim to family as something they had and something they wanted." See Kath Weston, introduction to *Love Makes a Family: Portraits of Lesbian, Gay, Bisexual, and Transgender Parents and Their Families*, ed. Peggy Gillespie (Amherst: University of Massachusetts Press, 1999), 4.

16. April Martin, "Afterword," in Gillespie, *Love Makes a Family*, 251.

17. In *Bowers v. Hardwick* (1986), the Supreme Court *upheld* the constitutionality of a Georgia anti-sodomy law. In *Romer v. Evans* (1996), the court *overturned* a state constitutional amendment in Colorado that prevented protected status based upon homosexuality or bisexuality, finding that the amendment did not satisfy the equal protection clause. See also Lillian Faderman, *The Gay Revolution: The Story of the Struggle* (New York: Simon and Schuster, 2015), 467.

18. Weston, introduction to *Love Makes a Family*, 5.

19. Martin, "Afterword," 251.

20. See this book's introduction for a summary of the arguments of traditional fatherhood advocates like Blankenhorn, Popenhoe, and Whitehead.

21. "APA on Children Raised by Gay Parents," American Psychological Association, 2012. Web.

22. Peggy Drexler, *Raising Boys without Men: How Maverick Moms Are Creating the Next Generation of Exceptional Men* (Emmaus, PA: Rodale Books, 2005), xvi.

23. Interestingly, Drexler's driving question is whether sons of maverick mothers will "grow to manliness," not the meaning of "manliness" and the gender essentialism that informs the notion. She concludes that the boys she studied "had a wider range of interests and friendships than the boys I studied from heterosexual parents, and they appeared more at ease in situations of conflict. They developed their 'boyishness' at a normal rate, but their sense of justice and fairness and their ability to express their feelings were off the charts. They admired many kinds of men, from scientists to sports heroes, and they accepted their own quirks and interests (and those around them) more readily than did boys from traditional families." See Drexler, *Raising Boys without Men*, xiv, 209.

24. Susan Golombok, Modern Families: Parents and Children in New Family Form (Cambridge, UK: Cambridge University Press, 2015), 196.

25. Melinda Cooper, Family Values: Between Neoliberalism and the New Social Conservatism (Brooklyn, NY: Zone Books, 2017, 9.

26. "While the focus of the Presidential Fatherhood Initiative has varied from Clinton to Bush to Obama, the crux of the proposal remains the same: helping fathers gain access to decent employment will help them to provide financially for their children, and in turn, become more socially involved with their children." See Diane Dixon Weaver, "The First Father: Perspectives on the President's Fatherhood Initiative," *Family Court Review* 50, no. 2 (April 2012): 301.

27. Weaver, "First Father," 302.

28. Michael Strautmanis, "Promoting Responsible Fatherhood and Healthy Families," White House. June 15, 2012. One offshoot of this initiative, "My Brother's Keeper," aimed to help "more young men of color facing especially tough odds to stay on track and reach their full potential" ("FACT SHEET: Opportunity for All: President Obama Launches My Brother's Keeper Initiative to Build Ladders of Opportunity for Boys and Young Men of Color," White House: Office of the Press Secretary, February 27, 2014.) Critics of the My Brother's Keeper initiative acknowledge the particular needs of Black boys and men. However, they question claims about the necessity of fathers and note that the focus on "brothers" is tantamount to an "abandonment of women of color." See Kimberlé Crenshaw, "The Girls Obama Forgot," *New York Times*, July 29, 2014. Their concerns led to the creation of the campaign #SayHerName: according to the African American Policy Forum website, "Launched in December 2014 by the African American Policy Forum (AAPF) and Center for Intersectionality and Social Policy Studies (CISPS), the #SayHerName campaign brings awareness to the often invisible names and stories of Black women and girls who have been victimized by racist police violence, and provides support to their families." Some Black writers also critique the focus on boys and men of color. In *Heavy: An American Memoir*, Kiese Laymon writes, "I'd never given much weight to the idea of present black fathers saving black boys . . . I respected my father but I never felt that I needed him or any other man in the house to show me how to be a present American man. And I couldn't imagine how those teachings would have made me healthier or more generous" (Laymon, *Heavy: An American Memoir* (New York: Scribner, 2018), 200).

29. Morrissette credits this shift to the lessening of the stigma of single motherhood in the early aughts. See Mikki Morrissette, *Choosing Single Motherhood: The Thinking Woman's Guide* (Boston: Houghton Mifflin, 2008), 2. To be clear, the "women" Morrissette imagines are likely white, as they do not perceive themselves to be potential targets of racialized

and racist thinking about single mothers, namely the assumption that they are "welfare queens." See chapter 1 for analysis of this racialized and racist construct.

30. Morrissette, *Choosing Single Motherhood*, xxii.

31. *Choosing Single Motherhood*, 2.

32. *Choosing Single Motherhood*, 337.

33. Mikki Morrissette, *Retrospective: Eighteen Years as a Choice Mom*, eGuide, Choice-Moms website, 2017, 2.

34. Morrissette, *Choosing Single Motherhood*, 64.

35. *Choosing Single Motherhood*, 65 (my italics).

36. *Choosing Single Motherhood*, 139–228.

37. *Choosing Single Motherhood*, 79.

38. *Choosing Single Motherhood*, 109.

39. *Choosing Single Motherhood*, xx.

40. *Choosing Single Motherhood*, xii.

41. *Choosing Single Motherhood*, xiii.

42. Jane Mattes, *Single Mothers by Choice: A Guidebook for Single Women Who Are Considering or Have Chosen Motherhood* (New York: Three Rivers Press, 1994), xvii.

43. Morrissette, *Choosing Single Motherhood*, xix.

44. *Choosing Single Motherhood*, xx.

45. *Choosing Single Motherhood*, 93, 136.

46. *Choosing Single Motherhood*, 78.

47. *Choosing Single Motherhood*, 122.

48. *Choosing Single Motherhood*, 137.

49. *Choosing Single Motherhood*, 85.

50. *Choosing Single Motherhood*, 80.

51. *Choosing Single Motherhood*, 116.

52. *Choosing Single Motherhood*, 132.

53. *Choosing Single Motherhood*, 117, 119.

54. *Choosing Single Motherhood*, 120.

55. *Choosing Single Motherhood*, 128.

56. *Choosing Single Motherhood*, 137.

57. *Choosing Single Motherhood*, 123.

58. *Choosing Single Motherhood*, 123 (my italics).

59. Louise Sloan, *Knock Yourself Up—No Man? No Problem! A Tell-All Guide to Becoming a Single Mom* (New York: Penguin, 2007), xi.

60. *Knock Yourself Up* addresses prospective single mothers who want to have a biological child that they gestate. Sloan describes her target readers as "women who not only want to raise a child but who, like so many other women, want the messy, scary, beautiful, animal experience of having a baby grew inside them, of giving birth, of knowing another human being from the moment of conception, and of having a deeply, biological connection to a child" (xv). She suggests that the experience of pregnancy and birth of one's genetic child fosters a distinctive connection, but some adoptive parents, as well as parents who use a surrogate, describe feeling a deeply physical connection to their child(ren) as well.

61. Sloan, *Knock Yourself Up*, xvi. I would argue that the inclusion of extensive research and illustrative personal narratives in Mattes's and Morrissette's guidebooks distinguish them from strictly practical "how-to books."

62. Sloan credits Vicky Iovine, whom she refers to as the "queen of the *Girlfriends' Guide* publishing empire," for inventing the genre of the "girlfriends' guide." *Knock Yourself Up*, xv. Sloan's use of the word "girlfriend" to connote the conviviality and trust of female

friendship is notable in that *Knock Yourself Up* presents reproductive strategies pioneered by literal girlfriends—that is, lesbian romantic partners.

63. Sloan, *Knock Yourself Up*, 9.

64. *Knock Yourself Up*, 19, 9.

65. *Knock Yourself Up*, 9.

66. *Knock Yourself Up*, 2.

67. *Knock Yourself Up*, 72.

68. *Knock Yourself Up*, 253.

69. *Knock Yourself Up*, 124.

70. *Knock Yourself Up*, 124.

71. *Knock Yourself Up*, 29.

72. *Knock Yourself Up*, 111.

73. *Knock Yourself Up*, 110–11.

74. *Knock Yourself Up*, 120.

75. *Knock Yourself Up*, 28.

76. *Knock Yourself Up*, 28–29.

77. *Knock Yourself Up*, 119.

78. *Knock Yourself Up*, 120.

79. *Knock Yourself Up*, 16.

80. *Knock Yourself Up*, 14.

81. *Knock Yourself Up*, 16.

82. *Knock Yourself Up*, 16.

83. *Knock Yourself Up*, 16.

84. *Knock Yourself Up*, 17.

85. *Knock Yourself Up*, 148.

86. *Knock Yourself Up*, 31.

87. *Knock Yourself Up*, x.

88. *Knock Yourself Up*, xii.

89. *Knock Yourself Up*, xiii.

90. *Knock Yourself Up*, xiii.

91. *Knock Yourself Up*, xiii.

92. *Knock Yourself Up*, xiii.

93. *Knock Yourself Up*, xiii.

94. *Knock Yourself Up*, 153.

95. *Knock Yourself Up*, x.

96. *Knock Yourself Up*, xii (my italics).

97. *Knock Yourself Up*, xviii.

98. *Knock Yourself Up*, xvii.

99. *Knock Yourself Up*, xviii, xvii.

100. *Knock Yourself Up*, xv, xiv.

101. *Knock Yourself Up*, x.

102. Alexandra Soiseth, *Choosing You: Deciding to Have a Baby on My Own* (Berkeley, CA: Seal Press, 2008), 189.

103. J. Jack Halberstam, *Gaga Feminism: Sex, Gender, and the End of Normal* (Boston: Beacon Press, 2012), 317.

CONCLUSION

1. Lindal Buchanan, *Rhetorics of Motherhood* (Carbondale: Southern Illinois University Press, 2013), 123.

2. John Schilb, *Rhetorical Refusals: Defying Audiences' Expectations* (Carbondale: Southern Illinois University Press, 2007).

3. Ross and Solinger, *Reproductive Justice*, 13–14 (see intro, n. 15). See also Jenna Vinson and Clare Daniel's compelling argument about the relevance and necessity of an RJ framework in approaches to teen pregnancy in "'Power to Decide' Who Should Get Pregnant: A Feminist Rhetorical Analysis of Neoliberal Visions of Reproductive Justice," *Present Tense: A Journal of Rhetoric in Society* 8, no. 2 (July 2020): 169.

4. Vinson, *Embodying the Problem*, 169 (my italics) (see intro, n. 127).

5. Vinson, *Embodying the Problem*, 148.

6. C. Nicole Mason, "A Black, Queer Single Mother on Why I Am Proud to Use the Term Single Mother by Choice." *Huffington Post*, December 6, 2016.

7. Mason, "Black, Queer Single Mother."

8. Mason.

9. Mason.

10. Griffin and Chávez, "Introduction," 11 (see intro, n. 126).

11. Schilb, *Rhetorical Refusals*, 3.

12. Schilb, 16.

13. Schilb, 18.

14. Schilb, 6.

15. Janice Fernheimer, "A Review of *Rhetorical Refusals: Defying Audiences' Expectations* by John Schilb," *Rhetoric Society Quarterly* 39, no. 1 (Winter 2009): 101 (original emphasis).

16. Stephanie Hartzell, "An (In)visible Universe of Grief: Performative Disidentifications with White Motherhood in the We Are Not Trayvon Martin Blog," *Journal of International and Intercultural Communication* 10, no. 1 (2017): 68.

17. V. Jo Hsu, "A Single Life Reinvented: Personal Writing as the Negotiation of Identity in Richard Rodriguez's Autobiographical Trilogy," *Rhetoric Review* 35, no. 4 (2016): 368.

18. Hsu, "Single Life Reinvented," 363.

19. Loretta J. Ross and Rickie Solinger, *Reproductive Justice: An Introduction* (Oakland: University of California Press, 2017), 227.

20. Loretta J. Ross et al., "Introduction," in *Radical Reproductive Justice: Foundation, Theory, Practice, Critique*, ed. Loretta J. Ross et al. (New York: Feminist Press, 2017), 14.

21. Ross et al., "Introduction," 14.

22. Kathleen M. de Onís, "Lost in Translation: Challenging (White, Monolingual Feminism's) 'Choice' with Justicia Reproductiva," *Women's Studies in Communication* 38, 1 (2015): 10. In the original title, "life" and "choice" appeared in angle brackets, but for typesetting purposes I render these as single quotation marks here.

23. Fernheimer, "Review of *Rhetorical Refusals*," 101.

24. Ross, "Conceptualizing Reproductive Justice Theory," 172.

25. Ross, "Conceptualizing Reproductive Justice Theory," 172.

26. Ross et al., "Introduction."

27. SisterSong Women of Color Reproductive Health Collective was founded in 1997 and was renamed the SisterSong Women of Color Reproductive Justice Collective in 2010. See Rachel Strickler and Monica Simpson, "A Brief Herstory of SisterSong," in Ross et al., *Radical Reproductive Justice*, 57; also, Abigail Abrams, "'We Are Grabbing Our Own Microphones': How Advocates of Reproductive Justice Stepped into the Spotlight," *Time*, November 21, 2019.

28. Ross et al., "Introduction," 14. In 2006 a group of women of color RJ theorists defined the criteria for RJ: "Is intersectional; Connects the local to the global; Based on the

human rights framework; Makes the link between the individual and community; Addresses government and corporate responsibility; Fights all forms of population control (eugenics); Commits to individual/community leadership development that results in power shifts; Puts marginalized communities at the center of the analysis; Understands that political power, participation of those impacted, and policy changes are necessary to achieve reproductive justice; Has its own intersectionality of involving theory, strategy, and practice; Applies to everyone." In Ross et al., "Introduction," 19–20.

29. Though the projected ambit of the National Welfare Rights Organization (NWRO), an umbrella group of welfare rights organizations which was active from 1966–1975, included all people (not just mothers), they prefigure those of RJ. Like RJ, NWRO insisted on people's right to access, respect, and autonomy, and they made explicit the connections between personal experience and socio-political forces, practices, and policies. NWRO "demanded welfare payments that provided an adequate income, dignified treatment, justice and democratic participation" (VCU Libraries Social Welfare History Project, "National Welfare Rights Organization," last modified August 29, 2022). Recognizing the divisiveness and damage enacted by "categories" of welfare recipients, NWRO disavowed them altogether. NWRO founder Johnnie Tillmon explains how NWRO's disavowal combats sexism: "We put together our own welfare plan, called Guaranteed Adequate Income (GAI), which would eliminate sexism from welfare. There would be no 'categories'—men, women, children, single, married, kids, no kids—just poor people who need aid. You'd get paid according to need and family size only and that would be upped as the cost of living goes up" ("Welfare Is a Women's Issue," *Ms.*, Spring 1972). See also Felicia Kornbluh's "The Goals of the National Welfare Rights Movement: Why We Need Them Thirty Years Later," *Feminist Studies* 24, no. 1 (Spring 1998): 65–78; *The Battle for Welfare Rights: Poverty and Politics in Modern America* (Philadelphia: University of Pennsylvania Press, 2007), and, with Gwendolyn Mink, *Ensuring Poverty: Welfare Reform in Feminist Perspective* (Philadelphia: University of Pennsylvania Press, 2018).

30. "Analyzing white supremacy is a cornerstone of reproductive justice." (In Ross's "Conceptualizing Reproductive Justice Theory," 173). Also, Reproductive Justice Theory "question[s] neoliberal discourses about individual rights and the marketplace of choices denied to the vulnerable members of our society." (In Ross's "Conceptualizing Reproductive Justice Theory," 223.) Elsewhere, Ross defines "white supremacy" as "a lethal body of ideas comprised of racism, Christian nationalism, homophobia, nativism, settler colonialism, transphobia, misogyny, and authoritarianism" (Ross, "Reproductive Justice as Intersectional Feminist Activism," in *Souls: A Critical Journal of Black Politics, Culture, and Society* 19, no. 3, (2017): 241.

31. Ross, "Reproductive Justice as Intersectional Feminist Activism," 301.

32. Ross, "Reproductive Justice as Intersectional Feminist Activism," 291.

33. See Sara Hayden's "Revitalizing the Debate Between 'Life' and 'Choice': The 2004 March for Women's Lives" in *Communication and Critical/Cultural Studies* 6, no. 2, June 2009, 111–31. In the original title, "life" and "choice" appeared in angle brackets, but for typesetting purposes I render these as single quotation marks here.

34. Andrea Smith, *Conquest: Sexual Violence and American Indian Genocide* (Cambridge, MA: South End Press, 2005), 166.

35. Osub Ahmed and Christy M. Gamble, "Reproductive Justice: What It Means and Why It Matters (Now More Than Ever)," Public Health Post, January 16, 2017.

36. For more on intensive mothering as the maternal ideology of postfeminist neoliberalism, see [D.] Lynn O'Brien Hallstein, "When Neoliberalism Intersects with Post-Second Wave Mothering: Reinforcing Neo-Traditional American Family Configurations and

Exacerbating the Post-Second Wave Crisis in Femininity," in *Mothering in the Age of Neoliberalism*, ed. Melinda Vandenbeld Giles (Bradford, ON: Demeter Press, 2014), 297–314.

37. See Susan Douglas and Meredith Michaels, *The Mommy Myth: The Idealization of Motherhood and How It Has Undermined All Woman* (New York: Free Press, 2004).

38. Whether mothers want to or should "intensively" mother is another question!

39. Monica Simpson quoted in Abrams, "'We Are Grabbing Our Own Microphones.'"

40. Ross, "Reproductive Justice as Intersectional Feminist Activism," 303.

41. Cindy L. Griffin and Karma Chávez, "Introduction: Standing at the Intersections of Feminisms, Intersectionality, and Communication Studies," in Chávez and Griffin, *Standing in the Intersection: Feminist Voices, Feminist Practices in Communication Studies* (Albany: SUNY Press, 2012), 11.

42. Karma R. Chávez, *Queer Migration Politics: Activist Rhetoric and Coalitional Possibilities* (Urbana: University of Illinois Press, 2013), 46–47.

BIBLIOGRAPHY

"14 Celebrities Who Adopted as Single Mothers." Ranker: Vote on Everything. October 13, 2018.

Abrams, Abigail. "'We Are Grabbing Our Own Microphones': How Advocates of Reproductive Justice Stepped into the Spotlight." *Time*, November 21, 2019.

Adams, Heather Brook. *Enduring Shame: A Recent History of Unwed Pregnancy and Righteous Reproduction.* Columbia: University of South Carolina Press, 2022.

———. "Rhetorics of Unwed Motherhood and Shame." *Women's Studies in Communication* 40, no. 1 (2016): 91–110.

Ahmed, Osub, and Christy M. Gamble. "Reproductive Justice: What It Means and Why It Matters (Now More Than Ever)." Public Health Post, January 16, 2017.

Anderson, Gillian, and Joseph G. Moore. "'Doing It All . . . and Making It Look Easy!': Yummy Mummies, Mompreneurs and the North American Neoliberal Crisis of the Home." In Giles, *Mothering in the Age of Neoliberalism*, 96–116.

"APA on Children Raised by Gay and Lesbian Parents: How Do These Children Fare?" American Psychological Association, 2012.

Aristotle. *On Rhetoric: A Theory of Civic Discourse.* Translated by George A. Kennedy. New York: Oxford University Press, 1991.

Armitstead, Claire. "My Life as a Story: Claire Armitstead on the Rise and Rise of the Memoir." *Guardian*, January 26, 2001. Web.

Arnold, Lorin Basden, and BettyAnn Martin, eds. *Taking the Village Online: Mothers, Motherhood, and Social Media.* Bradford, ON: Demeter Press, 2016.

Asen, Robert. "Imagining in the Public Sphere." *Philosophy and Rhetoric* 35, no. 4 (2002): 345–65.

Atwill, Janet M. *Rhetoric Reclaimed: Aristotle and the Liberal Arts Tradition.* Ithaca, NY: Cornell University Press, 2009.

Austin, Nefertiti. "Adoption's #PARENTINGSOWHITE Problem." *Mutha Magazine*, July 26, 2016.

———. *Motherhood So White: A Memoir of Race, Gender, and Parenting in America.* Naperville, IL: Sourcebooks, 2019.

Bandele, Asha. "Woman Up." In *One Big Happy Family*, edited by Rebecca Walker, 17–28. New York: Riverhead Books, 2009.

Banwart, Doug. "Jerry Falwell, the Rise of the Moral Majority, and the 1980 Election." *Western Illinois Historical Review* 5 (Spring 2013): 133–57.

Bartky, Sandra Lee. "Toward a Phenomenology of Feminist Consciousness." *Social Theory and Practice* 3, no. 4 (Fall 1975): 396–406.

Bawarshi, Anis S., and Mary Jo Reiff. *Genre: An Introduction to Theory, History, Research, and Pedagogy.* West Lafayette, IN: Parlor Press, 2010.

Bennett, Jessica. "Meet the Groundbreaking New Second Family." *New York Times*, January 17, 2021.

Benoit, William. "On Aristotle's Example." *Philosophy and Rhetoric* 20, no. 4 (1987): 251–67.

Berlant, Lauren, with Jay Prosser. "Intimate Publics: A Conversation." *Biography* 34, no. 1 (Winter 2011): 180–87.

Bernstein, Mary, and Renate Reimann. "Queer Families and the Politics of Visibility." In *Queer Families, Queer Politics: Challenging Culture and the State*, edited by Mary Bernstein and Renate Reimann, 1–20. New York: Columbia University Press, 2001.

Bitzer, Lloyd. "The Rhetorical Situation." *Philosophy and Rhetoric* 1, no. 1 (January 1968): 1–14.

Blackstone, Amy. *Childfree by Choice: The Movement Redefining Family and Creating a New Age of Independence*. New York: Dutton, 2019.

Blankenhorn, David. *Fatherless America: Confronting Our Most Urgent Social Problem*. New York: BasicBooks, 1995.

Bock, Jane D. "Doing the Right Thing: Single Mothers by Choice and the Struggle for Legitimacy." *Gender and Society* 14, no. 1 (February 2000): 62–86.

Bold, Christine. *The WPA Guides: Mapping America*. Jackson: University Press of Mississippi, 1999.

Bolick, Kate. "All the Single Ladies." *Atlantic*, November 2011.

Boyd, Susan B., Dorothy E. Chunn, Fiona Kelly, and Wanda Wiegers. *Autonomous Motherhood? A Socio-Legal Study of Choice and Constraint*. Toronto: University of Toronto Press, 2015.

Bradbury, Kelly, Envera Dukaj, and Paul Muhlhauser. "Refiguring Family: Rhetoric, Feminist Voices, and Digital Publishing." *Women and Language* 35, no. 2 (2012). (Archived online).

Briggs, Laura. *How All Politics Became Reproductive Politics: From Welfare Reform to Foreclosure to Trump*. Oakland, CA: University of California Press, 2018.

Britt, Elizabeth C. *Conceiving Normalcy: Rhetoric, Law, and the Double Binds of Infertility*. Tuscaloosa: University of Alabama Press, 2001.

Broad, K. L., Sarah L. Crawley, and Lara Foley. "Doing 'Real Family Values': The Interpretive Practice of Families in the GLBT Movement." *Sociological Quarterly* 45, no. 3 (Summer 2004): 509–27.

Brown, Ivana. "Mommy Memoirs: Feminism, Gender and Motherhood in Popular Culture." *Journal of the Association for Research on Mothering* 8, nos. 1 and 2 (Winter/Summer 2006): 200–12.

Brown, Wendy. "Neo-Liberalism and the End of Liberal Democracy." *Theory and Event* 7, no. 1 (January 2003). Web.

Buchanan, Lindal. *Rhetorics of Motherhood*. Carbondale: Southern Illinois University Press, 2013.

Bullock, Maggie. "The Abortion Doctor and His Accuser." *Atlantic*, March 2020.

Buss, Helen M. *Repossessing the World: Reading Memoirs by Contemporary Women Writers*. Waterloo, ON: Wilfred Laurier University Press, 2012.

Calhoun, Cheshire. *Feminism, the Family, and the Politics of the Closet: Lesbian and Gay Displacement*. Oxford, UK: Oxford University Press, 2003.

Callard, Agnes. *Aspiration: The Agency of Becoming*. New York: Oxford University Press, 2018.

Carasthatis, Anna. "The Concept of Intersectionality in Feminist Theory." *Philosophy Compass* 9, no. 5 (May 2014): 304–14.

———. *Intersectionality: Origins, Contestations, Horizons*. Lincoln: University of Nebraska Press, 2016.

Chávez, Karma R. *Queer Migration Politics: Activist Rhetoric and Coalitional Possibilities*. Urbana: University of Illinois Press, 2013.

Chávez, Karma R., and Cindy L. Griffin, eds. *Standing in the Intersection: Feminist Voices, Feminist Practices in Communication Studies*. Albany: SUNY Press, 2012.

Cho, Sumi, Kimberlé Williams Crenshaw, and Leslie McCall. "Toward a Field of Intersectionality Studies." *Signs* 38, no. 4 (Summer 2013): 785–810.

Chocano, Carina. "Baby Mama." *Los Angeles Times*. April 25, 2008.

Cloud, Dana L. "Queer Theory and 'Family Values': Capitalism's Utopias of Self-Invention." In *Marxism, Queer Theory, Gender*, 71–114. Syracuse, NY: Red Factory, 2001.

———. "The Rhetoric of Family Values: Scapegoating, Utopia, and the Privatization of Social Responsibility." *Western Journal of Communication* 62, no. 4 (June 2009): 387–419.

Cohen, Michael. *Live from the Campaign Trail: The Greatest Presidential Campaign Speeches of the Twentieth Century and How They Shaped Modern America*. New York: Walker, 2008.

Cole, Elizabeth R. "Coalitions as a Model for Intersectionality: From Practice to Theory." *Sex Roles* 59, nos. 5–6 (2008): 443–53.

Collins, Patricia Hill. "All in the Family: Intersections of Gender, Race, and Nation." *Hypatia* 13, no. 3 (Summer 1998): 62–82.

———. *Black Feminist Thought: Knowledge, Consciousness, and the Politics of Empowerment*. Revised tenth anniversary edition. New York: Routledge, 2000.

Coltrane, Scott. *Gender and Families*. Thousand Oaks, CA: Pine Forge Press, 1998.

Condit, Celeste M. *Decoding Abortion Rhetoric: Communicating Social Change*. Urbana: University of Illinois Press, 1990.

Coontz, Stephanie. *The Way We Never Were: American Families and the Nostalgia Trap*. New York: Basic Books, 1992.

Cooper, Melinda. *Family Values: Between Neoliberalism and the New Social Conservatism*. Brooklyn, NY: Zone Books, 2017.

Couser, G. Thomas. *Memoir: An Introduction*. New York: Oxford University Press, 2012.

Cramer, Beth, dir. *Plan B: Single Women Choosing Motherhood*. 2009; New York: Brave Films, 2009. DVD.

Crenshaw, Kimberlé Williams. "Demarginalizing the Intersection of Race and Sex: A Black Feminist Critique of Antidiscrimination Doctrine, Feminist Theory and Antiracist Politics." *University of Chicago Legal Forum* 1989, no. 8 (1989): 139–68.

———. "The Girls Obama Forgot." *New York Times*, July 29, 2014.

———. "Mapping the Margins: Intersectionality, Identity Politics, and Violence against Women of Color." *Stanford Law Review* 43, no. 6 (July 1991): 1241–99.

———. "Race to the Bottom: How the Post-Racial Revolution Became a Whitewash." *Baffler*, 35 (June 2017).

Curran, Laura, and Laura Abrams. "Making Men into Dads: Fatherhood, the State, and Welfare Reform." *Gender and Society* 14, no. 5 (October 2000): 662–78.

Dargis, Manhola. "Learning on the Job about Birthing Babies." *New York Times*, April 25, 2008.

———. "Love Means Having to Say I Feel." *New York Times*, April 22, 2010.

Daum, Meghan. *Selfish, Shallow, and Self-Absorbed: Sixteen Writers on the Decision Not to Have Kids*. New York: Picador, 2016.

Davenport, Nina, dir. *First Comes Love*. 2012. N.p.: Baby Pictures, 2012.

Davis, Angela. "Outcast Mothers and Surrogates: Racism and Reproductive Politics in the Nineties." In *American Feminist Thought at Century's End: A Reader*, edited by Linda S. Kauffman, 355 – 66. Cambridge, MA: Blackwell, 1993.

Dees, Richard H. "Moral Conversions." *Philosophy and Phenomenological Research* 56, no. 3 (September 1996): 531–50.

Demo, Anne Teresa, Jennifer L. Borda, and Charlotte H. Kroløkke, eds. *The Motherhood Business: Consumption, Communication, and Privilege*. Tuscaloosa: University of Alabama Press, 2015.

de Onís, Kathleen M. "Lost in Translation: Challenging (White, Monolingual Feminism's) 'Choice' with Justicia Reproductiva." *Women's Studies in Communication* 38, no. 1 (2015): 1–19.

DePaulo, Bella. *Singled Out: How Singles Are Stereotyped, Stigmatized, and Ignored, and Still Live Happily Ever After*. New York: St. Martin's, 2007.

Devitt, Amy. *Writing Genres*. Carbondale: Southern Illinois University Press, 2004.

Douglas, Susan, and Meredith Michaels. *The Mommy Myth: The Idealization of Motherhood and How It Has Undermined All Women*. New York: Free Press, 2004.

Dow, Dawn Marie. *Mothering while Black: Boundaries and Burdens of Middle-Class Parenthood*. Oakland: University of California Press, 2019.

Dowland, Seth. "'Family Values' and the Formation of a Christian Right Agenda." *Church History* 78, no. 3 (September 2009): 606–31.

Drexler, Peggy. *Raising Boys without Men: How Maverick Moms Are Creating the Next Generation of Exceptional Men*. Emmaus, PA: Rodale Books, 2005.

Dubriwny, Tasha N. "Consciousness-Raising as Collective Rhetoric: The Articulation of Experience in the Redstockings' Abortion Speak-Out of 1969." *Quarterly Journal of Speech* 91, no. 4 (2005): 395–422.

Dymond, Justine, and Nicole Willey. "Introduction: Creating the Collection." *Motherhood Memoirs: Mothers Creating/Writing Lives*, edited by Justine Dymond and Nicole Willey, 1–32. Bradford, ON: Demeter Press, 2013.

Edelman, Marian Wright. "Colorado College Baccalaureate Address." Colorado Springs, May 16, 1999. Iowa State University, Archive of Women's Political Communication.

Edin, Kathryn, and Maria J. Kefalas. *Promises I Can Keep: Why Poor Women Put Motherhood before Marriage*. Oakland: University of California Press, 2011.

Emig, Janet. *The Composing Processes of Twelfth Graders*. Urbana, IL: National Council of Teachers of English, 1971.

Enoch, Jessica. "Survival Stories: Feminist Historiographic Approaches to Chicana Rhetorics of Sterilization Abuse," *Rhetoric Society Quarterly* 35, no. 3 (Summer 2005): 5–30.

Faderman, Lillian. *The Gay Revolution: The Story of the Struggle*. New York: Simon and Schuster, 2015.

Faludi, Susan. *Backlash: The Undeclared War against American Women*. Fifteenth anniversary edition. New York: Three Rivers Press, 2006.

Ferguson, Michaele L. "Choice Feminism and the Fear of Politics." *Perspectives on Politics* 8, no. 1 (March 2010): 247–53.

Fernheimer, Janice. "A Review of *Rhetorical Refusals: Defying Audiences' Expectations* by John Schilb." *Rhetoric Society Quarterly* 39, no. 1 (Winter 2009): 99–102.

Fiske, John. *Media Matters: Everyday Culture and Political Change*. Minneapolis: University of Minnesota Press, 1994.

Fixmer-Oraiz, Natalie. "Contemplating Homeland Maternity." *Women's Studies in Communication* 38, no. 2 (2015): 129–34.

———. *Homeland Maternity: US Security Culture and the New Reproductive Regime*. Urbana: University of Illinois Press, 2019.

Flores, Lisa. "Between Abundance and Marginalization: The Imperative of Racial Rhetorical Criticism." *Review of Communication* 16, no. 1 (January 2016): 4–24.

Frankenberg, Ruth. *White Women, Race Matters: The Social Construction of Whiteness*. Minneapolis: University of Minnesota Press, 1993.

Fraser, Nancy. "The End of Progressive Neoliberalism." *Dissent Magazine*, January 2, 2017.

———. *The Old Is Dying and the New Cannot Be Born*. New York: Verso, 2019.

Freeman, Elizabeth. "Queer Belongings: Kinship Theory and Queer Theory." In Haggerty and McGarry, *Companion to Lesbian, Gay, Bisexual, Transgender, and Queer Studies*, 295–314.

Friedman, May. *Mommyblogs and the Changing Face of Motherhood*. Toronto: University of Toronto Press, 2013.

Friedman, May, and Shana L. Calixte. "Introduction." In *Mothering and Blogging*, 21–36.

———, eds. *Mothering and Blogging: The Radical Act of the MommmyBlog*. Toronto: Demeter Press, 2009.

Garbes, Angela. "Why Are We Only Talking about 'Mom Books' by White Women?" *Cut*, November 1, 2018.

Gere, Ann Ruggles. *Writing Groups: History, Theory, and Implications*. Carbondale: Southern Illinois University Press, 1987.

Gilder, George. "Freedom from Welfare Dependency." *Religion and Liberty* 4, no. 2 (March–April 1994): n.p.

———. *Men and Marriage*. Gretna, LA: Pelican, 1993.

Giles, Melinda Vandenbeld, ed. *Mothering in the Age of Neoliberalism*. Bradford, ON: Demeter Press, 2014.

Gillespie, Peggy, ed. *Love Makes a Family: Portraits of Lesbian, Gay, Bisexual, and Transgender Parents and Their Families*. Amherst: University of Massachusetts Press, 1999.

Gilmore, Leigh. *Tainted Witness: Why We Doubt What Women Say about Their Lives*. New York: Columbia University Press, 2017.

Gleiberman, Owen. "The Back-Up Plan." *Entertainment Weekly*, April 22, 2010.

———. "Best Friends Forever." *Entertainment Weekly*, August 20, 2010.

Golombok, Susan. *Modern Families: Parents and Children in New Family Form*. Cambridge, UK: Cambridge University Press, 2015.

Gore, Al, and Tipper Gore. *Joined at the Heart: The Transformation of the American Family*. New York: Henry Holt, 2002.

Grabill, Jeffrey T., and Stacey Pigg. "Messy Rhetoric: Identity Performance as Rhetorical Agency in Online Public Forums." *Rhetoric Society Quarterly* 42, no. 2 (2012): 99–119.

Graham, Susanna. "Choosing Single Motherhood: Single Women Negotiating the Nuclear Family Ideal." In *Families beyond the Nuclear Ideal*, edited by Daniela Cutas and Sarah Chan, 97–109. London: Bloomsbury, 2012.

Griffin, Cindy L., and Karma Chávez. "Introduction: Standing at the Intersections of Feminisms, Intersectionality, and Communication Studies." In Chávez and Griffin, *Standing in the Intersection*, 1–34.

Gurak, Laura, Smiljana Antonijevic, Lauire Johnson, Clancy Ratliff, and Jessica Reyman. "Introduction: Weblogs, Rhetoric, Community, and Culture." *Into the Blogosphere* (2004). Retrieved from the University of Minnesota Digital Conservancy.

Gutman, Herbert G. "Persistent Myths about the Afro-American Family." *Journal of Interdisciplinary History* 6, no. 2 (Autumn 1975): 181–210.

Haggerty, George E., and Molly McGarry, eds. *A Companion to Lesbian, Gay, Bisexual, Transgender, and Queer Studies*. New York: John Wiley and Sons, 2007.

Halberstam, J. Jack. "Forgetting Family." In Haggerty and McGarry, *Companion to Lesbian, Gay, Bisexual, Transgender, and Queer Studies*, 315–24.

———. *Gaga Feminism*. Boston: Beacon Press, 2012.

Halloran, Michael. "Aristotle's Concept of Ethos, or If Not His, Somebody Else's." *Rhetoric Review* 1, no. 1 (September 1982): 58–63.

Hallstein, [D.] Lynn O'Brien. *Bikini-Ready Moms: Celebrity Profiles, Motherhood, and the Body*. Albany: State University of New York Press, 2015.

———. "Introduction to Mothering Rhetorics." *Women's Studies in Communication* 40, no. 1 (2017): 1–10.

———. "When Neoliberalism Intersects with Post-Second Wave Mothering: Reinforcing Neo-Traditional American Family Configurations and Exacerbating the Post-Second Wave Crisis in Femininity." In Giles, *Mothering in the Age of Neoliberalism*, 297–314.

Hartzell, Stephanie. "An (In)visible Universe of Grief: Performative Disidentifications with White Motherhood in the We Are Not Trayvon Martin Blog." *Journal of International and Intercultural Communication* 10, no. 1 (2017): 62–79.

Hayden, Sara. "Revitalizing the Debate between 'Life' and 'Choice': The 2004 March for Women's Lives." *Communication and Critical/Cultural Studies* 6, no. 2 (2009): 111–31.

Hayden, Sara, and D. Lynn O'Brien Hallstein. *Contemplating Maternity in an Era of Choice: Explorations into Discourses of Reproduction*. Lanham, MD: Lexington Books, 2010.

Hayford, Sarah R., and Karen Benjamin Guzzo. "The Single Motherhood by Choice Myth." *Contexts* 14, no. 4 (Fall 2015): 70–72.

Hays, Sharon. *The Cultural Contradictions of Motherhood*. New Haven: Yale University Press, 1996.

Henke, Tracy. "The Choice to be Childfree: An Increasing Factor in U.S. Population Growth." Negative Population Growth, August 25, 2014. Web.

Hertz, Rosanna. "The Father as an Idea: A Challenge to Kinship Boundaries by Single Mothers." *Symbolic Interaction* 25, no.1 (2002): 1–31.

———. *Single by Chance, Mothers by Choice: How Women Are Choosing Parenthood without Marriage and Creating the New American Family*. New York: Oxford University Press, 2006.

Hesse, Doug, and Kathleen Blake Yancey. "Permission to Write." *Writing on the Edge* 25, no. 1 (Fall 2014): 13–29.

Hesse, Douglas D. "2005 CCC Chair's Address: Who Owns Writing?" *College Composition and Communication* 57, no. 2 (December 2005): 335–57.

Heyes, Cressida. *Self-Transformations: Foucault, Ethics, and Normalized Bodies*. New York: Oxford University Press, 2007.

Hirschmann, Nancy J. "Choosing Betrayal." *Perspectives on Politics* 8, no. 1 (March 2010): 271–78.

Hirshman, Linda. *Victory: The Triumphant Gay Revolution*. New York: HarperCollins, 2012.

Hogg, Charlotte. "Including Conservative Women's Rhetorics in an 'Ethics of Hope and Care.'" *Rhetoric Review* 34, no. 4 (2015): 391–408.

Holden, Stephen. "In a Baste and Switch, a New Father Is Born." *New York Times*, August 19, 2010.

Hsu, V. Jo. "A Single Life Reinvented: Personal Writing as the Negotiation of Identity in Richard Rodriguez's Autobiographical Trilogy." *Rhetoric Review* 35, no. 4 (2016): 361–73.

Hundley, Heather L., and Sara E. Hayden. *Mediated Moms: Contemporary Challenges to the Motherhood Myth*. New York: Peter Lang, 2015.

Hymowitz, Kay. "How Single Motherhood Hurts Kids." *New York Times*, February 8, 2014.

Hymowitz, Kay, Jason S. Carroll, W. Bradford Wilcox, and Kelleen Kaye. "The Great Crossover." In *Knot Yet: The Benefits and Costs of Delayed Marriage in America*, 17–19. Report produced for the National Marriage Project at the University of Virginia, the National Campaign to Prevent Teen and Unplanned Pregnancy, and the Relate Institute, 2013.

Ide, Michael Enku, Blair Harrington, Yolanda Wiggins, Tanya Rouleau Whitworth, and Naomi Gerstel. "Emerging Adult Sons and Their Fathers: Race and the Construction of Masculinity." *Gender and Society* 32, no. 1 (February 2018): 5–33.

Jensen, Robin. *Infertility: Tracing the History of a Transformative Term*. University Park: Penn State University Press, 2016.

Jolles, Marjorie. "Between Embodied Subjects and Objects: Narrative Somaesthetics." *Hypatia* 27, no. 2 (Spring 2012): 301–18.

Josephson, Jyl J., and Cynthia Burack. 1998. "The Political Ideology of the Neo-Traditional Family." *Journal of Political Ideologies* 3, no. 2 (June 1998): 213–31.

Juffer, Jane. *Single Mother: The Emergence of the Domestic Intellectual*. New York: NYU Press, 2006.

Katz, Judy, and Oren Rudavsky, dir. *And Baby Makes Two*. 1999; New York City: First Run Features, 1999.

Kerber, Linda K. "The Republican Mother." In *Women's America: Refocusing the Past*, edited by Linda K. Kerber and Jane Sherron De Hart, 119–28. 6th ed. New York: Oxford University Press, 2004.

Kingsolver, Barbara. *High Tide in Tucson: Essays from Now or Never*. New York: Harper, 1995.

Klinenberg, Eric. *Going Solo: The Extraordinary Rise and Surprising Appeal of Living Alone*. New York: Penguin Books, 2013.

Kohler, Will. "Gay History—June 19, 1983: Founder of the Moral Majority Jerry Falwell: 'AIDS Is God's Punishment for Homosexuals.'" Back2Stonewall, June 19, 2020.

Kornbluh, Felicia. "The Goals of the National Welfare Rights Movement: Why We Need Them Thirty Years Later." *Feminist Studies* 24, no. 1 (Spring 1998): 65–78.

———. *The Battle for Welfare Rights: Poverty and Politics in Modern America*. Philadelphia: University of Pennsylvania Press, 2007.

Kornbluh, Felicia, and Gwendolyn Mink. *Ensuring Poverty: Welfare Reform in Feminist Perspective*. Philadelphia: University of Pennsylvania Press, 2018.

Kotkin, Joel. *The Rise of Post-Familialism: Humanity's Future?* Singapore: Civil Service College, 2012.

Kranish, Michael. "In Bully Pulpit, Preaching Values." *Boston Globe*, December 10, 1993.

Lareau, Annette. *Unequal Childhoods: Class, Race, and Family Life*. 2nd ed. Berkeley: University of California Press, 2011.

Larson, Thomas. *The Memoir and the Memoirist: Reading and Writing Personal Narrative*. Athens, OH: Swallow Press, 2007.

Laymon, Kiese. *Heavy: An American Memoir*. New York: Scribner, 2018.

Lee, Amanda. "Single Mothers 'Bad for Society,' Pew Research Center's Latest Poll Finds." *Huffington Post*, February 21, 2011.

Lehmann-Haupt, Rachel. *DIY Mom: A Solo Parenting Adventure*. Bronx: She Writes Press, 2013. Ebook.

———. *In Her Own Sweet Time: Unexpected Adventures in Finding Love, Commitment, and Motherhood*. New York: Basic Books, 2010.

Lehr, Valerie. *Queer Family Values: Debunking the Myth of the Nuclear Family*. Philadelphia: Temple University Press, 1999.

Lind, Emily R. M. "Disruptive Speech: A Discursive Analysis of Single Mother Memoirs and the Challenge to Compulsory Heterosexuality." *Journal of the Motherhood Initiative for Research and Community Involvement* 7, no. 1 (2016): 52–63.

Lorde, Audre. "Age, Race, Class and Sex: Women Redefining Difference." In *Sister Outsider: Essays and Speeches*, 114–23. Repr., Berkeley, CA: Crossing Press, 1984.

Lotz, Amanda D. "Postfeminist Television Criticism: Rehabilitating Critical Terms and Identifying Postfeminist Attributes." *Feminist Media Studies* 1, no. 1 (2001): 105–21.

Ludtke, Melissa. *On Our Own: Unmarried Motherhood in America*. Berkeley: University of California Press, 1997.

Lugones, Maria. "From within Germinative Stasis: Creating Active Subjectivity, Resistant Agency." In *Entremundos/AmongWorlds: New Perspectives on Gloria Anzaldúa*, edited by AnaLouise Keating, 85–100. New York: Palgrave Macmillan, 2005.

Lumbiano, Wahneema. "Black Ladies, Welfare Queens, and State Minstrels: Ideological War by Narrative Means." In *Race-ing Justice, En-gendering Power: Essays on Anita Hill, Clarence Thomas, and the Construction of Social Reality*, edited by Toni Morrison, 323– 63. New York: Pantheon, 1992.

Mack, Katherine. "Do Two a Family Make? Hollywood Engages Intentional Single Motherhood." In *Motherhood and Single-Lone Parenting: A Twenty-First Century Perspective*, edited by Maki Motapanyane, 53–71. Bradford, ON: Demeter, 2016.

———. "I Am Murphy Brown: Race and Class in the Rhetoric of Single Mothers by Choice." *Rhetoric Review* 39, no. 3 (September 2020): 287–302.

Mack, Katherine, and Jonathan Alexander. "The Ethics of Memoir: Ethos in Uptake." *Rhetoric Society Quarterly* 49, no. 1 (2019): 49–70.

Mailloux, Steven. *Reception Histories: Rhetoric, Pragmatism, and American Cultural Politics*. Ithaca, NY: Cornell University Press, 1998.

Mamo, Laura. *Queering Reproduction: Achieving Pregnancy in the Age of Technoscience*. Durham, NC: Duke University Press, 2007.

Martin, April. Afterword in Gillespie, *Love Makes a Family*.

Marsh, Margaret, and Wanda Ronner. *The Empty Cradle: Infertility in America from Colonial Times to the Present*. Baltimore, MD: Johns Hopkins University Press, 1996.

———. *The Pursuit of Parenthood: Reproductive Technology from Test-Tube Babies to Uterus Transplants*. Baltimore: Johns Hopkins University Press, 2019.

Mason, Nicole C. "A Black, Queer Single Mother on Why I Am Proud to Use the Term Single Mother by Choice." *Huffington Post*, December 6, 2016.

———. "This Is Why I Identify as a Single Mother by Choice." Scary Mommy, January 5, 2017.

Mattes, Jane. *Single Mothers by Choice: A Guidebook for Single Women Who Are Considering or Have Chosen Motherhood*. New York: Three Rivers Press, 1994.

May, Elaine Tyler. *Barren in the Promised Land: Childless Americans and the Pursuit of Happiness*. New York: Basic Books, 1995.

May, Vivian. *Pursuing Intersectionality, Unsettling Dominant Imaginaries*. New York: Routledge, 2015.

McClain, Linda C. "A Diversity Approach to Parenthood in Family Life and Family Law." In McClain and Cere, *What Is Parenthood?*, 41–62.

McClain, Linda C., and Daniel Cere, eds. *What Is Parenthood? Contemporary Debates about the Family*. New York: NYU Press, 2013.

McClarin, Kim. *Womanish: A Grown Black Woman Speaks on Love and Life*. New York: Ig, 2019.

McGee, Michael Calvin. "The 'Ideograph': A Link between Rhetoric and Ideology." *Quarterly Journal of Speech* 66, no. 1 (February 1980): 1–16.

McGee, Micki. *Self-Help, Inc.: Makeover Culture in American Life*. New York: Oxford University Press, 2005.

McLanahan, Sara, and Christopher Jencks. "Was Moynihan Right? What Happens to Children of Unmarried Mothers." *Education Next* 15, no. 2 (Spring 2015): 14–20.

McRobbie, Angela. "Post-Feminism and Popular Culture." *Feminist Media Studies* 4, no. 3 (2004): 255–64.

Miller, Benita. "Mothering while Poor: Utilizing the Reproductive Justice Framework to Build the Capacities of Young Mothers." In Ross et al., *Radical Reproductive Justice*, 355–60.

Miller, Carolyn. "Genre as Social Action." *Quarterly Journal of Speech* 70 (1984): 151–67.

Miller, Carolyn R., and Dawn Shepherd. "Blogging as Social Action: A Genre Analysis of the Weblog." *Into the Blogosphere* (2004). Retrieved from the University of Minnesota Digital Conservancy.

Miller, Claire Cain. "The Divorce Surge Is Over, but the Myth Lives On." *New York Times*, December 2, 2014.

Miller, Nancy K. "But Enough about Me, What Do You Think of My Memoir?" *Yale Journal of Criticism* 13, no. 2 (Fall 2000): 421–36.

Moral Majority. "Family Manifesto." Jerry Falwell Library, 1988.

Morin, Rich. "Disapprove of Single Mothers." Pew Research Center, January 6, 2011.

Morrissette, Mikki. "2015 Choice Mom Survey Results." ChoiceMoms, 2015.

———. "2016 Choice Mom Survey Results: Finding Support." ChoiceMoms, 2016.

———. *Choosing Single Motherhood: The Thinking Woman's Guide*. Boston: Houghton Mifflin, 2008.

———. *Retrospective: Eighteen Years as a Choice Mom*. eGuide. ChoiceMoms. 2017.

Moynihan, Daniel. *The Negro Family: The Case for National Action*. Office of Policy Planning and Research, United States Department of Labor, March 1965.

Murray, Charles. "The Coming White Underclass." *Wall Street Journal*, October 29, 1993.

Negra, Diane. "Quality Postfeminism?: Sex and the Single Girl on HBO." *Genders* 39 (2004). Web.

Nicholson, Linda. "The Myth of the Traditional Family." In *Feminism and Families*, edited by Hilde Lindemann Nelson, 27–42. New York: Routledge, 1997.

O'Reilly, Andrea. "The Motherhood Memoir and the 'New Momism': Biting the Hand That Feeds You." In *From the Personal to the Political: Toward a New Theory of Maternal Narrative*, edited by Andrea O'Reilly and Sylvia Caporale Bizzini, 238–48. Selinsgrove, PA: Susquehanna University Press, 2009.

———. "We Need to Talk about Patriarchal Motherhood: Essentialization, Naturalization, and Idealization in Lionel Shriver's *We Need to Talk about Kevin*." *Journal of the Motherhood Initiative for Research and Community Involvement* 7, no. 1 (Spring/Summer 2016): 64–81.

O'Rourke, Shannon, dir. *Maybe Baby*. 2007; Beacon, NY: New Day Films, 2007. DVD.

Otis, Hailey Nicole. "Intersectional Rhetoric: Where Intersectionality as Analytic Sensibility and Embodied Rhetorical Praxis Converge." *Quarterly Journal of Speech* 105, no. 4 (October 2019): 369–89.

Owens, Kim Hensley. *Writing Childbirth: Women's Rhetorical Agency in Labor and Online*. Carbondale: Southern Illinois University Press, 2015.

Perry, Twila L. "Symposium, Family Values, Race, Feminism and Public Policy." *Santa Clara Law Review* 36 (1996): 345–74.

Pew Research Center. "Chapter 2: Public Views on Changing Gender Roles." May 29, 2013.

———. "The Decline of Marriage and the Rise of New Families." November 18, 2010.

Phillips, Michael. "The Back-Up Plan." *Los Angeles Times*, April 22, 2010.

Philyaw, Deeshaw. "Ain't I a Mommy: Why Are so Few Motherhood Memoirs Penned by Women of Color?" *bitchmedia*, February 23, 2016.

Plant, Rebecca Jo. *Mom: The Transformation of Motherhood in Modern America*. Chicago: University of Chicago Press, 2010.

Plato. *Gorgias*. Translated by James A. Arieti and Roger M. Barrus. Newburyport, MA: Focus Publishing, 2007.

Pogrebin, Letty Cottin. *Family Politics: Love and Family on an Intimate Frontier*. New York: McGraw Hill, 1983.

Popenhoe, David. "The Controversial Truth: Two-Parent Families Are Better." *New York Times*, December 26, 1992, 21.

———. *Life without Father: Compelling New Evidence that Fatherhood and Marriage Are Indispensable for the Good of Children and Society*. New York: Martin Kessler Books, 1996.

———. *War over the Family*. New Brunswick, NJ: Transaction Publishers, 2005.

Pruett, Kyle D. *Fatherneed: Why Father Care Is as Essential as Mother Care for Your Child*. New York: Broadway Books, 2001.

Quadagno, Jill. *The Color of Welfare: How Racism Undermined the War on Poverty*. New York: Oxford University Press, 1994.

Quayle, Dan. "Address to the Commonwealth Club of California." May 19, 1992. Dan Quayle website.

———. "Murphy Brown Speech." San Francisco, CA. May 19, 1992. Voices of Democracy. Web.

Rak, Julie. *Boom: Manufacturing Memoir for the Popular Market*. Waterloo, ON: Wilfred Laurier University Press, 2013.

Randles, Jennifer. "'Manning Up' to Be a Good Father: Hybrid Fatherhood, Masculinity, and U.S. Responsible Fatherhood Policy." *Gender and Society* 32, no. 4 (August 2018): 516–39.

Ratcliffe, Krista. "In Search of the Unstated: The Enthymeme and/of Whiteness." *JAC* 27, nos. 1/2 (2007): 275–90.

Ravitz, Jessica. "Out of Wedlock Births Hit Record High." CNN, April 8, 2009.

Reddy, Nancy. "We Need to Talk about Whiteness in Motherhood Memoirs." Electric Literature, December 4, 2018.

Reid-Brinkley, Shanara Rose. "Mammies and Matriarchs: Feminine Style and Signifyin(g) in Carol Moselet Braun's 2003–2004 Campaign for the Presidency." In Chávez and Griffin, *Standing in the Intersection*, 35–58.

Renegar, Valerie R., and Kirsti K. Cole. "'Evil Is Part of the Territory:' Inventing the Stepmother in Self-Help Books." *Women's Studies in Communication* 42, no. 4 (2019): 511–33.

Reynolds, Nedra. "Ethos as Location: New Sites for Understanding Discursive Authority." *Rhetoric Review* 11, no. 2 (Spring 1993): 325–38.

Rich, Adrienne. *Of Woman Born: Motherhood as Experience and Institution.* 2nd ed. New York: W. W. Norton, 1986.

———. "Motherhood in Bondage (1976)." In *On Lies, Secrets, and Silence: Selected Prose, 1966–1978*, 195–97. New York: W. W. Norton, 1979.

Roberts, Dorothy. *Killing the Black Body: Race, Reproduction, and the Meaning of Liberty.* New York: Vintage Books, 1997.

Roberts-Miller, Patricia. *Deliberate Conflict: Argument, Political Theory, and Composition Classes.* Carbondale: Southern Illinois University Press, 2004.

Robillard, Amy E. "Seeking Adequate Rhetorical Witness for Life Writing." *Rhetoric Society Quarterly* 49, no. 2 (2019): 185–92.

Ross, Loretta J. "Conceptualizing Reproductive Justice Theory: A Manifesto for Activism." In Ross et al., *Radical Reproductive Justice*, 170–232.

———. "Reproductive Justice as Intersectional Feminist Activism." *Souls* 19, no. 3 (July–September 2017): 286–314.

Ross, Loretta, Lynn Roberts, Erika Derkas, Whitney Peoples, and Pamela Bridgewater Toure, eds. *Radical Reproductive Justice: Foundation, Theory, Practice, Critique.* New York: Feminist Press, 2017.

Ross, Loretta, and Rickie Solinger. *Reproductive Justice: An Introduction.* Oakland: University of California Press, 2017.

Rowe, Aidan. "Same-Sex Marriage: An Alternative Gay Liberation Viewpoint." *Redline* (blog), August 23, 2013.

Royster, Jacqueline Jones, and Gesa E. Kirsch. *Feminist Rhetorical Practices: New Horizons for Rhetoric, Composition, and Literacy Studies.* Carbondale: Southern Illinois University Press, 2012.

Ruggles, Steven. "The Origins of African-American Family Structure." *American Sociological Review* 59, no. 1 (February 1994): 136–51.

Schilb, John. *Rhetorical Refusals: Defying Audiences' Expectations.* Carbondale: Southern Illinois University, 2007.

Schwarzbaum, Lisa. "Baby Mama." *Entertainment Weekly*, April 25, 2008.

Scott, Joan W. "The Evidence of Experience." *Critical Inquiry* 17, no. 4 (Summer 1991): 773–97.

Sehgal, Parul. "In a Raft of New Books: Motherhood from (Almost) Every Angle." *New York Times*, April 24, 2018.

Self, Robert O. *All in the Family: The Realignment of American Democracy since the 1960s.* New York: Hill and Wang, 2012.

Siegel, Marika. *The Rhetoric of Pregnancy.* Chicago: University of Chicago Press, 2014.

Silbergleid, Robin. "'Oh Baby!' Representations of Single Mothers in American Popular Culture." *Americana: The Journal of American Popular Culture* 1, no. 2 (Fall 2020): n.p.

Single Mothers by Choice. (Blog hosted by the Single Mothers by Choice website).

Sloan, Louise. *Knock Yourself Up—No Man? No Problem! A Tell-All Guide to Becoming a Single Mom.* New York: Penguin, 2007.

Smith, Andrea. *Conquest: Sexual Violence and American Indian Genocide.* Cambridge, MA: South End Press, 2005.

Smith, Ben, "The Conservative Pundit with a Legacy From 1994," *New York Times*, August 31, 2020, B1.

Smith, Sidonie, and Julia Watson. *Reading Autobiography: A Guide for Interpreting Life Narratives.* Minneapolis: University of Minnesota, 2010.

Soiseth, Alexandra. *Choosing You: Deciding to Have a Baby on My Own*. Berkeley, CA: Seal Press, 2008.

Solinger, Rickie. *Beggars and Choosers: How the Politics of Choice Shapes Adoption, Abortion, and Welfare in the United States*. New York: Hill and Wang, 2002.

———. *Wake Up Little Susie: Single Pregnancy and Race before Roe v. Wade*. New York: Routledge, 1992.

Solomon, Andrew. *Far from the Tree: Parents, Children, and the Search for Identity*. New York: Scribner, 2012.

Stacey, Judith. *In the Name of the Family*. Boston: Beacon Press, 1996.

Stonesifer, Jené. *When Baby Makes Two: Single Mothers by Chance or by Choice*. Los Angeles: Lowell House, 1994.

Strautmanis, Michael. "Promoting Responsible Fatherhood and Healthy Families." White House. June 15, 2012.

Strickler, Rachel, and Monica Simpson. "A Brief Herstory of SisterSong." In Ross et al., *Radical Reproductive Justice*, 50–57.

Stubblefield, Anna. "'Beyond the Pale': Tainted Whiteness, Cognitive Disability, and Eugenic Sterilization." *Hypatia* 22, no. 2 (Spring 2007): 162–81.

Sullivan, Andrew. "Here Comes the Groom: A (Conservative) Case for Gay Marriage." *New Republic*, August 27, 1989.

Swanson, Kara W. *Banking on the Body: The Market in Blood, Milk, and Sperm in Modern America*. Cambridge, MA: Harvard University Press, 2014.

Thompson, Julie M. *Mommy Queerest: Contemporary Rhetorics of Lesbian Maternal Identity*. Amherst: University of Massachusetts Press, 2002.

Tillmon, Johnnie. "Welfare Is a Women's Issue." *Ms.*, Spring 1972.

Traister, Rebecca. *All the Single Ladies: Unmarried Women and the Rise of an Independent Nation*. New York: Simon and Schuster, 2016.

Tucker, Judith Statman. "Small World: Maternal Blogging, Virtual Friendship, and the Computer-Mediated Self." Foreword to Friedman and Calixte, *Mothering and Blogging*, 1–20.

Vandenberg-Daves, Jodi. *Modern Motherhood: An American History*. New Brunswick, NJ: Rutgers University Press, 2014.

Vanguri, Star Medzerian, ed. *Rhetorics of Names and Naming*. New York: Routledge, 2018.

VCU Libraries Social Welfare History Project. "National Welfare Rights Organization." Last modified August 29, 2022. Web.

Villarosa, Linda. "The Long Shadow of Eugenics in America." *New York Times Magazine*, June 12, 2022.

Vinson, Jenna. *Embodying the Problem: The Persuasive Power of the Teen Mother*. New Brunswick, NJ: Rutgers University Press, 2017.

Vinson, Jenna, and Clare Daniel. "'Power to Decide' Who Should Get Pregnant: A Feminist Rhetorical Analysis of Neoliberal Visions of Reproductive Justice." *Present Tense: A Journal of Rhetoric in Society* 8, no. 2 (July 2020). Web.

Vivian, Bradford. "The Threshold of the Self." *Rhetoric and Philosophy* 33, no. 4 (2000): 303–18.

Warner, Michael. "Introduction: Fear of a Queer Planet." *Social Text*, no. 29 (1991): 3–17.

———. *Publics and Counterpublics*. New York: Zone Books, 2005.

———. *The Trouble with Normal: Sex, Politics, and the Ethics of Queer Life*. Cambridge, MA: Harvard University Press, 2000.

Weaver, Diane Dixon. "The First Father: Perspectives on the President's Fatherhood Initiative." *Family Court Review* 50, no. 2 (April 2012): 297–309.

Welter, Barbara. "The Cult of True Womanhood: 1820–1860." In *The American Family in Social-Historical Perspective*, edited by Michael Gordon, 224–50. New York: St. Martin's Press, 1973.

Weston, Kath. *Families We Choose: Lesbians, Gays, and Kinship (Between Men—Between Women)*. New York: Columbia University Press, 1997.

———. "Introduction: Capturing More Than the Moment: Lesbian/Gay Families in the Making." In Gillespie, *Love Makes a Family*, 3–11.

Whitehead, Barbara Dafoe. "Dan Quayle Was Right." *Atlantic*, April 1993.

Wilkinson, Stephanie, and Jennifer Niesslein. "Tales from the (Mother) Hood: Motherhood in Book Publishing." *Brain, Child*, Spring 2005.

Wines, Michael. "Riots in Los Angeles: The President; White House Links Riots to Welfare." *New York Times*, May 5, 1992.

Winkler, Celia. "Redefining Single Motherhood: The 1990s Child Support Discourse and the Dismantling of the U.S. Welfare State." In Giles, *Mothering in the Age of Neoliberalism*, 255–78.

Yancey, Kathleen Blake. *Writing in the 21st Century*. Report, the National Council of Teachers of English. February 2009. Web.

Yancy, George. *Look, a White! Philosophical Essays on Whiteness*. Philadelphia: Temple University Press, 2012.

Yi, Youngjoo, and Tuba Angay-Crowder. "Self-Sponsored Writing." *TESOL Encyclopedia of English Language Learning*. January 18, 2018.

Yi, Youngjoo, and A. Hirvela. "Technology and 'Self-Sponsored' Writing: A Case Study of a Korean-American Adolescent." *Computers and Composition* 27, no. 2 (June 2010): 94–111.

Young, Iris Marion. *Intersecting Voices: Dilemmas of Gender, Political Philosophy, and Policy*. Princeton, NJ: Princeton University Press, 1997.

Zinsser, William. *Inventing the Truth: The Art and Craft of Memoir*. Boston: Houghton Mifflin, 1998.

INDEX